By curiously focusing on disbanded organizations and the emotions of the actors involved, rather than their imputed reasons or interests, Kleres' research opens new vistas of analysis and theorizing. This is an important book, innovative and insightful.

Jack Barbalet, *Department of Sociology, Hong Kong Baptist University, Hong Kong*

The Social Organization of Disease

Empirically, this book is a case-study analysis of dissolution processes in German AIDS organizations. Indeed, why is it that civic organizers start out with a commitment to a cause but end up dissolving their organization? This question is exactly what Kleres seeks to tackle within *The Social Organization of Disease*.

Focusing on the emotional bases of dissolved German AIDS organizations to develop a typology of civic action and organizing, Kleres presents a perspective on non-profit organizations that analyses organizational development through the emotional sensemaking of individual organizers, within the light of larger political processes and cultural contexts. To this end, this volume develops and applies a new methodology for researching emotions empirically, expanding the scope of narrative analysis. However, parallel to this, *The Social Organization of Disease* also explores how shifting discursive processes establish emotional climates and thus impact on state policies and the evolution of AIDS organizing.

The book would appeal to sociologists and political scientists working in the field of social movements and non-profit organisations: but it would also appeal to those who are interested in the sociology of emotions. It would potentially be of interest to non-profit scholars who consider community-based organizations, volunteerism and advocacy, and secondarily, to medical sociologists interested in AIDS service organizations, Sociology, International relations, Social Work and Political Science. It may also be of interest to NGO-activists and/or employees and leadership.

Jochen Kleres holds a PhD in sociology from the University of Leipzig and is currently a research fellow at Scuola Normale Superiore (Firenze, Italy)

Routledge Advances in Sociology

216 **The Sociology of Postmarxism**
Richard Howson

217 **The Precarious Generation**
A Political Economy of Young People
Judith Bessant Rys Farthing and Rob Watts

218 **Human Rights, Islam and the Failure of Cosmopolitanism**
June Edmunds

219 **New Generation Political Activism in Ukraine**
2000–2014
Christine Emeran

220 **Turkish National Identity and Its Outsiders**
Memories of State Violence in Dersim
Ozlem Goner

221 **Composing Processes and Artistic Agency**
Tacit Knowledge in Composing
Tasos Zembylas and Martin Niederauer

222 **Islamic Environmentalism**
Activism in the United States and Great Britain
Rosemary Hancock

223 **Mediating Sexual Citizenship**
Neoliberal Subjectivities in Television Culture
Anita Brady, Kellie Burns and Cristyn Davies

224 **The Social Organization of Disease**
Emotions and Civic Action
Jochen Kleres

225 **Migration to Rural and Peripheral Destinations**
Transnationalism, Integration, and Acculturation on the Margins
Ruth McAreavey

226 **Open Borders, Unlocked Cultures**
Romanian Roma Migrants in Western Europe
Edited by Yaron Matras and Daniele Viktor Leggio

The Social Organization of Disease

Emotions and Civic Action

Jochen Kleres

LONDON AND NEW YORK

First published 2018
by Routledge
2 Park Square, Milton Park, Abingdon, Oxon OX14 4RN

and by Routledge
711 Third Avenue, New York, NY 10017

Routledge is an imprint of the Taylor & Francis Group, an informa business

© 2018 Jochen Kleres

The right of Jochen Kleres to be identified as author of this work has been asserted by him in accordance with sections 77 and 78 of the Copyright, Designs and Patents Act 1988.

All rights reserved. No part of this book may be reprinted or reproduced or utilized in any form or by any electronic, mechanical, or other means, now known or hereafter invented, including photocopying and recording, or in any information storage or retrieval system, without permission in writing from the publishers.

Trademark notice: Product or corporate names may be trademarks or registered trademarks, and are used only for identification and explanation without intent to infringe.

British Library Cataloguing in Publication Data
A catalogue record for this book is available from the British Library

Library of Congress Cataloging in Publication Data
A catalog record for this book has been requested

ISBN: 978-1-138-89804-2 (hbk)
ISBN: 978-1-315-70881-2 (ebk)

Typeset in Times New Roman
by Wearset Ltd, Boldon, Tyne and Wear

Printed and bound in Great Britain by
TJ International Ltd, Padstow, Cornwall

For my parents

Contents

List of figures xii
Acknowledgments xiii

1 Introduction 1

Conceptual problems 2
Theoretical problems 5
Theories of volunteerism 6
Advances: theories of social movements 7
Conceptual problems revisited: empowering distinctions 9
A framework 12
Structure of the book: on studying disbanded AIDS organizations 12

2 Towards a political sociology of AIDS service organizations 22

A first premise: the social construction of AIDS 23
The (non-)emergence of AIDS organizations 24
A second premise: the evolution of public health 27
Queer corporatism 29
Professionalization and its discontents 32
Power in the field: the field of AIDS organizing 33
AIDS service organizations as political and discursive agents 35
Conclusion: AIDS service organizations as a form of power 37

3 AIDS organizations in Germany 42

Parallels: a brief note on the AIDS discourse in Germany 42
The role of identity: the emergence of AIDS relief organizations 43

*The power of discourse: the evolution of AIDS policies in
    Germany 44*
The stakes of AIDS organizing and of its political inclusion 52
The evolution and transformation of AIDS relief 54
The normalization of AIDS 56
Differences—the German case in contrast 58
Conclusion 63

4 Making sense of neo-corporatism and neo-institutionalism 68

Neo-corporatism—principle considerations 68
The rationalist premises of neo-corporatism 69
Neo-institutionalism 72
Key assumptions of neo-institutionalism 72
Neo-institutionalism and social change 74
The sensemaking approach 78
Sensemaking: the process of organizing 78
Seven characteristics and some sources of sensemaking 79
Conclusion 80

5 Sensemaking, narrative analysis and emotions 87

Narrative methodology and analysis 87
Convergences: sensemaking and narrative analysis 88
Emotions and narrative analysis 89
The narrativity of emotions 90
Towards narrative emotion analysis 94
Other linguistic manifestations of emotions 98
A note on realism in narrative interviewing 100
Non-conscious emotions 101
Sensemaking and emotions 102

6 Activists, volunteers and small town adversities 109

Paul's activism: moral shocks in a climate of adversity 110
Volunteerism: Sandra and Claudia 117
Volunteerism vs. activism 121
Conclusion 127

7 AIDS politics between compassion and pity 133

Peter: volunteerism, political inclusion and self-confidence 134
Alfons: pity and avoiding narration 142
Conclusion 149

8 Cuddly easterners, professionalism and the west 153

Professionalization as a tragedy of activism: Adam 154
Professionalism: Erwin 164
Solidarity and communal organizing: Benjamin 171
Conclusion 175

9 Professionalism and the limits of migrantic activism 179

Medical professionalism: Sarah 179
Professional volunteerism: Onur 186
Hybrid activism: Anıl 191
Conclusion 198

10 Conclusion: the meaningful, emotional and powered nature of nonprofits 202

A different take on nonprofits 202
Three modes of civic action 204
Modes of civic action, narrativity and sensemaking 205
Hybridity and interrelatedness 206
Contexts and conditions 207
Modes of civic action and civic organizations 208
Demise 209
Coda 211

Appendix 1: reflections on fieldwork 213
Appendix 2: transcription system 216
Index 217

Figures

1.1	Total number of local member organizations of German AIDS Relief	14
3.1	Visuals from the campaign of the Federal Center for Health Education	46
3.2	Visuals from DAH campaigns	48
3.3	Poster fostering gay life in non-urban settings	57
3.4	"He is a son, patient, employee, customer"	57
3.5	"Laughing, loving, fighting"	58
3.6	"Okay: I am gay"	59
3.7	DAH visual addressing the gay leather/fetish scene	61
3.8	Excerpt from DAH brochure	62

Acknowledgments

This book is the outcome of my dissertation project at the University of Leipzig, Germany. The dissertation it is based on would never have been written without the generous support and patience of a number of people to whom I feel tremendous gratitude. Chief among them is my thesis supervisor, Helena Flam, who let me benefit in many ways from her wealth of knowledge while always giving greatest respect to my autonomy. Beyond the immediate work on my dissertation, she gave me numerous opportunities to develop my research, present it to scholarly audiences, publish my ideas and become a part of academic communities.

Second, I am greatly indebted to Eron Witzel who shared his life with me during the dissertation work. I would never have managed to finish it without his love, humor, care and companionship as well as his emotional and material support. He also carefully polished my English.

I would like to thank my parents who, I know, I can always fall back on. It is to them that I would like to dedicate this book.

A number of people have given me invaluable feedback in the course of this project. Donatella della Porta was the second reader at my defense and her insight has helped me improve the manuscript for the publication of this book. Benno Gammerl read the entire manuscript and gave me great advice and fruitful challenges. Deborah Gould helped me improve Chapter 2. Helmut Kuzmics and Charlotte Bloch contributed stimulating ideas to the article on which the methods chapter is based. The same article also benefited from Jack Barbalet's support and the input of two anonymous reviewers of the *Journal for the Theory of Social Behaviour*. I also received stimulating feedback at a colloquium at Ersta Sköndal Högskolan, Stockholm. Finally, several groups of students in seminars at the University of Leipzig, Germany, at Karlstad University, Sweden and at Gothenburg University, Sweden, have helped me reflect my findings and ideas. Finally, I received helpful comments from three anonymous reviewers at Routledge.

Deutsche AIDS Hilfe and Rainer Herrn helped me identify disbanded AIDS organizations and their organizers and shared their impressions of and insights about these organizations. Deutsche AIDS Hilfe and Bundeszentrale für Gesundheitliche Aufklärung also kindly allowed me to use some of their visuals.

My research was kindly supported by a scholarship from the Heinrich Böll Foundation.

My love goes to my friends, especially Robert Prekel and Ruti Ungar. The friendship with Åsa Wettergren, Pia Andersson and Öncel Naldemirci grew while I was working on the manuscript for this book. Peter Mihelj visited me wherever I lived to share his teasing and companionship with me from when I left my small-town roots. The wonderful presence of all of them in my life has sustained me throughout the work on this project and beyond.

But most of all, I owe a huge debt of gratitude to the many civic organizers who trusted me to generously share their stories with me. I hope I have managed to do justice to their experience and wish that this book will help future organizers in their efforts.

J.K.
Florence, December 2016

Chapter 1

Introduction

This study is an exploration into the nature of AIDS (acquired immune deficiency syndrome) organizations as civil society actors. In theoretical terms, it is a critical appraisal of the theories of nonprofit organizations, that provide us with insufficient answers to the question of what nonprofits are as a distinct sociological category. This study therefore aims at contributing to a positive theory of nonprofit organizations. Empirically, for reasons explained below, I will use disbanded AIDS organizations as cases in point. In this introductory chapter I will engage with nonprofit and social movement theories to advance the principal perspective of this book. I will do this in five steps:

1. *Conceptual problems*: definitions of nonprofits/nongovernmental organizations (NGOs)/the third sector only tell us what these are not. Thus they capture a rather heterogeneous range of organizations.
2. *Theoretical problems*: third sector theories are quasi-functionalist and thus hardly compensate for the conceptual problems. They lack grounding in individual action.
3. *Theories of volunteerism* are too rationalistic to fill this gap. Other bodies of research can give fruitful input here:
4. *Related theories*: social movement theorizing provides an expanded scope of analytical tools that allows us to move beyond this rationalistic focus and connect theories of volunteerism with nonprofits.
5. *Power and emotions*: however, movement theories cannot conceptualize other forms of civic action. A power and emotions perspective can serve as an inclusive framework to map different kinds of civic action.

In the next two chapters, I synthesize existing research on AIDS organizations in the US and Germany in order to open up new perspectives on nonprofits. I also describe the history of the field of AIDS organizing, how it emerged and evolved and which discourses were relevant. I will use elements of neo-corporatism, neo-institutionalism and discourse analysis as well as sociological approaches to emotions for this but will not focus on either of these theories.

For the main part, this study starts from the tail end: four case studies of German AIDS organizations that have ceased to exist. How did it come about that key organizers who had once been committed to a cause later disband their organization? While itself an interesting paradox, more importantly, such turning points in the life of an organization can reveal much about the organization beyond the immediate dissolution process—fundamental aspects of organizing, otherwise hidden as routine, everyday social life.[1] In particular, analyses of the conditions underlying members' collective decision to disband sheds light on the specific civic nature of the organizations. As it turns out this decision is often much less a matter of sheer necessity, even though it may appear so, but in fact it rests on contingent social, specifically emotional premises that constitute organizational realities in specific ways.[2] For this reason the empirical part of this study does not analyze the political process affecting the organizations (e.g., the reasons for cuts in subsidies). Rather, taking such contexts as givens, what is of interest here is the question what members of an organization do if, for example, funding decreases, how this matters to them and which consequences they draw or do not draw from it. This will show how they relate to dominant forms of power and how this is in turn mediated by more subtle, discursive-emotional forms of power inscribed into different paradigms of civic action and AIDS discourses which shape their motives for their civic action and its limits.[3]

This study focuses on a specific kind of AIDS organization. Rather than on more radical and also better researched kinds of AIDS organizations (specifically ACT UP; see, for example, Gould 2009), the focus will be on AIDS service organizations (ASOs). These have become predominant at least in the industrialized world where they form an integral element of the public health policies. These can be briefly characterized as NGOs offering services like primary, secondary and/or tertiary prevention via a combination of volunteers and paid professionals (cf. Patton 1990: 12). This paradigm of AIDS organizing has historically evolved from an initially predominant grassroots approach. ASOs differ from their predecessors in that they have typically entered relatively stable relations with state agencies which provide more or less of their resources in exchange for fulfilling defined functions within public health policies. Formally, the focus on service provision, their professionalized, formalized and bureaucratized structure, and their co-operative relation to state agencies sets them apart from other forms of AIDS organizing, like ACT UP, that focus on direct action, grassroots principles, informality and a highly politicized, oppositional stance.

Conceptual problems

Thesis

What are nonprofit organizations as a sociological category? And how does this theoretical concept relate to others in the social sciences? Closer inspection reveals fundamental problems with definitions of nonprofits. They do little more than roughly demarcate what is a diverse field. What is more, the relation with other, related concepts in the social sciences remains insufficiently specified.

NGOs/nonprofits[4]

Despite the less than uniform use of the term NGO—a problem in itself[5]—definitions share as a common denominator the idea that they are organizations which are neither formally part of the state nor of the economic sphere either. The very term *nongovernmental* organization indicates this. The central problem is the negative definitional logic. It only establishes what NGOs are not but says nothing about what they are in positive terms. This problem persists to date. Martens (2002: 282; cf. also, for example, Eliasoph 2013: 96), for instance, defines NGOs as: "formal (professional) independent societal organizations whose primary aim is to promote common goals at the national or international level." To be sure, there have been numerous attempts to differentiate the concept further but none has succeeded in an encompassing, uniform definition (Brand 2000: 21) and none overcomes the negative logic. To date, "the world of NGOs contains a bewildering variety of labels" (Lewis 2010: 1057). What is more, such efforts typically emphasize selected aspects of subgroups of NGOs while either leaving others—or at least some outliers—uncharted (e.g., focus on advocacy in Hirsch 2001) or resulting in rather abstract definitions (such as volunteerism or solidarity as the essential characteristics of NGOs; e.g., Glagow 1993). Others focus on function or structure (e.g., education, advice, representation, etc.) or the role of the state, while still others contrast various grassroots organizations, North vs. South NGOs, etc. (see Brand 2000). These difficulties at establishing valid subcategories point at the problematic consequences of the negative definitional logic, lumping together an otherwise rather heterogeneous range of organizations (see also Lewis 2010: 1058). It seems highly unlikely that any definitional effort will succeed as long as the fundamental negative logic is retained.

The third sector

Definitions of the third sector suffer from essentially identical problems—the negative definitional logic. Thus the third sector is made up of private, non-statutory organizations, whose core objective is not the production of economic benefit for organizational stake holders, but the pursuit of public welfare (e.g., Salamon and Anheier 1996). In fact the definition is so similar that it doesn't require separate discussion. Propositions for a unique logic of the sector—altruism and solidarity (cf., for example, Seibel and Anheier 1990: 12)—remain too vague. However, to add to the conceptual confusion, some distinguish NGOs and (other parts of) the third sector but fail to spell out (satisfying) criteria for such distinctions.[6] Finally, third sector research has drawn attention to the difficulties of contrasting the third sector with the other two sectors, state and economy, as the borders have become increasingly blurry empirically (see, for example, Andrews and Edwards 2004: 484; Ott 2000; Seibel and Anheier 1990: 9; Smith and Lipsky 1993).[7]

Social movements

Strikingly, many authors distinguish NGOs and social movements. But their criteria remain implicit and/or they employ diverse or problematic ones. Typically, they fail to fully acknowledge that organizations are a—more or less—important element of movements in modern social movement theories (see, for example, Della Porta and Diani 2015; McCarthy and Zald 1977; Melucci 1995). In this vein some have contrasted movements with the allegedly more formal, persistent or institutionalized NGOs (e.g., Martens 2002: 281; Take 2002; Wahl 1996), or oppose organizations and movements entirely (see the discussion in Brand 2000: 29)—not valid criteria for movement theorists (see Flam 2002). This also glosses over the possibility of NGOs emerging from non-movement contexts or, where this possibility is acknowledged, non-movement-related NGOs remain unconceptualized (e.g., Roth 2001: 50).

To map civic action inductively

A fundamental reason for these problems is in the genesis of the term NGO. It emerged first as a legal term in UN-contexts and only subsequently turned into a category of social analysis. Social movements, by contrast, have traditionally been analyzed in national contexts. This is to say that the distinction between both has not been introduced within a common theoretical framework but has rather rested on the implicit criterion of geographic scope. Only globalization has brought previously independent scholarly discourses in touch with each other and engendered analyses of NGOs in national/local contexts as well as of transnational social movements. This has raised the issue of how to relate both concepts. Yet attempts at explicating any such distinction are caught up in the formerly separated theorizing and the lack of an encompassing conceptual framework. Thus attempts at developing this distinction tend to assume pre-existing, intuitive and often vague notions of NGOs and social movements as a basis for the selection of empirical cases which are then used to pin down differences. Inevitably, this ends up reproducing implicit preconceptions of both NGOs and social movements. Strikingly, hardly any research tries to identify differences empirically and comparatively in an inductive manner (with the exception perhaps of Eliasoph 1998; or Diani and Bison 2004, discussed below). What is more, reflections about the purposes of (relational) definitions are largely missing. For instance, do we need the distinction to understand different social processes; to explain different causal mechanisms; or to address normative issues of democracy theories? Instead, this is to say, we should develop this difference inductively from empirical cases within a common theoretical framework with a keen eye for the purposes of such an endeavor.

Theoretical problems

Thesis

Third sector theories do little more to help us understand the nature of nonprofit organizations. This is chiefly because of quasi-functionalist arguments and a lacking conception of individual action in such organizations.

Synopsis

Economic theories wonder why *homo oeconomicus* is so seemingly irrational as to set up nonprofits (see the overviews in Hansmann 1987; also James 1989; Ortmann and Brhlikova 2010; Steinberg 2008; Zimmer and Scholz 1992). Their answer to this paradox is, basically, that nonprofits would fill the gaps where other mechanisms (market, state) fail at the provision of certain goods. *Market failure* theorists (Hansmann 1989) focus on goods (e.g., Third World aid) whose quality is difficult to control by the buyer (distant donor). How can the buyer be sure that donations will be used for the specified purposes? Contrasting with businesses, nonprofits would have no incentive to use money for other purposes as, by definition, backed by tax exemption laws, they do not aim at distributing profits to organizational stakeholders—a structural condition for buyers'/donors' trust. Nonprofits would thus be set up to meet the demand for certain goods in a satisfactory way. The theory of *state failure* (Weisbrod 1989; see also Toepler and Anheier 2010) addresses the less than satisfactory state provision of public goods. This is so because democratic, i.e., public-dependent, political actors tend to cater to the average citizen, ignoring other than median interests. Such outlier interests would then be served by nonprofit organizations—their theoretical *raison d'être*. Among political approaches (see also Seibel 2010), the theory of *third-party government* (Salamon 1987, 1996) sees state and nonprofits as interdependent: nonprofits provide decentralized services while the state supplies resources for this. This functions to avoid a number problems of independent service provision by either side—such as insufficiency, amateurishness, etc. of entirely donor-dependent nonprofits—as the state ensures resources, sets priorities, monitors quality, etc. while avoiding the shortcomings of bureaucratic service provision. The theory of *functional dilettantism* (Seibel 1989, 1991; Seibel and Anheier 1990) sees nonprofits as a means of symbolic politics: the state relies on them where social problems (e.g., violence against women or sufficient health care) seem unsolvable within the existing (market economic) social order. This would create the impression of the state taking measures about these problems, while employed nonprofits—structurally problem-ridden or dilettantish, it is argued, as they are—fail to really solve them but instead shield state institutions against damages to their legitimacy.

The need for an actors-based theory of nonprofits

A key point of criticism is the functionalism implicit in the idea that the failure of market or state to produce certain goods will result in the formation of nonprofit organizations. This appears rather automatic, as a theory of why individual actors would set up nonprofits and work or volunteer in them remains wanting, especially given that *homo oeconomicus* will not be able to extract profits from them (Zimmer and Scholz 1992: 33).[8] An adequate theory of individual action in nonprofits is equally wanting in political theories as they effectively explain nonprofits primarily by recourse to the state (Zimmer and Scholz 1992).[9]

We need to base a theory of nonprofit organizations in an adequate conception of individual action. Mere unmet needs fail to account for the existence of nonprofits. This is in fact the foundational insight of all modern social movement theories which have looked for factors mediating between grievances and protest. State policies may certainly play a role, but they too must resonate with nonprofit actors lest we reduce nonprofits to mere appendices of the state.

Theories of volunteerism

Thesis

Theories of volunteerism would seem to fill in this gap. However, their decidedly rationalist bent means that they fail to capture volunteerism's complexity. What is more, they do not account for the organizational aspect of volunteering.

A briefest look at these theories (Musick and Wilson 2008; see also, for example, Anheier and Scherer 2015: 501–3; Smith 1994; Wilson 2000) illustrates a rationalist emphasis on socio-technical aspects: some look at how human capital (education, workload, income) facilitates handling the burdens of volunteer work. Others discuss benefits received in exchange for volunteering. Finally, there is a focus on social capital (networks, family status, social status, etc.) conducive to the production of trust, the spreading of information, the improvement of one's chances of being asked to volunteer and other facilitating conditions.

While they may or may not elucidate conditions of volunteering, little attention is paid to the richness in cultural meaning of, and the emotions involved in, volunteering. Meaningfulness is conceptualized away, for instance, by "explaining" volunteerism with altruistic attitudes and sympathy for a certain cause ("purposive incentive") (Smith 1994: 251), rather than treating altruism and sympathy as something to be explained. Quite general demographic traits are taken as explanations and it thus appears as if people volunteer *because*, for example, they are married, have children, earn a certain amount of income, are employed (part-time) and are white men(!). What is more, the organizational contexts of volunteering are rarely considered (see also Stirling 2007: 10)[10] nor, conversely, how volunteer action constitutes nonprofit organizations. Theories of individual volunteering and of nonprofit organizations have developed, and remain to date, largely independent from each other, which is one reason why third sector theories are insufficiently grounded in a conception of individual actors.

The need for more complex theories

Overall, theories of volunteerism only provide us with the analytical tools to identify socio-technical determinants and demographic correlates of volunteer action. The embeddedness of volunteerism in culture evidenced by a limited and scattered body of research (Eliasoph 1998, 2011; Jakob 1993; Stirling 2007; Wuthnow 1991, 1995; but see also Wilson 2000) therefore falls out of the theoretical picture. These must be included to arrive at an adequate understanding of volunteerism; and this must include a consideration of the link between volunteer action and nonprofit organizing.

Advances: theories of social movements

Thesis

By comparison, social movement research has developed a much broader array of analytical tools and has moved beyond rationalist arguments. Theories of volunteerism have remained surprisingly uninformed by this (see, for example, Musick and Wilson 2008), but can arguably benefit from a theoretical cross-over.

Movement theorizing places a strong focus on social movement organizations, starting out with resource mobilization theories (Edwards and McCarthy 2004; Jenkins 2001; e.g., McCarthy and Zald 1977). Adding to considerations of organizational resources, subsequent theorizing focused on political opportunity structures for and political process contexts of such organizing (e.g., Eisinger 1973; Kitschelt 1986; Kriesi 2004; McAdam 1999; Meyer 2004; Meyer and Minkoff 2004) as well as the strategic construction of mobilizing frames by organizational actors (e.g., Benford and Snow 2000; Snow et al. 1986). There is arguably some potential in applying these principle perspectives to nonprofit, i.e., non-contentious organizations. Incidentally, existing research has pointed at aspects of political opportunity structures for nonprofits such as depoliticizing effects of US tax exemption laws on nonprofits (Clemens 2006) or analyses of engagement politics (Olk et al. 2010). The analysis in Chapters 2 and 3 present aspects of a discourse and emotion-focused version of political process. Comparing AIDS organizations in the US and Germany (Chapter 3) points at the formative significance of different patterns of nonprofit–state relations. Such findings await systematic study and theorizing—something I will not be able to do here. This is because in their emphasis on organizations these movement theories tend to relegate individual activists to a marginal theoretical position. Second, a rationalist (except for framing theory) and strategic conception of social action predominates in these theories. Other social movement theories might thus be better suited to address the outlined problems of nonprofit theorizing.

The collective-identity approach asks how a collective actor/identity constitutes itself in the context of social conflicts. Melucci (1995) conceives this as an interactive process among a multitude of actors in cultural contexts, including as one element social movement organizations. However, this link is not further developed into an organization theory. The process characteristic is crucial here. He emphasizes that this process comprises and connects a diverse range of actors and orientations without entirely leveling such differences. This makes for an inherently dynamic, reflexive and interactively meaning-making conception of social movements. Crucially, this distinguishes the approach from its appropriations into pre-existing, strategic action-based theories. These view collective identity rather as a public good that functions as an incentive for recruitment and/or that is primarily forged by social movement organizations (rather than emerging from larger, informal interaction networks; see, for example, Flesher Fominaya 2010: 396–8; Hunt *et al*. 1994; Snow 2001).

Crucially, this comprises discourses, narrative and emotions. A narrative perspective (see also Daphi 2010: 15–18; e.g., Flam 1998; Nepstad 2001; Polletta 2006) seems particularly adequate to capture the process quality not just of activism but civic identities more generally (Somers 1995). The empirical part of this study will demonstrate that and how three forms of civic action—activism, volunteerism, professionalism—emerge narratively. Given the inherent diversity of any (part of a) collective actor together with notions of narrativity the question arises as to whether collective identity is more of an analytical category than an empirical phenomenon (cf. the discussion in Flesher Fominaya 2010: 399; McDonald 2002; Saunders 2008). For Melucci (1995: 50) collective identity "is not a thing, but a system of relations and representations." What binds people together in social movements and motivates their participation may rather be interlaced representations of emotions, relations and experiences (Flam 1990a, 1990b, 2000: 6). Collective identity theorizing (e.g., Melucci 1995) has acknowledged emotions in principle but has not squarely integrated them (cf., for example, Polletta and Jasper 2001) What is more, much like with the notion of collective identity, there is a tendency to subsume emotions under pre-existing, strategic action-based analytical categories. Limiting emotions to something strategically manipulable (e.g., Jasper 2011) eschews their *sui generis* causal and formative force. It is thus more promising to view collective action as an effort at wrestling with dominant, and pushing for alternative, feeling rules (e.g., Flam 1990a, 2005). The concept of feelings rules, derived as it is from organization research (Hochschild 1979, 1983), would specifically help to integrate the organizational aspect into theorizing.

Although feeling rules may be conveyed in the concrete in and through movements and organizations, they are ultimately embedded in wider cultural contexts (Hochschild 1979, 1983). This alerts us to the interdependent relation between movement organizations and the larger cultural processes that animate both social movements as well as the formation of emotions and identities. This raises the crucial issue, whether nonprofit organizations may be equally informed by, and formative of, cultural processes. From this perspective then, nonprofit organizations would be constituted by cultural processes of meaning construction and emotions and they would in turn feed back into them. Wolfe (2001) provides a useful starting point for this: he views volunteerism as constituted by actors' motives and emotions which are embedded in social contexts of culture (providing meaning systems) and organizations. By extension, we could argue that volunteers and their cultural backgrounds in turn co-constitute nonprofit organizations. Volunteerism and nonprofit organizations mutually constitute each other. Nonprofit *organizing* can be understood as a process through which the shape and content of both concrete instances of volunteer action and of nonprofit organizations as such are being continuously forged.

This notion of a dynamic co-constitution of civic action and civic organizations would transcend the tendency in social movement research of focusing on organizations as the primary loci of agency as criticized above. Importantly, this perspective would also depart from the quasi-functionalism of third sector theories. Nonprofits can be understood through the lens of individual actors embedded into culture and organizations: both nonprofits and volunteerism constitute each other. Social movement theory, where it focuses on cultural dynamics of identity, discourse, emotions, etc., provides valuable tools to analyze this and conceptualize the link between culture, volunteer action and organization. What is more, common analytical tools for movements and nonprofits would open perspectives to inductively distinguish meaningfully social movements from nonprofits through a focus on different identities, meanings and emotions.

Conceptual problems revisited: empowering distinctions

Definitions of social movements might equally help in distinguishing nonprofit organizations. However, as I will argue here, movement theorists do not define social movements in relation to other forms of civic action. A critical appraisal of this can help us outline an integrative analytical framework for such conceptual distinctions.

Synthesizing the major theoretical approaches to social movements, Diani (1992: 13) arrived at the following definition (my emphases): "A social movement is a *network* of informal interactions between a plurality of individuals, groups and/or organizations, engaged in a political or cultural *conflict*, on the basis of a shared *collective identity*" (see also Diani and Bison 2004; Diani and della Porta 1999: 13–20).

I will consider each of these criteria in turn. Diani's notion of *conflict* is rather inclusive, comprising systemic, non-systemic and institutionalized conflicts. Arguably, however, not every political conflict could meaningfully be said to constitute social movements (cf. Burstein 1998). After all, conflict is an essential element of most forms of politics, not all of which can plausibly be referred to as social movements.[11] Also the notion that social movements would pursue such conflict outside established channels of influence (e.g., Eliasoph 2013; Walker 2013) fails to capture many instances of collective action that would be intuitively described as social movements, and indeed Diani (1992) includes institutionalized conflicts.[12] The question thus remains, what kind of conflict would be distinctive of social movements.[13] Second, he essentially makes an argument about size when he talks about interaction *networks*. To be sure it is important to recognize that social movements may extend beyond their organizations (contra resource mobilization theory) (cf. also Walker 2013), but there is no reason why the theoretical concept of social movements should be limited to processes of a certain minimal complexity and scope—and where would that minimum be? Questions of growth and spread, decline, and of degrees of formalization and organizational structure of social movements are theoretical-explanatory rather than conceptual problems (cf. Andrews and Edwards 2004: 485–6). Movements could thus be very small as in turn nonprofits may be based in constituent communities.[14] The argument about *collective identity* (contrasting mere organizational identity; Diani 1992) also relates to that about size, and analogous objections can be made (see also Saunders 2008). More importantly, however, it precludes conceptualizing social movements relative to other forms of civic action: if activism is constituted and driven by collective identity, then what would volunteerism be about? The only answer possible from this perspective is in a negative logic: it would not be based in collective identity. What it would be based in instead, however, cannot be conceived. The notion of collective identity is hence ill-suited to map other forms of collective action.[15]

This has to do with a fundamental premise that has remained largely implicit in pertinent theorizing to date. This is the fact that the classic problem of collective action (Olson 1965) has been constitutive of much modern social movement theories (see, for example, McCarthy and Zald 1977; Melucci 1995). In contrast, volunteerism is generally not understood as collective action. Pertinent theories rather focus on individual acts rather than on why individuals join together (see Musick and Wilson 2008). Yet this glosses over the fact that volunteerism, too, typically operates as collective action, especially in and through (sometimes very large, sometimes networks of) organizations (e.g., Anheier and Scherer 2015).

I want to argue here that an emotion-centered approach allows us to better specify movement-constituting conflicts. And it provides an inclusive frame for mapping different kinds of civic action/organizations.

Ad hoc understandings of social movements highlight protest, resistance and disobedience, etc., that is, the central significance of power. This is why there is ample discourse of liberation in social movement theory. Concepts such as cognitive (McAdam 1999) or emotional liberation (Flam 1993, 2005) refer to people breaking with their compliance in being ruled.[16] Movement-constituting conflicts are then about the refusal to comply with hegemonic power, challenging this power through "deviant" courses of action and about efforts by powerful actors to assert their power. This should not be reduced to formal characteristics of social movements. What is essential are the orientations and motives of the movement, that is whether or not it stops challenging or stops maintaining the orientation to possibly challenge hegemonic power, which could in principle be retained despite episodes of formal co-operation with hegemonic actors.

This leads to the second aspect. Emotions are particularly indicative of how people relate to power. Crucially, emotions are at the basis of all forms of collective action ranging from social movements to corporate action (Flam 1990b, 1990a). Emotions (together with cognitions) are also the basis for structures of hegemonic power and it is through emotional and cognitive liberation that people come to form social movements (Flam 1993, 2005; McAdam 1999), hence, for instance, the prominent, yet not exclusive, role of anger in social movements (e.g., Flam 2004; Jasper 1998). Anger, distrust, disappointment, etc. have a strong potential to propel disengagement with hegemonic power structures and to produce an oppositional, rather than just reformative, stance. This study argues that distinctive sets of emotions are at the basis of different forms of civic action. It is precisely because of these different emotional bases that some forms of civic action take on a non-oppositional character and do not challenge hegemonic power structures. Compassion or pity, for instance, may inspire to help others without challenging power structures. This focus on the broad range of emotions in civic action and their intertwining with dominant power promises a positive theory of volunteer action and nonprofit organizing as distinct from social movements.

Empirical analysis in this study (Chapters 6–9) will focus on the central emotions underlying the engagement of civic actors in disbanded AIDS organizations in order to determine how they related to—challenged or complied with—hegemonic power structures. Three modes of civic actions emerge, each based in different, emotionally mediated relations to power structures. Activism goes farthest in challenging hegemonies as indicated, for instance, through specific forms of solidarity, resentment or anger. Volunteerism was found to be based in feelings such as compassion or pity, and to some extent, pride in enacting a socially valued ideal of the committed citizen. A third type—professionalism—entails pride (professional prestige) along with compassion and rationality. Crucially, respective emotional bases of engagement led civic actors to construct organizational realities in different degrees of politicization. It is crucial, however, to see that emotions only function here as a lens to bring into focus how civic actors relate to power structures. It is this latter aspect that distinguishes modes of civic action. Although there are affinities between certain emotions and modes of civic action, this link should probably not be considered binding. Future research will have to apply and test the typology developed here.

A framework

I have argued here that existing definitions of nonprofits are blurry and that the literature on volunteerism is not very helpful. While definitions of social movements are more developed, movement theorizing fails to propose an inclusive framework that would encompass related concepts like nonprofit organizing and that would avoid a negative logic in characterizing differences between social movement organizations and NGOs. A number of principal premises for a theory of nonprofit organizing emerge from these arguments:

1 *Linking nonprofit organizing and volunteerism*: nonprofit theories need to be based in a notion of individual organizing action.
2 *Beyond rationalist theorizing*: an adequate theory of individual organizers would heed social-cultural complexity. The analytical tools of social movement research—specifically discourses, identities and emotions—go a long way towards filling this gap.
3 *An inclusive framework*: in conceptual respects, nonprofit theorizing needs to start out from an inclusive theoretical framework that allows the inductive specification of different forms of civic action. The relation of civic action to hegemonic power is a central dimension here in order to construct differential categories including social movement and nonprofit organizations.
4 An *emotions perspective* provides both a lens for the analysis of how actors relate to hegemonic power and an inclusive framework within which different forms of civic action can be mapped and characterized in a positive definitional logic.

These premises will be the foundation of the exploration of the civic nature of AIDS organizations advanced in this study. In the following I will provide a brief outline of this book and a description of my empirical investigations.

Structure of the book: on studying disbanded AIDS organizations

The main part of this study analyzes AIDS organizations as civic actors, i.e., as negotiated, processual and constituted by their members, using case studies of four disbanded AIDS organizations in Germany (Chapters 6–9). But before I can turn to this, it is first necessary to contextualize current paradigms of AIDS organizing. What are typical forms of AIDS organizing, how have they emerged and evolved, who are key actors in them? This will produce important findings in itself as it highlights the connections between shifting AIDS discourses, state policies and AIDS organizing within a field perspective as well as the emotional politics embedded in it. Beyond this, however, it will provide the necessary basis and contexts for the empirical analysis of disbanded AIDS organizations and help to link micro-analyses of single AIDS organizations with wider social contexts.

I will first address this by synthesizing research about North American AIDS organizing in Chapter 2. There are a number of reasons for this. The first AIDS organizations emerged in the US and there is a significant scope of available research, which overall provides a fine grained picture of the evolving formation of AIDS organizing. This allows for a synthesis of existing research that opens up initial inroads into a different understanding of nonprofits, responding to the critique of third sector theorizing advanced in this introductory chapter. Thus, American AIDS organizing becomes an orienting point of reference and comparison for analyzing its counterpart in Germany (Chapter 3). Pertinent research on Germany is scant. Though it has generally not squarely focused on AIDS *organizing*, it nevertheless provides pertinent data on organizations. Together with published discourse of German AIDS organizations themselves, it is possible to consider the German case comparatively in light of the key findings from the US. This will be supplemented by visuals produced by AIDS organizations, for example, for their prevention campaigns. Overall, both these chapters establish typical aspects of AIDS organizing as a sound basis for later analyses of dissolution processes.

The synthesis advanced in Chapters 2 and 3 has more than a preparatory function for the empirical case studies. In addressing some of the problems of nonprofit theories it aims at developing central aspects of a political sociology of AIDS organizations. Contrasting third sector theories I will show how AIDS nonprofits—their emergence, development and decline—are instead contingent on evolving dominant AIDS discourses and the emotional climates they constitute. AIDS organizing thus emerges as fundamentally meaningful and emotional. I will also show how AIDS service organizing relates to dominant power processes and in turn constitutes a power structure itself. To this end I will rely on theoretical elements of neo-corporatism, neo-institutionalism, discourse analysis and the sociology of emotions without, however, focusing on just one of them. The comparative perspective will add further nuances to this.

However, while useful for the purposes of highlighting the contingencies and power aspects of nonprofit organizing, neo-corporatism and neo-institutionalism are rather limited with respect to how individual organizers engage in creating, sustaining or disbanding nonprofits—the problem of a micro-foundation of nonprofit theory. How do they relate to dominant discourses, emotional climates and power processes? Chapter 4 will discuss the potentials and limitations of neo-corporatism and neo-institutionalism for nonprofit theorizing and advance an organization theoretical framework—based on sensemaking—that allows to address this question in the empirical case studies.

Given the issues I have raised in this introductory chapter, the empirical part of this study will not be about analyzing overall trends towards dissolution or otherwise within the field of AIDS organizations in Germany. In fact, as Figure 1.1 shows, the field of AIDS organizations in Germany has overall been relatively stable, oscillating around an average of 121 local member organizations of German AIDS Relief. Rather the focus is on single organizations—case studies of four German AIDS organizations that have disbanded. Reconstructing the field of AIDS organizations in Germany helped to structure the empirical research and select organizations (see Appendix 1).

To be able to analyze interviews not only with respect to the meaningful dimension of nonprofit organizing but also its emotional bases, I had to develop a new methodology. Pre-existing methodologies were largely mute on the matter of emotions (but see recently Flam and Kleres 2015). Chapter 5 translates the organization theoretical framework into a suitable methodology relying on narrative analysis but extending it with analytical tools to bring emotions into relief. To this end I developed a narrative notion of emotions. In addition I incorporated linguistic analytical tools.

With these bases, Chapters 6 to 9 present four case studies of dissolved AIDS organizations. A key task here is to identify the (hidden) preconditions and premises that prefigure the quite often seemingly self-evident decision of actors to disband. It is crucial to undo the taken-for-grantedness and seeming inevitablity of this decision. Emotion analysis proves particularly useful in characterizing modes of civic action in positive terms, thus avoiding a negative definitional logic. This allows for the construction of three such modes: activism, volunteerism

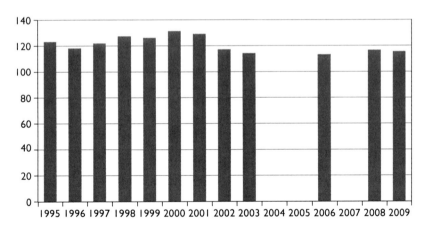

Figure 1.1 Total number of local member organizations of German AIDS Relief.
Source: annual reports of German AIDS Relief.

Notes
There is a peak of 131 in 2000 and a low of 113 in 2006. Available data for 2004, 2005 and 2007 was incomplete and has been omitted. Note that a relative decline need not be due to dissolutions. Some organizations merely left German AIDS Relief but continued to operate independent of it.

and professionalism. Each of these modes—through their emotional bases—entails specific ways of constructing organizational reality. Each of these have specific potentials and limitations for civic action. This becomes clear in the course of organizational dissolution. Finally, Chapter 10 summarizes conclusions for a theory of nonprofit organizations.

Notes

1 Cf. Flam (1998) for a similar research strategy.
2 This also contrasts with the practically context-free automatism that Hirschman (1982) ascribed to demobilization. He rightly pointed out that success or failure of engagement do not in themselves suffice to explain demobilization. But this led him to abandon the issue, focusing instead on how civic actors tend to invest more time than they anticipated which somewhat inevitably leads to frustration and retreat.
3 In this sense I depart from existing research on the dissolution of nonprofit organizations that focuses precisely on lacking financial or social capital, age and size of the organization, etc. as explanations of organizational demise (e.g., Hager *et al.* 1996).
4 I use 'NGO' and 'nonprofit' interchangeably.
5 Complaints about the disparate use of the term NGO recur in the literature (Martens 2002; Roth 2001; Rucht 1996: 31; Windfuhr 1999: 521).
6 Glagow (1993: 305), for instance, separates NGOs from large welfare associations and institutions of cultural life, science and education which are all a part of the third sector. Wahl (1996: 39, 43) distinguishes them from unions and (traditional) associations. Messner (1996: 19) differentiates NGOs from other civil society actors like interest associations. Only Brand (2000: 34) indicates an explicit criterion. His characterization of large associations as "*not necessarily* voluntary" (my emphasis) indicates, however, that this allows at best for a vague distinction. And in the vast majority of cases, membership is in fact voluntary.
7 Nonprofits may carry out state policies and receive government funding or may even have been initiated by state agencies; professionalization may introduce characteristics of business organizations. Together with their empirical heterogeneity this has resulted in a sometimes amusing inflation of sub-categories, like GONGOs (government organized NGOs), GRINGOs (government run/inspired NGOs), QUANGOs (quasi NGOs), PONGOs (profit oriented NGOs), etc. (Take 2002: 39; Windfuhr 1999: 522).
8 This also goes for historical accounts or historically informed theories of nonprofits (Sachße 2000; Salamon and Anheier 1996).
9 The chief exception to be mentioned here are entrepreneur theories of nonprofits. These focus on how organizational entrepreneurs, already equipped with a mission, set out to recruit and mobilize others by, for example, setting selective incentives, being eager to maximize non-monetary returns (see overview in Toepler and Anheier 2010). This puts the formation of organizational causes into a "black box"—the entrepreneur—and can thus reduce mobilization to nonprofits to a mere rational choice.
10 Few other exceptions exist but tend to focus on rather limited aspects, for instance: linking personal importance, prestige or value congruence with volunteer role identity (Grube and Piliavin 2000); general psychological factors like, for example, altruism, excitement about beginning as a volunteer, etc. (Haski-Leventhal and Bargal 2008); informal organizational rules for political conversations (Perrin 2005); different organizational hierarchies between volunteers and professionals (Nadai *et al.* 2005); or the general socializing role of organizations (disciplining, incentive setting, role defining, co-ordinating, etc.) (Wuthnow 1995).

11 Diani (1992) employs here the same reifying empiricist strategy found in other efforts to distinguish nonprofits and social movements: empirical social movements are first identified to be then used for deriving arguments about the nature of social movements. This strategy reifies implicit preconceptions. See also Eliasoph (2013) for a similar operation.
12 Criteria, such as the non-routine qualities of social movement organizations and their operation outside established channels of political influence remain too vague. As metaphors they have some ad hoc plausibility, but they fail to spell out what exactly constitutes non-routine political action outside the established channels. Even institutionalization remains underspecified as Andrews and Edwards (2004: 483) illustrate.
13 Eliasoph (2013: Ch. 2) equally mentions conflicts as a distinguishing mark of activists vs. volunteers, but equally does not specify what kind of political conflicts constitute a social movement. She suggests that naming and constructing an issue as a human-made problem is characteristic of activism. Yet as we will see nonprofits equally involve definitions of social problems as such and as requiring human intervention.
14 AIDS service organizations, often community-based, provide an excellent case in point (e.g., Altman 1994). Second, it is tautological to distinguish movement organizations from other kinds of civic organizations by the connectedness of the former with other social movement organizations (e.g., Diani and Bison 2004) or by their orientation towards "mobilizing movement networks" (Klein *et al.* 2005: 60).
15 The few arguments that squarely address the difference between NGOs and social movement organizations essentially share this problem of operating on a positive definition of social movements with NGOs as a residual, only negatively defined category (e.g., Demirovic 1998; Walk and Brunnengräber 2000: 217).
16 Liberation, however, should not be understood in absolute terms. Activism may in itself operate on the basis of certain power structures while challenging others.

References

Altman, Dennis. 1994. *Power and Community*. London, Bristol: Taylor and Francis.
Andrews, Kenneth T. and Bob Edwards. 2004. "Advocacy Organizations in the US Political Process." *Annual Review of Sociology* 30: 479–506.
Anheier, Helmut K. and Nikolas Scherer. 2015. "Voluntary Actions and Social Movements." Pp. 494–510 in *The Oxford Handbook of Social Movements*, edited by D. Della Porta and M. Diani. Oxford: Oxford University Press.
Benford, Robert D. and David A. Snow. 2000. "Framing Processes and Social Movements: An Overview and Assessment." *Annual Review of Sociology* 26: 611–39.
Brand, Ulrich. 2000. *Nichtregierungsorganisationen, Staat und ökologische Krise: Konturen kritischer NRO-Forschung am Beispiel der biologischen Vielfalt*. Münster: Westphälisches Dampfboot.
Burstein, Paul. 1998. "Interest Organizations, Political Parties, and the Study of Democratic Politics." Pp. 39–56 in *Social Movements and American Political Institutions*, edited by A. N. Costain and A. S. McFarland. Boston, Oxford: Rowman & Littlefield Publishers.
Clemens, Elizabeth S. 2006. "The Constitution of Citizens: Political Theories of Nonprofit Organizations." Pp. 207–20 in *The Nonprofit Sector: A Research Handbook*, edited by W. W. Powell and R. Steinberg. New Haven, London: Yale University Press.
Daphi, Priska. 2010. *The Literature on Social Movements and Collective Identity: A Review*. Berlin: Berlin Graduate School of Social Sciences, Humboldt Universität.

Della Porta, Donatella and Mario Diani, eds. 2015. *The Oxford Handbook of Social Movements*. Oxford: Oxford University Press.
Demirovic, Alex. 1998. "NGOs and Social Movements: A Study in Contrasts." *Capitalism, Nature, Socialism* 9(3): 83–92.
Diani, Mario. 1992. "The Concept of Social Movement." *The Sociological Review* 40(1): 1–25.
Diani, Mario and Ivano Bison. 2004. "Organizations, Coalitions, and Movements." *Theory and Society* 33(3): 281–309.
Diani, Mario and Donatella della Porta. 1999. *Social Movements: An Introduction*. Blackwell Publishers.
Edwards, Bob and John D. McCarthy. 2004. "Resources and Social Movement Mobilization." Pp. 116–52 in *The Blackwell Companion to Social Movements*, edited by D. A. Snow, S. A. Soule and H. Kriesi. Malden, Oxford, Carlton: Blackwell Publishing.
Eisinger, Peter K. 1973. "The Conditions of Protest Behavior in American Cities." *American Political Science Review* 67(1): 11–28.
Eliasoph, Nina. 1998. *Avoiding Politics: How Americans Produce Apathy in Everyday Life*. Cambridge, New York, Melbourne, Madrid: Cambridge University Press.
Eliasoph, Nina. 2011. *Making Volunteers: Civic Life after Welfare's End*. Princeton, Oxford: Princeton University Press.
Eliasoph, Nina. 2013. *The Politics of Volunteering*. Cambridge, Malden: Polity Press.
Flam, Helena. 1990a. "Emotional 'Man': I. The Emotional 'Man' and the Problem of Collective Action." *International Sociology* 5(1): 39–56.
Flam, Helena. 1990b. "Emotional 'Man': II. Corporate Actors as Emotion-Motivated Emotion Managers." *International Sociology* 5(2): 225–34.
Flam, Helena. 1993. "Die Erschaffung und der Verfall oppositioneller Identität." *Forschungsjournal Neue Soziale Bewegungen* 2: 83–97.
Flam, Helena. 1998. *Mosaic of Fear*. Boulder: East European Monographs.
Flam, Helena. 2000. "Soziologie der Emotionen. Struktur—Norm—Individuum." Pp. 285–304 in *Biographische Sozialisation. Der Mensch als soziales und personales Wesen*, edited by E. M. Hörning. Stuttgart: Lucius & Lucius Verlagsgesellschaft.
Flam, Helena. 2002. "National-Global: Zentraleuropa seit 1989." Unpublished presentation at 31st Congress of the German Society of Sociology, Leipzig.
Flam, Helena. 2004. "Anger in Repressive Regimes: A Footnote to Domination and the Arts of Resistance by James Scott." *European Journal of Social Theory* 7(2): 171–88.
Flam, Helena. 2005. "Emotions' Map: A Research Agenda." Pp. 19–40 in *Emotions and Social Movements*, edited by H. Flam and D. King. London, New York: Routledge.
Flam, Helena and Jochen Kleres, eds. 2015. *Methods of Exploring Emotions*. London, New York: Routledge.
Flesher Fominaya, Cristina. 2010. "Collective Identity in Social Movements: Central Concepts and Debates." *Sociology Compass* 4(6): 393–404.
Glagow, Manfred. 1993. "Die Nicht-Regierungsorganisation in der Internationalen Entwicklungszusammenarbeit." Pp. 304–26 in *Handbuch der Dritten Welt. Band 1: Grundprobleme, Theorien, Strategien*, edited by D. Nohlen and F. Nuscheler. Bonn: Verlag J. H. W. Dietz Nachf.
Gould, Deborah. 2009. *Moving Politics: Emotion and ACT UP's Fight against AIDS*. Chicago: University of Chicago Press.
Grube, Jean A. and Jane Allyn Piliavin. 2000. "Role Identity, Organizational Experiences, and Volunteer Performance." *Personality and Social Psychology Bulletin* 26(9): 1108–19.

Hager, Mark, Joseph Galaskiewicz, Wolfgang Bielefeld and Joel Pins. 1996. "Tales from the Grave: Organizations Accounts of Their Own Demise." *American Behavioral Scientist* 39(8): 975–94.

Hansmann, Henry B. 1987. "Economic Theories of Nonprofit Organizations." Pp. 27–42 in *The Nonprofit Sector: A Research Handbook*, edited by W. W. Powell. New Haven: Yale University Press.

Hansmann, Henry B. 1989. "The Role of Nonprofit Enterprise." Pp. 57–84 in *The Economics of Nonprofit Institutions*, edited by S. Rose-Ackerman. New York, Oxford: Oxford University Press.

Haski-Leventhal, Debbie and David Bargal. 2008. "The Volunteer Stages and Transitions Model: Organizational Socialization of Volunteers." *Human Relations* 61(1): 67–102.

Hirsch, Joachim. 2001. "Des Staates neue Kleider. NGOs im Prozess der Internationalisierung des Staates." Pp. 13–43 in *Nichtregierungsorganisationen in der Transformation des Staates*, edited by U. Brand, A. Demirovic, C. Görg and J. Hirsch. Münster: Westphälisches Dampfboot.

Hirschman, Albert O. 1982. *Shifting Involvements*. Princeton, NJ: Princeton University Press.

Hochschild, Arlie R. 1979. "Emotion Work, Feeling Rules, and Social Structure." *American Journal of Sociology* 85(3): 551–75.

Hochschild, Arlie R. 1983. *The Managed Heart: Commercialization of Human Feeling*. Berkeley: University of California Press.

Hunt, Scott A., Robert D. Benford and David A. Snow. 1994. "Identity Fields: Framing Processes and the Social Construction of Movement Identities." Pp. 185–208 in *New Social Movements: From Ideology to Identity*, edited by E. Laraña, H. Johnston and J. R. Gusfield. Philadelphia: Temple University Press.

Jakob, Gisela. 1993. *Zwischen Dienst und Selbstbezug: Eine biographieanalytische Untersuchung ehrenamtlichen Engagements*. Opladen: Leske + Budrich.

James, Estelle. 1989. "Economic Theories of the Nonprofit Sector: A Comparative Perspective." Pp. 21–30 in *The Third Sector. Comparative Studies of Nonprofit Organizations*, edited by W. Seibel and H. K. Anheier. Berlin, New York: Walter de Gruyter.

Jasper, James M. 1998. "The Emotions of Protest: Affective and Reactive Emotions In and around Social Movements." *Sociological Forum* 13(3): 397–424.

Jasper, James M. 2011. "Emotions and Social Movements: Twenty Years of Theory and Research." *Annual Review of Sociology* 37: 285–303.

Jenkins, Craig. 2001. "Social Movements: Resource Mobilization Theory." Pp. 14368–71 in *International Encyclopedia of the Social and Behavioral Sciences*, edited by N. J. Smelser and P. B. Baltes. Oxford: Elsevier.

Kitschelt, Herbert P. 1986. "Political Opportunity Structures and Political Protest: Anti-Nuclear Movements in Four Democracies." *British Journal of Political Sociology* 16: 57–85.

Klein, Ansgar, Heike Walk and Achim Brunnengräber. 2005. "Mobile Herausforderer und alternative Eliten. NGOs als Hoffnungsträger einer demokratischen Globalisierung?" Pp. 10–79 in *NGOs im Prozess der Globalisierung. Mächtige Zwerge—umstrittene Riesen*, edited by A. Brunnengräber, A. Klein and H. Walk. Bonn: Bundeszentrale für politische Bildung.

Kriesi, Hanspeter. 2004. "Political Context and Opportunity." Pp. 67–90 in *The Blackwell Companion to Social Movements*, edited by D. A. Snow, S. A. Soule and H. Kriesi. Malden, Oxford, Carlton: Blackwell Publishing.

Lewis, David. 2010. "Nongovernmental Organizations, Definition and History." Pp. 1056–62 in *International Encyclopedia of Civil Society*, edited by H. K. Anheier and S. Toepler. New York: Springer Publishing.

Martens, Kerstin. 2002. "Mission Impossible? Defining Nongovernmental Organizations." *Voluntas. International Journal of Voluntary and Nonprofit Organizations* 13(3): 271–85.

McAdam, Doug. 1999. *Political Process and the Development of Black Insurgency, 1930–1970*. Chicago, London: University Of Chicago Press.

McCarthy, John D. and Mayer N. Zald. 1977. "Resource Mobilization in Social Movements: A Partial Theory." *American Journal of Sociology* 82(6): 1212–41.

McDonald, Kevin. 2002. "From Solidarity to Fluidarity: Social Movements beyond 'Collective Identity'. The Case of Globalization Conflicts." *Social Movement Studies* 1(2): 109–28.

Melucci, Alberto. 1995. "The Proces of Collective Identity." Pp. 41–63 in *Social Movements and Culture*, edited by H. Johnston and B. Klandermans. Minneapolis, London: University of Minnesota Press, UCL Press.

Messner, Dirk. 1996. "Politik im Wandel. NGOs in der Irrelevanzfalle oder NGOisierung der Weltpolitik." Pp. 39–48 in *Globale Trends und internationale Zivilgesellschaft. Oder: Die NGOisierung der Weltpolitik*, edited by Friedrich-Ebert-Stiftung. Bonn: Friedrich-Ebert-Stiftung.

Meyer, David S. 2004. "Protest and Political Opportunities." *Annual Review of Sociology* 30: 125–45.

Meyer, David S. and Debra C. Minkoff. 2004. "Conceptualizing Political Opportunity." *Social Forces* 82(4): 1457–92.

Musick, Marc A. and John Wilson. 2008. *Volunteers: A Social Profile*. Bloomington, Indianapolis: Indiana University Press.

Nadai, Eva, Peter Sommerfeld, Felix Bühlmann and Barbara Krattiger. 2005. *Fürsorgliche Verstrickung: Soziale Arbeit zwischen Profession und Freiwilligenarbeit*. Wiesbaden: VS Verlag für Sozialwissenschaften.

Nepstad, Sharon Erickson. 2001. "Creating Transnational Solidarity: The Use of Narrative in the U.S.–Central America Peace Movement." *Mobilization: An International Quarterly* 6(1): 21–36.

Olk, Thomas, Ansgar Klein and Birger Hartnuß, eds. 2010. *Engagementpolitik. Die Entwicklung der Zivilgesellschaft als politische Aufgabe*. Wiesbaden: VS Verlag für Sozialwissenschaften.

Olson, Mancur. 1965. *The Logic of Collective Action: Public Goods and the Theory of Groups*. Cambridge, MA, London: Harvard University Press.

Ortmann, Andreas and Petra Brhlikova. 2010. "Theories of Nonprofit Organization, Economic." Pp. 1521–7 in *International Encyclopedia of Civil Society*, edited by H. K. Anheier and S. Toepler. New York: Springer Publishing.

Ott, J. Steven, ed. 2000. *The Nature of the Nonprofit Sector: An Overview*. Boulder: Westview Press.

Patton, Cindy. 1990. *Inventing AIDS*. New York, London: Routledge.

Perrin, Andrew J. 2005. "Political Microcultures: Linking Civic Life and Democratic Discourse." *Social Forces* 84(2): 1049–82.

Polletta, Francesca. 2006. *It Was Like a Fever: Storytelling in Protest and Politics*. Chicago, London: University of Chicago Press.

Polletta, Francesca and James M. Jasper. 2001. "Collective Identity and Social Movements." *Annual Review of Sociology* 27: 283–305.

Roth, Roland. 2001. "NGO und transnationale Bewegungen: Akteure einer 'Weltzivilgesellschaft'?" Pp. 43–63 in *Nichtregierungsorganisationen in der Transformation des Staates*, edited by U. Brand, A. Demirovic, C. Görg and J. Hirsch. Münster: Westphälisches Dampfboot.

Rucht, Dieter. 1996. "Multinationale Bewegungsorganisationen. Bedeutung, Bedingungen, Perspektiven." *Forschungsjournal Neue Soziale Bewegungen* 9(2): 30–41.

Sachße, Christoph. 2000. "Freiwilligenarbeit und private Wohlfahrtskultur in historischer Perspektive." Pp. 75–88 in *Engagierte Bürgerschaft. Traditionen und Perspektiven*, edited by A. Zimmer and S. Nährlich. Opladen: Leske + Budrich.

Salamon, Lester M. 1987. "Partners in Public Service: The Scope and Theory of Government-Nonprofit Relations." Pp. 99–117 in *The Nonprofit Sector: A Research Handbook*, edited by W. W. Powell. New Haven: Yale University Press.

Salamon, Lester M. 1996. "Third Party Government. Ein Beitrag zu einer Theorie der Beziehung zwischen Staat und Nonprofit-Sektor im modernen Wohlfahrtsstaat." Pp. 79–102 in *Wohlfahrtspluralismus: Vom Wohlfahrtsstaat zur Wohlfahrtsgesellschaft*, edited by A. Evers and T. Olk. Opladen: Westdeutscher Verlag.

Salamon, Lester M. and Helmut K. Anheier. 1996. "Social Origins of Civil Society: Explaining the Nonprofit Sector Cross-Nationally." *Voluntas. International Journal of Voluntary and Nonprofit Organizations* 9(3): 213–48.

Saunders, Clare. 2008. "Double-Edged Swords? Collective Identity and Solidarity in the Environment Movement." *The British Journal of Sociology* 59(2): 227–53.

Seibel, Wolfgang. 1989. "The Function of Mellow Weakness: Nonprofit Organizations as Problem Nonsolvers in Germany." Pp. 177–92 in *The Nonprofit Sector in International Perspective: Studies in Comparative Culture and Policy*, edited by E. James. New York, Oxford: Oxford University Press.

Seibel, Wolfgang. 1991. *Der Funktionale Dilettantismus. Zur Politischen Soziologie von Steuerungs- und Kontrollversagen im "Dritten Sektor" zwischen Markt und Staat.* Baden-Baden: Nomos.

Seibel, Wolfgang. 2010. "Theories of Nonprofit Sector, Political." Pp. 1533–7 in *International Encyclopedia of Civil Society*, edited by H. K. Anheier and S. Toepler. New York: Springer Publishing.

Seibel, Wolfgang and Helmut K. Anheier. 1990. "Sociological and Political Science Approaches to the Third Sector." Pp. 7–20 in *The Third Sector: Comparative Studies of Nonprofit Organizations*, edited by W. Seibel and H. K. Anheier. Berlin, New York: Walter de Gruyter.

Smith, David Horton. 1994. "Determinants of Voluntary Association Participation and Volunteering: A Literature Review." *Nonprofit and Voluntary Sector Quarterly* 23(3): 243–63.

Smith, Steven Rathgeb and Michael Lipsky. 1993. *Nonprofits for Hire: The Welfare State in the Age of Contracting*. Cambridge, MA, London: Harvard University Press.

Snow, David A. 2001. "Collective Identity and Expressive Forms." Pp. 2212–19 in *International Encyclopedia of the Social and Behavioral Sciences*, edited by N. J. Smelser and P. B. Baltes. Oxford: Elsevier.

Snow, David A., E. Burke Rochford, Jr., Steven K. Worden and Robert D. Benford. 1986. "Frame Alignment Processes, Micromobilization, and Movement Partipication." *American Sociological Review* 51(4): 464–81.

Somers, Margaret R. 1995. "Narrating and Naturalizing Civil Society and Citizenship Theory: The Place of Political Culture and the Public Sphere." *Sociological Theory* 13(3): 229–74.

Steinberg, Richard. 2008. "Economic Theories of Nonprofit Organizations." Pp. 117–39 in *The Nonprofit Sector: A Research Handbook*, Second Edition, edited by W. W. Powell and R. Steinberg. New Haven: Yale University Press.
Stirling, Christine. 2007. *The Volunteer Citizen, Health Services and Agency: The Identity Work of Australian and New Zealand Ambulance Volunteers.* PhD thesis, University of Tasmania.
Take, Ingo. 2002. *NGOs im Wandel. Von der Graswurzel auf das diplomatische Parkett.* Wiesbaden: Westdeutscher Verlag.
Toepler, Stefan and Helmut K. Anheier. 2010. "Theories of Nonprofit Sector, Economic." Pp. 1527–33 in *International Encyclopedia of Civil Society*, edited by H. K. Anheier and S. Toepler. New York: Springer Publishing.
Wahl, Peter. 1996. "NGOs in der Weltpolitik. Zwischen (Selbst-)Überschätzung und Realismus." Pp. 39–48 in *Globale Trends und internationale Zivilgesellschaft. Oder: Die NGOisierung der Weltpolitik*, edited by Friedrich-Ebert-Stiftung. Bonn: Friedrich-Ebert-Stiftung.
Walk, Heike and Achim Brunnengräber. 2000. *Die Globalisierungswächter. NGOs und ihre transnationalen Netze im Konfliktfeld Klima.* Münster: Westphälisches Dampfboot.
Walker, Edward T. 2013. "Voluntary Associations and Social Movements." Pp. 1385–8 in *The Blackwell Encyclopedia of Social and Political Movements*, edited by D. A. Snow, D. Della Porta, B. Klandermans and D. McAdam. New York: Blackwell.
Weisbrod, Burton A. 1989. "Toward a Theory of the Voluntary Sector in a Three-Sector Economy." Pp. 1–44 in *The Economics of Nonprofit Institutions*. New York, Oxford: Oxford University Press.
Wilson, John. 2000. "Volunteering." *Annual Review of Sociology* 26: 215–40.
Windfuhr, Michael. 1999. "Der Einfluss von NGOs auf die Demokratie." Pp. 520–48 in *Demokratie in Ost und West*, edited by W. Merkel and A. Busch. Frankfurt am Main: Suhrkamp.
Wolfe, Alan. 2001. "What is Altruism?" Pp. 320–30 in *The Nature of the Nonprofit-Sector*, edited by J. S. Ott. Boulder, Oxford: Westview Press.
Wuthnow, Robert. 1991. *Acts of Compassion: Caring for Others and Helping Ourselves.* Princeton: Princeton University Press.
Wuthnow, Robert. 1995. *Learning to Care: Elementary Kindness in an Age of Indifference.* New York, Oxford: Oxford University Press.
Zimmer, Annette and Martina Scholz. 1992. "Ökonomische und politologische Theorieansätze. Der dritte Sektor zwischen Markt und Staat." *Forschungsjournal Neue Soziale Bewegungen* 5(4): 21–39.

Chapter 2

Towards a political sociology of AIDS service organizations

In the following I will tackle some of the issues of nonprofit theorizing raised in the previous chapter on the basis of existing research on AIDS organizing. This research allows us to explore the many ways in which discourses and the emotions inscribed into them have constituted and shaped AIDS organizing. It amply illustrates the meaningful-emotional nature of nonprofit organizing in contrast to the quasi-functionalist failure arguments of third sector theories. Synthesizing existing research also allows us to identify different forms of power running through the field of AIDS organizing as well as different ways in which AIDS organizations relate to these power structures. This results in a general framework which identifies typical pressures, trajectories and transformations, actors and rationales, etc.

Keeping with the overall focus of this study, analysis in this chapter will primarily look at AIDS service organizations (ASOs) as a specific, yet in most industrialized countries predominant, form of civic AIDS organizing. Ad hoc understanding would categorize them as nonprofit organizations rather than social movement organizations, which makes them an interesting case in light of the theoretical issues raised. AIDS service organizations can be characterized by their focus on service delivery (counseling, prevention, medical advice, testing, advocacy, etc.) as well as structurally through their combination of a professionalized staff profile with a volunteer base that links them to a constituent community (Patton 1990: 12). This formal characterization already sets them apart from other forms of AIDS organizing, such as ACT UP, with a focus on direct, political action and grassroots organizing principles. It also sets them apart from their beginnings, which, as for the first AIDS organizations, typically hark back to the gay movement. For the most part I will therefore use the generic term 'AIDS organizing' as a catch-all category to capture these different forms of AIDS organizations and activism. This will bring into focus differences, specifically in how they relate to hegemonic power.

Although more pertinent research is available for the US than for Germany, it is still relatively scattered and fragmented. Some research looks at society-wide trends (e.g., Patton 1990), other work even compares a number of industrialized countries (e.g., Baldwin 2005), including the US, or describes phenomena of a global or transnational scope (e.g., Altman 1994). Next we find studies focusing on different cities and/or social groups (Chambré 2006; e.g., Lune 2007; Stoller 1998), regions or single (sets of) organizations (Cain 1993; e.g., Rosenthal 1996). Together, however, this disparate body of research forms a coherent picture in several respects that allows us to address a number of issues of nonprofit theorizing, even though this picture will have to remain incomplete (e.g., regional and local differences). This lacuna is especially acute as different levels of the state in the federal system of the US responded quite differently. While the federal government, especially under Reagan, was notoriously passive about AIDS, cities like New York or San Francisco, on the other hand, were more active, especially with respect to involving civic AIDS organizations. The literature on AIDS organizing is largely mute on the role of such differences. Whereas some have an explicitly local or regional focus, others simply discuss generically the role of "the state." However, this is less of a problem for considering a number of overarching trends (e.g., professionalization) and specifically we can draw a number of synthesizing conclusions for the evolution of AIDS organizing that bear on the outlined issues of nonprofit theory.

A first premise: the social construction of AIDS

Two premises are fundamental to the development of AIDS organizing: the social construction of AIDS and the historical evolution of public health policies. This section develops the constructionist premise while the next applies it to the emergence of AIDS organizations before I look into the second premise.

Despite the pervasive dominance of a medico-biological view of illness, from a social and cultural point of view, AIDS—and illness more generally—is the product of social constructions rather than an objective given. This aims not at disputing the truth of medico-scientific theories but rather at opening a perspective that brings into focus the complex aspects of AIDS as a social phenomenon—how it is as such constituted through, and how it operates in, society. Susan Sontag (1990 [1977, 1988]) was the first to explore the metaphorical dimension of cancer and later of AIDS. Her aim was to free these diseases of their metaphorical, stigmatizing content and to reduce them to their essence as mere diseases. This ambition was subsequently criticized. As Treichler has argued, the very idea of something being a disease is inherently metaphorical: "illness *is* metaphor" (1988: 34, original emphasis; see also Brandt 1988). In her view, AIDS is the result of necessary sensemaking work, without which there would be no social understanding of AIDS and thus indeed no AIDS *as such*. Crucially, this sensemaking is rather contingent on social conditions. For instance, as she shows, AIDS has been constituted and informed by various other discourses like gender, ethnicity and sexuality. Epstein (1996) has described the contingent social processes involved in establishing the theory of AIDS as a retroviral infectious disease.

Research shows how different ways of constructing the epidemic have specific social consequences. In fact, AIDS discourse has served as a vehicle for calibrating social categories of difference (Pulver 1999). Crucially, AIDS discourses do so by constituting an emotional climate.[1] Discourses define objects, subjectivities, characters and their relations in the AIDS narrative and thus calibrate how one can or indeed does feel about it. A few selective points will have to suffice here. Fear is arguably central as AIDS has overall operated as a dreaded and stigmatized disease (Bleibtreu-Ehrenberg 1989; Doka 1997; Sontag 1990; see also Treichler 1988). In many ways, this extends beyond the fear of death. AIDS-related fears have been greatly magnified by the discursive equation of HIV with death (the terror of an inevitable, difficult, dehumanizing death) and the contrasting of HIV/AIDS with life and hope (Jones 1992: 442; Sontag 1990: 112, 126; Wießner 2003: 57). Another key feature is the construction of social others (othering): by constructing AIDS in terms of already marginalized social groups (gays, drug users, etc.) or distant global regions and the ethnicities they symbolize (e.g., the "dark"(!) continent Africa) AIDS discourse constitutes them as "others" to a moral majority, which reassures itself this way of its supremacy (see, for example, Devine *et al.* 1999; Gilman 1988a, 1988b; Jones 1992; Patton 1990, 2002; Sontag 1990; Treichler 1988; Weingart 2002; Wießner 2003). This othering has cast AIDS as an outside—physical and moral—threat to the collective body (Jones 1992: 442; Weingart 2002: 31; Wießner 2003). Fears of these—deviant/othered—groups have been attached to AIDS, and AIDS in turn—though not invariably—has increased the fears and stigmatization of these groups at least for certain periods (Devine *et al.* 1999: 1213; Weingart 2002: 24; Wießner 2003). The image of AIDS as a polluting invasion (Sontag 1990: 134) has also attributed fault, guilt and shame to the polluter and conversely assumes that polluting people are in turn wrong (Sontag 1990: 136). Guilt and shame are further induced, as AIDS is "linked to an imputation of guilt" (Sontag 1990: 112–13; Devine *et al.* 1999: 1218; Jones 1992; Wießner 2003: 35, 47, 51): infection is readily explained in common view through group identity and concomitant deviant behaviors, casting AIDS as the tangible sign of intrinsic sickness (Weingart 2002: 58).

What is crucial for the present purpose is that these discourses and their emotional climates equally shape forms of social responses to AIDS. This is evident as hegemonic AIDS discourse has historically changed over time. This chapter will thus show how AIDS organizing—its emergence and ongoing evolution—has been intimately intertwined with the tides of AIDS discourse. AIDS discourse constitutes and shapes AIDS organizing, which in turn buttresses, or challenges, specific understandings of AIDS.

The (non-)emergence of AIDS organizations

The first AIDS organizations in the US emerged from the gay movement/community and later evolved into what has since become the dominant paradigm of AIDS organizing. This simple fact of the gay roots of AIDS organizing may seem all too self-evident. However, it rested to a considerable extent on hegemonic AIDS discourse, which equated AIDS with being gay.

AIDS emerged in dominant discourse first as a gay disease. This in turn rendered it a threat to gay communities (resonating, as it later did, with the high incidence of infection and death among gays). Experience of neglect by government and other dominant social institutions, framed by the gay community as homophobia (Gould 2009: 57; Kayal 1993: 5–7), both reflected and amplified the sentiment of a community under siege. This included, for instance, proposals for coercive public health measures or cutting research funds. Lune (2007: 25–8) describes how the federal government's inaction continued for the first 12 years of the epidemic between Reagan and Bush. Recommendations of presidential advisory committees were routinely ignored, such as calls for supporting community organizations, for federal leadership or for adequate funding. Given the construction of AIDS as a gay disease and the meanings this bestowed on government policies it is thus not coincidental that early AIDS organizing formed along lines of gay sexual identity. The very name of the first formal AIDS organization is indicative of this: Gay Men's Health Crisis (GMHC)—established in January 1982 in New York City (e.g., Chambré 2006: 15; see also Kayal 1993; Lune 2007). Set up by a group of gay men, it grew to epitomize the gay community: "Until 1988, AIDS, GMHC, and the gay community had been coterminous with each other. […] For a time, it seemed that to be identifiably gay in New York meant to be affiliated with GMHC" (Kayal 1993: 3; cf. Lune 2007: 8).

Just as fundamental as the high death toll of AIDS in gay communities, AIDS discourse, the construction of AIDS as gay, thus formed one of the most basic conditions for mobilization. From the start, this construct had been but a contingency: before it drew medical attention, street vernacular had already coined the term "junky pneumonia" for what came to be known as AIDS. Only after it began affecting otherwise healthy young gay men—rather than junkies, a group seen as intrinsically sick and doomed to die—did it come into focus and the construction of AIDS began along perceived epidemiological lines of sexuality (Chambré 2006: 75; Crimp 1988: 249; Patton 1990: 27–8).[2] This highlights the possibility of alternative forms of organizing, for instance, involving alliances with other marginalized groups or organizing just for everybody. However, this would have been predicated on a more inclusive construction of AIDS.[3] Rather, because of the more exclusive understanding, AIDS came to be experienced at a gay community level as a shared threat necessitating a collective gay response. What is more, it also gave significance to state inaction: while "state failure" to address the issues of AIDS (see above) was evidently a factor in the early AIDS mobilizing (Gould 2009: 57; Kayal 1993; e.g., Lune 2007) this gained mobilizing force only within a frame of AIDS as a gay disease. Far from the quasi-functionalist automatism suggested by nonprofit theory, "state failure" is not sufficient. "State failure" has to be made an issue, amplified by discourses and their social resonance.

Examples where discursive links between group identities and HIV/AIDS were missing further buttress this argument. In these cases, AIDS organizing had tremendous difficulties in taking off. For instance, Stoller (1998: 9–32) provides a startling account of how women with HIV/AIDS in the early phases of the epidemic tried to gain access to AIDS organizations and their services to no avail. The initial AIDS construct, informed as it was by sexist and homophobic discourses (e.g., Treichler 1988), did not allow for the very thought that women might be affected by HIV and AIDS. Their asking for help was literally incomprehensible.

Constructions of who is affected by HIV and AIDS also impeded AIDS organizing among/for Asian Americans: writing about San Francisco, Stoller (1998: 63–79) relates this to discourses on AIDS as a white, gay disease and concomitantly a myth of Asians' immunity to AIDS. These were in turn based on racist notions of a "model minority," whose members, by implication, would not engage in seedy practices. AIDS organizing only took off when the weight of scientific studies worked to refute such notions of immunity.

Chambré (2006: 73–91) describes how the construction of AIDS as a gay disease, as a sexually transmitted disease, and later as related to intravenous drug use, hampered AIDS organizing among/for African Americans and Hispanics in New York City. Ethnic organizing around AIDS would have inscribed the discursive luggage of AIDS and its emotional climate onto already stigmatized ethnic identities, e.g., in terms of deviant sexualities or drug use; and given the construction of AIDS as a sexually transmitted disease, it would have amplified the pre-existing image of hypersexuality that racist discourse has ascribed to blacks (Baldwin 2005: 198; Cohen 1996). Racist discourses on alleged black/African sexualities loom large in the context of AIDS on a much broader, global level (e.g., Packard and Epstein 1992; Patton 2002; Treichler 1992). It was also for such larger discursive contexts that messages of African Americans being at risk failed to resonate with ethnic minorities as AIDS discourse operated on a linking of AIDS with black people and Africa (Chambré 2006: 81).[4] Arguably then, ethnic minorities navigated the emotional climate of AIDS discourses—the attribution of shame and guilt—in their shying away from AIDS organizing.

But this leaves a crucial question unanswered: why was the inscription of risk and AIDS into gay identities relatively unproblematic while being resisted by ethnic minorities? Some (e.g., Chambré 2006; Stoller 1998) would explain this by referring to certain traits of these ethnic minorities, such as homophobia, machismo, strong religiosity, traditions or the value of family—factors that all attribute blame for failing to mobilize to the ethnic groups themselves (cf. Flam and Kleres 2016). However, (white) gays in principle also had to organize in the context of homophobia, patriarchal structures, a predominantly Christian culture and adverse middle-class moral values. An alternative view refers to the fact that the meaning of AIDS—a collective crisis or otherwise—has been quite different in gay than in ethnic communities (Baldwin 2005: 198–9; cf. also Cohen 1997; Rofes 1998: 85–8). For white, middle-class gay men living in an urban center AIDS appeared as the single most central social problem they were facing as a collective—simply because there were no other social problems of a similarly devastating magnitude. In contrast, some ethnic minorities in the US have already suffered collectively from a range of severe social problems, like unemployment, poverty, drugs, criminality, lack of health care, etc. In this context, AIDS does not appear as the single threat to the community but rather as only another one of many social ills.

In sum, then, a crucial condition for AIDS organizing can be found in the specific ways in which AIDS is inscribed into identities by dominant AIDS discourses and in the ways minorities navigate the emotional climate of AIDS discourse. This spurred activism in the case of gays, but failed to have the same effect on ethnic minorities. In the case of women, the non-inscription of AIDS entailed the initial insensitivity to their AIDS-related needs.

These findings form a stark contrast to third sector theories. These theories predict the emergence of nonprofit organization wherever social needs are unmet by either the state or the market. While this has some analytical purchase in the case of gay AIDS organizing, as indeed state failure was a key context for it, analysis in this section has demonstrated in many ways the fundamental contingency of nonprofit organizing in situations of system failures: it matters quite fundamentally how social problems are constructed and how these constructs reverberate in the life-worlds of actual people. Clearly, there is no automatic link between an unmet need for social services and the emergence of nonprofits.

What is more, even where a perception of state failure plays a role among nonprofit organizers, specific organizational responses may vary. Gay AIDS organizing neatly illustrates this: where GMHC came to opt for a politically limited approach focusing mainly on service provision, perceptions of "government failure" later inspired angered, radical AIDS activism in the form of ACT UP (Gould 2009). Contingent social conditions thus mediate the specific nonprofit/activist response to unmet needs—some of which will be explored later in this chapter.

A second premise: the evolution of public health

A second fundamental precondition for AIDS organizing is the evolution of public health, that is, longer historical lines predating the AIDS epidemic. This involved intertwined discourses on disease and health—the parallel evolution of dominant conceptions of disease and public health policies (Baldwin 2005: 11–19; see also Lupton 1995: 16–47). Historically there have been three alternate notions of disease—contagion through an infectious agent; unhealthy environments; and personal dispositions. These correspond to three paradigms of public health: interrupting transmission of contagious agents (quarantinism); improving noxious environments (sanitationism); and finally, encouraging healthy habits in individuals and discouraging unhealthy ones. Baldwin (2005) describes the history of public health in these terms. Crucial shifts set in early in the twentieth century—after the Middle Ages' quarantinism and nineteenth-century sanitationism—when the discovery of bacteria heralded yet another policy change towards avoiding exposure to microbes. This set the stage for modern public health. It entailed an individualization of public health as the new scientific knowledge made individual hygiene focal. This involved abandoning coercive means of quarantinism in favor of strategies of mass persuasion and education—health education, promotion of domestic hygiene, etc. Epidemiological shifts further contributed to this individualization: successes of public health policies and medical progress made infectious diseases increasingly unproblematic, leaving chronic and lifestyle diseases as unresolved public health issues (Baldwin 2005: 16). These added additional weight to the significance of individual behavior and personal responsibility, as medical knowledge attributed diseases such as obesity, heart disease or some cancers to poor diet, tobacco use, alcohol consumption, insufficient physical exercise, etc. Voluntary individual behavior changes became focal to public health.

What appeared to be a loosening of (coercive) social controls in fact relied on their internalization by moralizing health. Desirable health behavior became linked to a democratic ethos of good citizenship as a signifier of being a good burgher: "Sneezing and suffrage were linked" (Baldwin 2005: 15). There has been an ongoing process of moralization of health, with health increasingly taking on moral valence and replacing other forms of morality as regulators and signifiers of the good life (Crawford 1994; e.g., Lupton 1995; Petersen and Lupton 1997).

> Voluntarily adopted by citizens rather than imposed on subjects, it [social control] remained as strong as ever. Indeed the behavioral precepts of modern life were arguably stricter than before. The new individualized approach, with its emphasis on wholesome habits, has been caricatured as the reign of the monogamous jogger or, most extremely, dismissed as 'health fascism.' Such an individualized strategy, it is argued, ignores how any given choice [over health related behaviors] springs from broader social forces.
>
> (Baldwin 2005: 16)

These trends and transformations converged in the public health paradigm known as new public health. Instead of coercive means of health promotion it fosters voluntary behavior changes. Most importantly for the present purposes, a key element is to rely on civil society as a partner for promoting public health. By the time AIDS emerged, public health had taken on a particular shape characterized by moralization, individualization and voluntarism. In this way, the stage was set for developing responses to AIDS. To be sure, the move to new public health was nevertheless far from straightforward in the context of AIDS. Though fallen into disuse, old public health measures were still codified in laws. AIDS let the illusion of victory over infectious diseases collapse. In this context, the question re-emerged as to whether old public health measures needed to be applied to the AIDS epidemic—a question that was to be decided politically, "once the nature of the disease was better understood, once powerful groups of its initial victims organized in defense of their rights, and once the public health sector considered its options" (Baldwin 2005: 48).

Queer corporatism[5]

Political responses to AIDS varied over time. Fundamental to these changes were transformations of the dominant conceptions of AIDS (Baldwin 2005: 27–32): the latter shifted from gay disease (hence the early name GRID—Gay Related Immune Deficiency—in use before the name AIDS was conventionalized in 1982); to a disease of certain risk-groups;[6] to infectious disease spreading outside of risk groups; to a phase of normalization (Rofes 1998; Rosenbrock *et al.* 1999), where AIDS came to be seen as a chronic, manageable disease[7] and, again, as a disease of the marginalized. The political response evolved in parallel. The "minority disease" construct made it initially possible to neglect it more or less. Coercive measures were discussed and to a limited extend implemented (Baldwin 2005: 51–98). Only in the mid-1980s did the idea become dominant that AIDS spreads outside so-called risk-groups. This was the point when new public health became implemented on a larger scale within AIDS policies.

For AIDS organizations this was the decisive turning point as they now became integrated into public policy. Before, they had existed largely independent from and to a certain extent in opposition to the state. As the generalized conception of AIDS became dominant in society, symbolized by the death of Rock Hudson, powerful social strata now placed demands on the state for action and expertise. At that point, existing AIDS organizations already were in place as relatively exclusive carriers of (social) expertise and as potential carriers of prevention and so they now began to receive increasing amounts of public subsidies (Patton 1990). This is the beginning of the political inclusion of AIDS organizations. This pivotal moment for AIDS organizations entailed their growth, spread and their specific further evolution. A transformation of dominant AIDS discourses initiated changes in public policy and thus affected political opportunity structures for AIDS organizing which pre-existing AIDS organizations, by and large, were eager to capitalize on.

The transformations of AIDS discourse and the concomitant political inclusion of gay AIDS organizations can be understood as a change in the emotional climate around AIDS: constructing AIDS in othering terms—equating it with marginalized groups—has essentially been a project of mainstream society to manage fears of AIDS. If AIDS is only a disease of "the others," the "normal" can deem themselves safe. Together with attributions of blame and guilt inherent in this discourse, this allowed for a politics of relative ignorance regarding AIDS. These all too neat separations crumbled in the mid-1980s as the notion of AIDS as a general, infectious disease widely took hold. AIDS-related fears could no longer be purged from mainstream society. Reconstructed as an epidemiological "vector" or source, the so-called risk-groups now posed an acute threat to dominant social groups both in terms of physical and moral contagion. The political inclusion of AIDS organizations was thus fundamentally motivated by fear. By helping so-called risk-groups prevent the spread of HIV powerful social strata essentially engaged in another strategy of fear management: containment, the channeling of the threat posed by others away from themselves (Barbalet 1998: 159–60). Essentially, containment is a conservative move aiming at maintaining a status quo. This also goes for the political inclusion of AIDS organizing as will become clear if we take a more detailed look at the workings of this inclusion.

Neo-corporatist theory is particularly helpful in bringing into relief the minute terms of this inclusion and the forms of power operating in it. Neo-corporatism can briefly be described as a system of interest mediation where strong more or less centralized associations are granted privileged participation in the political process and/or monopolize interest representation (e.g., Czada 1998; see Chapter 4). They negotiate the specific shape of policies with each other or with the state (Lehmbruch 1979a: 54, 1979b: 150).

In the case of AIDS, negotiations concerned the political response to the epidemic. At stake was the use of new vs. old public health strategies. A number of pragmatic arguments were employed in favor of new public health, including, for instance, the danger of driving affected communities underground, their alienation from and hence unreachability by state institutions, the lack of state expertise about gay life-worlds etc. (Baldwin 2005: 125–34).[8]

More tacitly, however, the meaning of AIDS was also at stake. Different approaches to AIDS organizing—each premised on a specific understanding of the disease—had existed in the US when state agencies began to look for civic partners, so that, in selecting these, state institutions gave preference to and fostered very specific forms of AIDS organizing and ways of understanding AIDS while excluding others (Patton 1990: 5–23): for instance, African American communities initially included AIDS to some extent into pre-existing social organizations. This was premised on the conception of AIDS as only one part of a complex set of racist and other conditions. They thus preferred a full-plate approach, addressing a range of social problems, which would aim at social-political change based on a political analysis. Crucially, however, state funding contributed to the legitimacy, growth and spread of gay organizations. This helped establish a specific form of AIDS organizing as paradigmatic and concomitantly a relatively depoliticized, unchallenging conception of AIDS: gay organizations assumed individual behavior to be the focal problem based on the medical conception of AIDS. They preferred this understanding—among other reasons—for the morally neutralizing effects against the additional stigmatization of their lives through a disease constructed as a (gay) sexually transmitted disease (Baldwin 2005: 191; Patton 1990). It was thus a way of navigating the shaming aspects of AIDS discourse. The conservative aspect of fear-driven containment policies is particularly tangible here.

Neo-corporatist negotiations operate as bargain exchanges. One fundamental element of this is the abdication of the state from any direct and independent regulation of a policy area, which nevertheless remains a principle possibility throughout (Streeck and Schmitter 1985: 19–20). This functions as a "whip in the window" (Schmitter 1984: 16) as neo-corporatism aims at having social groups behave out of self-interest/in self-regulation in accordance with public interest. From this perspective, it emerges as a pivotal condition for AIDS organizing that coercive public health measures have variously remained a legal and political possibility. The political inclusion of AIDS organizations has thus been contingent on successful changes in group customs and on slowing the spread of HIV. Condoms became a precondition of freedom (Baldwin 2005: 129). However, not only the state has a whip. Neo-corporatism rests on the shared realization of interdependence (Lehmbruch 1984: 67). In the case of AIDS, this realization, as we have seen, was contingent on a shift in the dominant meaning of AIDS, when mainstream society realized it might be at risk of infection as well. AIDS-ridden gay communities were now not only a threat but also a *sine qua non* in the effort to contain HIV—there was a realization at the time that limiting the spread of HIV would not function without the co-operation of those viewed as its epidemiological source; that coercive means would not only be ineffective but also counter-productive (Baldwin 2005; Patton 1990). Arguably, then, a climate of mutual fear has been the driving force behind the neo-corporatist inclusion of AIDS organizations: fear of AIDS-ridden gay communities and their potential to spread HIV into the straight world, backed by credible arguments that coercive means would not be effective, as well as fear of state interventions, possibly including those very coercive means.

Neo-corporatism makes another argument that is helpful here. This is the idea of associations functioning as "private interest governments" (Streeck and Schmitter 1985): they play an active and instrumental role in ensuring that their constituencies abide by the terms of the deal with the state. They function as producers of group interests and identities. Indeed, a transformation of gay identity itself was at stake with the political inclusion of AIDS organizations (Baldwin 2005: 189–96; Padgug and Oppenheimer 1992: 261–3): the gay movement had rendered gay sex more than just sex by attaching to it a transgressive quality, a difference beyond the mere object of desire. This gave a heightened meaning to such things as promiscuity, anal sex, bathrooms, public backrooms, saunas, parks, etc.:

> Implicitly, gays were being asked to rein in their animal spirits in return for a consensual preventive approach. [...] At the moment of their incipient incorporation into mainstream society, gays were asked to make the choice that had been posed to all citizens with the start of democratic politics: be healthy or be a pariah. [...] For many gays, epidemiologically bad habits were also civil and personal liberties. For others, such change was worth the price of full membership in the larger community.
> (Baldwin 2005: 195–6)

AIDS organizations were the social sites where the specifics and extents of such transformations of gay identity were internally negotiated and spread to gay communities. That is to say, the prevention work of publicly funded AIDS organizations was not only about implanting new norms of sexual conduct in communities, but also about promoting a transformation of gay identity.

Professionalization and its discontents

Evolving state relations entailed fundamental changes in the enrolled AIDS organizations. Initially, they had a decidedly informal, egalitarian grassroots structure and empowerment orientation owing to their roots in the gay movement. This began to give way to an increasingly formal, hierarchical internal structure based on an internal functional differentiation of the roles of professionals, volunteers and clients (Cain 1993; MacLachlan 1992; Patton 1990). The process was tantamount to a re-distribution of power within AIDS organizations: informal egalitarian structures meant that *in principle* ownership of the organization resided with all members and with the constituent communities at large. This ownership was now increasingly transferred to organizational elites; and where all members had had the ability to speak for themselves, rank-and-file interests were now represented only vicariously by organizational elites (MacLachlan 1992). This allowed for in part new considerations to seep into decision making processes, such as organizational concerns or professional aspirations. This had effects, for instance, on the interpretation of experience of people with HIV/AIDS, the definition of needs and identities of clients, the access to information for rank-and-file members, the selection and design of services offered, the representation of people with HIV/AIDS, available forums for debate and the access to policy making (MacLachlan 1992). While this certainly did not eliminate the possibility for clients and rank-and-file members to speak for themselves, it did curb the practical import of their deliberations.

How can we account for this transformation? Arguably, there is more to it than Michelsian iron-law-automatism (as argued by, for example, Altman 1994; Stoller 1998). Empirical case studies have described professionalization as deliberately pursued by organizational elites and thus focused on their legitimizing rationales. In one study (Cain 1993), these legitimations included a perceived pressure to be accountable (despite only loosely defined state stipulations); the goal of service reliability, credibility and viability; keen concerns about the public image and respectability; and staff preferences for a professional work life. In another study (Rosenthal 1996) similar legitimations referred to an effort to secure private funding and hence to appeal to mainstream society. In both cases this resulted in a de-gaying of the organizations (cf. Cain 1994). Crucially, it also meant that opposing stakeholders—people with HIV/AIDS, gays and lesbians and more politically minded issue-activists—were marginalized in the process. Effectively, this loosened ties with constituent communities and restructured organizations into professional service agencies.

It is important to note the socially constructed nature of these legitimations. Significantly, both studies list examples where perceived external demands were in fact not backed by, and were even contradictory to, external actors. Public agencies had sometimes explicit preferences for greater representation of people with HIV/AIDS in the organization, where these were instead marginalized. This raises the question of pervasive cultural underpinnings that animated legitimations and made them powerful. As both studies (Cain 1993; Rosenthal 1996) point out, this had to do with the increasing dominance of the notion that HIV infection was a medical condition not restricted to gay men instead of a social problem impacting gay communities: this notion increased the weight of medical-professional vis-à-vis other forms of expertise. It also allowed for a re-orientation for appealing to mainstream society rather than specific communities. Professionalization involved the marginalization of opposing stakeholders and with them other conceptions of AIDS and their related forms of expertise, authority and organizing. This also had disempowering effects on the affected constituents (Cain 1993, 1994, 2001; MacLachlan 1992).

We can conclude that professionalized AIDS organizations are sites that are not only premised on specific meanings of AIDS, but, again, where those meanings (and their organizational cognates) are made hegemonic for constituent communities. By having fundamental consequences for how clients' experience, needs and interests would be interpreted, professionalization contributed to establishing the individualizing, relatively apolitical medical understanding of HIV/AIDS that it was itself premised on. This is much in line with the notion of private interest government and the organizational constitution of identities and interests.

Power in the field: the field of AIDS organizing

Another approach to organizations, neo-institutionalism, helps to analyze other dynamics. It looks at how institutionalized, legitimized, that is, taken-for-granted knowledge shapes organizations (see Chapter 4). For now, I would like to focus on one specific aspect. This concerns the fact that institutionalization occurs in organizational fields. As they evolved, AIDS organizations too came to constitute fields, that is together with other relevant actors "a recognized area of institutional life" structured by increased interaction, patterns of coalition and domination, increased information load and mutual awareness among involved actors (DiMaggio and Powell 1991: 64–5). Organizational fields come with strong conceptions of legitimate ways of organizing, leading to increasing resemblance among organizations within the field—what neo-institutionalism calls isomorphism (DiMaggio and Powell 1991). This became a crucial condition for their further development and for future AIDS organizations and helps me highlight aspects of organizational diffusion and power relations

Lune (2007) studied the process of field-formation in New York City. In a context of fundamental uncertainty and lack of knowledge on what was emerging as AIDS, the field of AIDS organizing first had to be innovated (Lune 2007:

42; see also Chambré 1996; Patton 2002: Ch. 1). Early organizers first had to establish AIDS as a recognizable, valid and legitimate social problem (Lune 2007: 42). What is more, state agencies and other social organizations largely neglected the social issues of AIDS (Perrow and Guillén 1990). Thus AIDS activism initially emerged in something of a vacuum allowing for degrees of organizational innovation. Gay Men's Health Crisis (GMHC) became emblematic of this. It soon left its street identity behind and developed an organizational service provision model, where AIDS is no longer seen as a political issue, but rather as a health issue to be addressed by professionals. Professionals, together with volunteers and clients made up the internal role structure (Patton 1990). Field formation thus entailed not only the emergence of specific roles and identities but established these as paradigmatic. AIDS work and AIDS organizing became institutionalized in that there were established ways of thinking and talking about AIDS, organizing around it and addressing the issues it raised through specific forms of AIDS work (Lune 2007: 47–8). As the field took shape as such, these social responses to AIDS became the legitimate ways of dealing with AIDS.

While early AIDS organizations, as innovators in marginal positions, had a certain amount of freedom in establishing what came to be legitimate forms of AIDS work, this legitimacy was a pre-given condition for any subsequent effort at AIDS organizing. Neo-institutionalism analyzes this as isomorphism, the convergence of organizations in a field towards similar organizational forms. This occurs through three mechanisms (DiMaggio and Powell 1991): professional organizers, through their training, have similar *normative* ideas of how to organize; organizations emulate other organizations seen as successful (*mimetic isomorphism*); finally, the state may exert *coercive* pressures to adopt specific organizational paradigms. This was also evident among AIDS organizations. In New York, professionals involved in AIDS organizing for ethnic minorities had often worked earlier for organizations like GMHC, bringing with them the paradigms of AIDS organizing to new organizations (Lune 2007: 78). At other times emerging, marginal AIDS organizations managed to associate themselves with, and emulate, established, professional ones, thus capitalizing on their legitimacy: this way, burgeoning ethnic minority AIDS organizations in New York managed to gain access to state and city administrations and receive funding (Chambré 2006: 85; Lune 2007: 72). An emerging organization for drug users in New York also explicitly modeled itself on GMHC (Chambré 2006: 85). The State of New York also molded the field through the AIDS Institute which functioned as a public funding agency. Through funding requirements and political oversight it promoted the bureaucratized GMHC model (Chambré 1995, 1996; Lune 2007: 72; Rosenthal 1996).

The formation of a field of AIDS organizing meant that specific forms of AIDS organizations—i.e., ways of talking and thinking about AIDS issues— became institutionalized, that is, as the taken-for-granted ways of doing AIDS work. This became an unavoidable context for subsequent organizations where pioneering organizations developed with some liberty. In this sense, the field of AIDS work operated as a power structure, promoting specific organizational forms, approaches and understandings of AIDS. Organizational fields can thus be understood as an enforced vehicle for establishing and retaining specific AIDS constructs.

In terms of nonprofit theorizing, fields constitute a specific opportunity structure, but also a constraint, for new organizational efforts. We have already seen how the institutionalization of gay AIDS organizations through state policy inclusion worked to the detriment of different paradigms of AIDS organizing in ethnic minorities (see section on Queer corporatism). Failure theories fall short of capturing the contingencies constituted by field dynamics. A field perspective can also help explain to some extent the shape and approach of organizational newcomers where failure theories could do little more than predict a generic nonprofit nature of emerging organizations. Also, AIDS organizations emerge from this perspective as structured by powerful meaning systems—an aspect that is equally missed by dominant nonprofit theories that make a simple link between needs and nonprofit emergence.

AIDS service organizations as political and discursive agents

The perspective on AIDS service organizations developed thus far needs to be amended in two ways: empirical research into AIDS professionalism adds a more nuanced view to the critique of professionalism as disempowering and depoliticizing. Second, AIDS organizations may assume degrees of discursive agency as creative agents in the field rather than passive recipients of AIDS discourse.

Empirical research on the distinctive characteristics of professionalism in AIDS work has advanced interesting arguments about the significant role of collective identities in it. Deverell (1997, 2001), for instance, argued that AIDS workers often share the collective identity of their clients (e.g., as gay men). This would secure clients' trust in the professional—a constitutive element of the professional relationship in general. The necessity for trust in the professional relation stems from the fact that clients cannot evaluate professional services themselves, as these are based in *exclusive* expertise.[9] While professional competence, i.e., trustworthiness, is generally indicated by credentials of formal expertise, shared collective identifications—being gay, HIV infection, history of drug use, gay/AIDS activism etc.—may supplement or even substitute for formal expertise. Through shared identities, professional AIDS workers are at the same time part of the very target group of their work. Brown (1997: 87–100) similarly argues that being gay, for instance, may in fact be one part of the qualifications needed for AIDS work. In addition, he points out, some may become professionals to pursue their political, activist goals or offer their services and expertise as an expression of their political orientations. In some cases, formal employment may be virtually the only practicable way to pursue this while still being able to make a living. Further, professionals may have worked as volunteers in the same field before and they may continue to volunteer beside their work. Finally, Brown argues, professionals may be exposed through their work to politicizing experiences.

These findings may be further illustrated and elaborated by Lune's (2007: 59–81) analysis of AIDS organizations for ethnic minorities in New York City. These organizations had a difficult and delayed take off and "had an embryonic existence until they received public funding" (Chambré 1997: 475; cf. Lune 2007: 67, 68, 75). In contrast, by the mid-1980s the AIDS organizations of gay white men had become the dominant form of AIDS organizing and had managed to establish some degree of access to, and co-operation with, public agencies. In effect, gay white men had become the face of AIDS in New York City and this was successfully embodied and marketed by their organizations (Lune 2007: 61). This alone indicates discursive agency on behalf of the dominant white AIDS organizations.

The emergence of organizations implying a not so exclusively gay construction of AIDS necessitated a great deal of discursive entrepreneurship and agency by nascent organizations, directed both at their own ethnic minority communities and at outside agents (public agencies, other AIDS organizations). The key impetus for these projects was first to "prove that this was an issue" (Ports quoted in Lune 2007: 65), and second to define an appropriate response. As both the support by and resonance in ethnic minority communities and by public agencies was wanting, social service *professionals* assumed discursive agency and initiated several AIDS organizations for ethnic minorities. That is to say, nonprofit organizing and, through it, civic action about AIDS in ethnic minority communities became possible only via the successful work of professionals. In this sense, professionalism had an empowering effect (albeit only within the confines of the professionalized ASO paradigm).

In a way then, the emergence of minority AIDS organizations could be accounted for in terms of (1) state failure amended, however, by (2) what could be termed volunteer, dominant, white organizational failure (neglect by established ASOs). But the degree of discursive entrepreneurship necessary to get the ethnic minority organizations off the ground refutes the automatism implied in "failure" theories, for clearly, the existence of unmet needs is not by itself sufficient to account for the emergence of a new set of nonprofits. These needs first have to be constructed as such. Their existence, legitimacy, urgency, etc. first had to be established in a dialog with public agencies, established ASOs and communities—a modification of dominant AIDS discourse. Professionals played an active part in this. Their role cannot be stressed enough here, just as the fact that they were neither amateurs nor mere professionals but volunteer professionals, becoming involved on behalf of and as advocates of hitherto marginalized, neglected groups. Clearly then, their work in this case must be understood as civic action.

In sum, there are a number of ambiguities and contingencies that are at odds with any simple and clearcut evaluation of professionalization as disempowering. While in principle disempowering relative to the grassroots ideal, some AIDS organizations may have an explicit or implicit policy of hiring gay men or people with HIV/AIDS, whereas others try to self-limit their dominant role in the organization (Cain 1993, 1994; e.g., Rosenthal 1996). Equally, whether or not professional work has a politicizing effect on the professional depends on many empirical contingencies that still need to be investigated. For one, ideas of what professional social work should and should not imply are far from monolithic and there are many different approaches to it. Some social workers may be proponents of empowerment strategies (Lupton 1995; but see for critical perspectives, for example, Terpe and Paierl 2010), while others may tend to see themselves as acting by virtue of some kind of superior expertise. This also means that the analysis of professional civic action cannot be reduced to formal characteristics. Rather it needs to focus on kinds of professional mindsets. This is also one reason why any distinction between movement organizations and nonprofits cannot be based on the mere presence or absence of formal professional structures.

These arguments notwithstanding, the basic critique of professionalization as displacing ordinary members (e.g., MacLachlan 1992) still stands. Direct expression and pursuit of interest is replaced by principles of consultation, vicarious pursuit of interest and representation.

Conclusion: AIDS service organizations as a form of power

This analysis responds to a number of the problems of nonprofit theorizing outlined in the introductory chapter. While the state (and the market) clearly failed in providing help for people affected by HIV/AIDS, this chapter has shown that failure theories fall short of explaining the emergence and evolution of AIDS organizing. Rather, AIDS discourse and its emotional climate turned out to be fundamental. It was the basis for both organizing efforts, public policies and the interaction between both. AIDS organizing thus emerged as a way of engaging with, or averting from, the meaning of HIV and AIDS in its complex ramifications and emotional implications. Nonprofit organizing is thus a deeply meaningful and emotional endeavor.

I have argued in the introductory chapter that we should differentiate different categories of civic organizing by how they relate to hegemonic power. Here we have seen that AIDS service organizations emerge from this analysis as an element of hegemonic power structures. I have shown how this power has its fundamental basis in AIDS discourses. It thus extends far beyond lines of explicit authority that would come into focus from a formalistic perspective on the inclusion of ASOs into public policies and their dependence on public funding. What is more, the evolution of dominant forms of AIDS organizing can be linked in complex ways to the changing paradigms of AIDS thought. Rather than being mere recipients of such discursive conditions, however, AIDS organizations are also active participants in the operation of this kind of power. In sum, the fundamental forms of power, pertinent to considering ASOs relation to hegemonic power, are ultimately of a discursive nature. This further underlines the meaningful nature of nonprofit organizing and precludes a merely formalistic analysis of how they relate to dominant power.

Notes

1 Barbalet defines emotional climates as configurations of group relations, which structure group emotions. These emotions need not necessarily be shared by all members of the group.

> Yet in their relations they will each contribute to the feelings of the group *qua* group, to its emotional formation or climate. […] Emotional climates are sets of emotions or feelings which are not only shared by groups of individuals implicated in common social structures and processes, but which are also significant in the formation and maintenance of political and social identities and collective behavior.
>
> (1998: 159, original emphasis)

2 Comparisons with hepatitis—traditionally constructed as a mere communicable disease—show that even the nature as an STD is a contingent construct (Altman 1994: 2).
3 In addition, solidarity between well-to-do gay men and drug users and other affected groups would have required overcoming social differences of class, ethnicity, etc.
4 Past experiences of medical racism, such as in the Tuskegee syphilis studies, further contributed to distrust against dominant institutions (Chambré 2006: 49–50).
5 I borrow the term from Cindy Patton (1997: xv).
6 These were initially the so-called '4-Hs': homosexuals, heroin addicts, hemophiliacs and Haitians.
7 This is in fact an older discourse that has partly also been proactively advanced by affected communities (Beaudin and Chambré 1996; Chambré 1996).
8 Essentially these rationales correspond to what neo-corporatist theories described as mutual benefits both sides can extract from entering a co-operative relationship (see, for example, Streeck 1994; Streeck and Kenworthy 2003; Streeck and Schmitter 1985).
9 Theories of professions has variously emphasized this: e.g., Freidson (1994: 157–163, 174); Macdonald (1995: 30); Merton (1957: 73–4, 1976: 65–72); or Parsons' (1975, 1991) notion of the professional's fiduciary responsibility.

References

Altman, Dennis. 1994. *Power and Community*. London, Bristol: Taylor and Francis.
Baldwin, Peter. 2005. *Disease and Democracy: The Industrialized World Faces AIDS*. Berkeley, Los Angeles, London: University of California Press.
Barbalet, Jack M. 1998. *Emotion, Social Theory, and Social Structure: A Macrosociological Approach*. Cambridge, New York, Melbourne, Madrid, Cape Town, Singapore, Sao Paulo: Cambridge University Press.
Beaudin, Christy L. and Susan M. Chambré. 1996. "HIV/AIDS as a Chronic Disease: Emergence from the Plague Model." *American Behavioral Scientist* 39(6): 684–706.

Bleibtreu-Ehrenberg, Gisela. 1989. *Angst und Vorurteil. AIDS-Ängste als Gegenstand der Vorurteilsforschung*. Reinbek bei Hamburg: Rowohlt Taschenbuch Verlag.
Brandt, Allan M. 1988. "AIDS and Metaphor: Toward the Social Meaning of Epidemic Disease." *Social Research* 55(3): 413–32.
Brown, Michael P. 1997. *RePlacing Citizenship: AIDS Activism and Radical Democracy*. New York, London: The Guilford Press.
Cain, Roy. 1993. "Community-Based AIDS Services: Formalization and Depoliticization." *International Journal of Health Services* 23(4): 665–84.
Cain, Roy. 1994. "Managing Impressions of an AIDS Service Organization: Into the Mainstream or Out of the Closet?" *Qualitative Sociology* 17(1): 43–61.
Cain, Roy. 2001. "The Involvement of People Living with HIV/AIDS in Community-Based Organizations: Contributions and Constraints." *AIDS Care* 13(4): 421–32.
Chambré, Susan M. 1995. "Creating New Nonprofit Organizations as Response to Social Change: HIV/AIDS Organizations in New York City." *Policy Studies Review* 14(1/2): 118–26.
Chambré, Susan M. 1996. "Uncertainty, Diversity, and Change: The AIDS Community in New York City." *Research in Community Sociology* 6: 149–90.
Chambré, Susan M. 1997. "Civil Society, Differential Resources, and Organizational Development: HIV/AIDS Organizations in New York City, 1982–1992." *Nonprofit and Voluntary Sector Quarterly* 26(4): 466–88.
Chambré, Susan M. 2006. *Fighting for Our Lives: New York's AIDS Community and the Politics of Disease*. New Brunswick, New Jersey, London: Rutgers University Press.
Cohen, Cathy J. 1996. "Contested Membership: Black Gay Identities and the Politics of AIDS." Pp. 362–394 in *Queer Theory/Sociology*, edited by S. Seidman. Cambridge, MA, Oxford: Blackwell Publishers.
Cohen, Peter F. 1997. "'All They Needed': AIDS, Consumption, and the Politics of Class." *Journal of the History of Sexuality* 8(1): 86–115.
Crawford, Robert. 1994. "The Boundaries of the Self and the Unhealthy Other: Reflections on Health, Culture and AIDS." *Social Science and Medicine* 38(10): 1347–65.
Crimp, Douglas. 1988. "How to Have Promiscuity in an Epidemic." Pp. 237–71 in *AIDS: Cultural Analysis/Cultural Activism*, edited by D. Crimp. Cambridge, MA, London: The MIT Press.
Czada, Roland. 1998. "Korporatismus/Neo-Korporatismus." Pp. 365–70 in *Wörterbuch Staat und Politik*, edited by D. Nohlen. Bonn: Bundeszentrale für politische Bildung.
Deverell, Katie. 1997. "Professionalism and Sexual Identity in Gay and Bisexual Men's HIV Prevention." Pp. 142–69 in *AIDS: Activism and Alliences*, edited by P. Aggleton, P. Davies and G. Hart. London, Bristol: Taylor and Francis.
Deverell, Katie. 2001. *Sex, Work and Professionalism: Working in HIV/AIDS*. London, New York: Routledge.
Devine, Patricia, E. Ashby Plant and Kristen Harrison. 1999. "The Problem of 'Us' versus 'Them' and AIDS Stigma." *American Behavioral Scientist* 42(7): 1212–28.
DiMaggio, Paul J. and Walter W. Powell. 1991. "The Iron Cage Revisited: Institutional Isomorphism and Collective Rationality in Organizational Fields." Pp. 63–82 in *The New Institutionalism in Organizational Analysis*, edited by P. J. DiMaggio and W. W. Powell. Chicago, London: Chicago University Press.
Doka, Kenneth J. 1997. *AIDS, Fear, and Society: Challenging the Dreaded Disease*. Washington, London: Taylor and Francis.

Epstein, Steven. 1996. *Impure Science: AIDS, Activism, and the Politics of Knowledge*. Berkeley, Los Angeles, London: University of California Press.
Flam, Helena and Jochen Kleres. 2016. "Inequality and Prejudice: German Social Scientists as Producers of Feeling Rules." *Sociological Research Online* 21(1): 13.
Freidson, Eliot. 1994. *Professionalism Reborn: Theory, Prophecy, and Policy*. Cambridge: Polity Press.
Gilman, Sander L. 1988a. "AIDS and Syphilis: The Iconography of Disease." Pp. 87–107 in *AIDS. Cultural Analsis/Cultural Activism*, edited by D. Crimp. Cambridge, MA, London: MIT Press.
Gilman, Sander L. 1988b. *Disease and Representation: Images of Illness from Madness to AIDS*. Ithaca, London: Cornell University Press.
Gould, Deborah. 2009. *Moving Politics: Emotion and ACT UP's Fight against AIDS*. Chicago: University of Chicago Press.
Jones, James W. 1992. "Discourses on and of AIDS in West Germany, 1986–90." *Journal of the History of Sexuality* 2(3): 439–68.
Kayal, Philip M. 1993. *Bearing Witness: Gay Men's Health Crisis and the Politics of AIDS*. Boulder, San Francisco, Oxford: Westview Press.
Lehmbruch, Gerhard. 1979a. "Consociational Democracy, Class Conflict, and the New Corporatism." Pp. 53–61 in *Trends toward Corporatist Intermediation*, edited by P. C. Schmitter and G. Lehmbruch. Beverly Hills, London: SAGE.
Lehmbruch, Gerhard. 1979b. "Liberal Corporatism and Party Government." Pp. 147–83 in *Trends Toward Corporatist Intermediation*, edited by P. C. Schmitter and G. Lehmbruch. Beverly Hills, London: SAGE.
Lehmbruch, Gerhard. 1984. "Concertation and the Structure of Corporatist Networks." Pp. 60–80 in *Order and Conflict in Contemporary Capitalism*, edited by J. H. Goldthorpe. Oxford: Clarendon Press.
Lune, Howard. 2007. *Urban Action Networks HIV/AIDS and Community Organizing in New York City*. Lanham: Rowman & Littlefield.
Lupton, Deborah. 1995. *The Imperative of Health: Public Health and the Regulated Body*. London, Thousand Oaks, New Delhi: SAGE.
Macdonald, Keith M. 1995. *The Sociology of the Professions*. London, Thousand Oaks, New Delhi: SAGE.
MacLachlan, John. 1992. "Managing AIDS: A Phenomenology of Experiment, Empowerment and Expediency." *Critique of Anthropology* 12(4): 433–56.
Merton, Robert K. 1957. "Some Preliminaries to a Sociology of Medical Education." Pp. 3–79 in *The Student-Physician: Introductory Studies in the Sociology of Medical Education*, edited by R. K. Merton, G. G. Reader and P. L. Kendall. Cambridge, MA: Commonwealth Fund, Harvard University Press.
Merton, Robert K. 1976. *Sociological Ambivalence and Other Essays*. New York: Free Press.
Packard, Randall M. and Paul Epstein. 1992. "Medical Research on AIDS in Africa: A Historical Perspective." Pp. 346–76 in *AIDS: The Making of a Chronic Disease*, edited by E. Fee and D. M. Fox. Berkeley, Los Angeles, Oxford: University of California Press.
Padgug, Robert and Gerald M. Oppenheimer. 1992. "Riding the Tiger: AIDS and the Gay Community." Pp. 245–78 in *AIDS: The Making of a Chronic Disease*, edited by E. Fee and D. M. Fox. Berkeley, Los Angeles, Oxford: University of California Press.
Parsons, Talcott. 1975. "The Sick Role and the Role of the Physician Reconsidered." *The Milbank Memorial Fund Quarterly: Health and Society* 53(3): 257–78.
Parsons, Talcott. 1991. *The Social System*. London: Routledge.

Patton, Cindy. 1990. *Inventing AIDS*. New York, London: Routledge.
Patton, Cindy. 1997. "Foreword." Pp. ix–xx in *RePlacing Citizenship: AIDS Activism and Radical Democracy*, by Michael P. Brown. New York, London: The Guilford Press.
Patton, Cindy. 2002. *Globalizing AIDS*. Minneapolis, London: University of Minnesota Press.
Perrow, Charles and Mauro F. Guillén. 1990. *The Aids Disaster: The Failure of Organizations in New York and the Nation*. New Haven, London: Yale University Press.
Petersen, Alan and Deborah Lupton. 1997. *The New Public Health: Discourses, Knowledges, Strategies*. London, Thousand Oaks, New Delhi: SAGE.
Pulver, Marco. 1999. *Tribut der Seuche oder: Seuchenmythen als Quelle sozialer Kalibrierung. Eine Rekonstruktion des AIDS-Diskurses vor dem Hintergrund von Studien zur Historizität des Seuchendispositivs*. Frankfurt am Main, Berlin, Bern, New York, Paris, Wien: Peter Lang Verlag.
Rofes, Eric. 1998. *Dry Bones Breathe: Gay Men Creating Post-AIDS Identities and Cultures*. New York, London: Harrington Park Press.
Rosenbrock, Rolf, Doris Schaeffer, Françoise Dubois-Arber, Martin Moers, Patrice Pinell and Michel Setbon. 1999. *The AIDS Policy Cycle in Western Europe: From Exceptionalism to Normalization*. Berlin: Wissenschaftszentrum Berlin für Sozialwissenschaften.
Rosenthal, Donald B. 1996. "Who 'Owns' AIDS Service Organizations? Governance Accountability in Non-Profit Organizations." *Polity* 24(1): 97–118.
Schmitter, Philippe C. 1984. *Neo-Corporatism and the State*. Florence: European University Institute, Working Paper 106.
Sontag, Susan. 1990. *Illness as Metaphor and AIDS and Its Metaphors*. New York: Picador.
Stoller, Nancy E. 1998. *Lessons from the Damned: Queers, Whores, and Junkies Respond to AIDS*. New York, London: Routledge.
Streeck, Wolfgang. 1994. "Einleitung des Herausgebers. Staat und Verbände: Neue Fragen. Neue Antworten?" Pp. 7–34 in *Staat und Verbände*. Opladen: Westdeutscher Verlag.
Streeck, Wolfgang and Lane Kenworthy. 2003. "Theories and Practices of Neo-Corporatism." Pp. 441–60 in *A Handbook of Political Sociology: States, Civil Society and Globalization*, edited by T. Janoski, R. R. Alford, A. M. Hicks and M. Schwarz. New York: Cambridge University Press.
Streeck, Wolfgang and Philippe C. Schmitter. 1985. "Community, Market, State—and Associations? The Prospective Contribution of Interest Governance to Social Order." Pp. 1–29 in *Private Interest Government: Beyond Market and State*, edited by P. C. Schmitter and W. Streeck. Beverly Hills: SAGE.
Terpe, Sylvia and Silvia Paierl. 2010. "From Bureaucratic Agencies to Modern Service Providers: The Emotional Consequences of the Reformation of Labour Administration in Germany." Pp. 209–29 in *Emotionalizing Organizations and Organizing Emotions*, edited by B. Sieben and Å. Wettergren. Basingstoke: Palgrave Macmillan.
Treichler, Paula A. 1988. "AIDS, Homophobia, and Biomedical Discourse: An Epidemic of Signification." Pp. 31–70 in *AIDS: Cultural Analysis/Cultural Activism*, edited by D. Crimp. Cambridge, MA, London: The MIT Press.
Treichler, Paula A. 1992. "AIDS and HIV Infection in the Third World: A First World Chronicle." Pp. 377–412 in *AIDS: The Making of a Chronic Disease*, edited by E. Fee and D. M. Fox. Berkeley, Los Angeles, Oxford: University of California Press.
Weingart, Brigitte. 2002. *Ansteckende Wörter. Repräsentationen von AIDS*. Frankfurt am Main: Suhrkamp.
Wießner, Peter. 2003. "AIDS als moderner Mythos." Pp. 19–71 in *AIDS im Wandel der Zeiten. Teil 1*, edited by Deutsche AIDS Hilfe. Berlin: Deutsche AIDS Hilfe.

Chapter 3
AIDS organizations in Germany

In contrast to the US, when it comes to Europe, and Germany specifically, AIDS organizations have received much more scanty scholarly attention. Rather, "a double bias, either micro or macro, seems to exist in the literature on HIV/AIDS" (Kenis and Marin 1997: 5): social research on AIDS either focuses on political-administrative action by state agencies (e.g., Kirp and Bayer 1994; Weilandt *et al.* 2001) or on individual risk-related behavior. This notwithstanding, and however disparate, existing German and comparative European research allows for a synthesizing description and analysis of the development of German AIDS organizations to address the central question of this chapter: do the core findings from the previous chapter also apply to German AIDS organizations? As I will show, similar shifts in AIDS discourses and their emotional climates precipitated equal shifts in AIDS organizing as in the US. Neo-corporatism will help here, too, to carve out pertinent power structures.

Parallels: a brief note on the AIDS discourse in Germany

A few, selective remarks on German AIDS discourse must suffice here in oder to indicate fundamental parallels to the American AIDS discourse (but see, for example, Jones 1992; Kruse 1987; Pulver 1999; Rühmann 1985: 2; Weingart 2002; Wießner 2003). Comparative studies of AIDS policies in the US, France, Germany and Sweden (Baldwin 2005) point at the same phases of AIDS discourse in these countries as outlined in the previous chapter—a gay disease, a risk-group disease, a threat to the general population, normalization. Studies on Germany support this finding but also point at some specificities (Wießner 2003): the notion of a gay disease was thus supplemented by additional othering elements, such as the idea of both American and (on an epidemiological route via the US) African origins of HIV (on the anti-American element in this, see also Przygoda 1990). This was later on inflated into apocalyptic scenarios affecting the entire society/nation with the thus identified "others" as threatening culprits. Othering, then, forms an equally important element in German discourse. Eventually, however, German AIDS discourse has calmed down and has entered a phase of normalization. The normalization-diagnosis enjoys great popularity in German AIDS discourse. The ubiquitousness of the arguments of Rosenbrock and collaborators can serve as an indicator here (see, for example, Rosenbrock and Schaeffer 2003; Rosenbrock *et al.* 2000).

Given these discursive parallels, the emotional climate around AIDS evolved along similar lines as in the US. A central feature also of German AIDS discourse, othering functioned as a means of dominant social strata to manage fears of AIDS. Fears of AIDS went rampant when othering as an *absolute*[1] relegation of AIDS to marginalized social groups stopped working and large strata of society realized that they were in principle at risk of infection as well.

These fundamental parallels are indicative of the global nature of AIDS discourse—something that has hitherto been noted only with respect to developing countries (e.g., Altman 1998, 1999; Karnik 2001), but equally holds for the industrialized world as well. When the AIDS epidemic took hold in Germany it already came with a symbolic luggage that had originated in the US. It is there that the basic meanings of AIDS were first carved out. German gays first learned via personal contacts with the US (friends, travels) of the new disease that seemed to concern gay men (Schilling 2000: 82).[2] The fact that othering in German AIDS discourse took on a specific form as anti-Americanism is particularly indicative of these discursive-geographic origins of AIDS discourse when it came to Germany.

The role of identity: the emergence of AIDS relief organizations

The predominant form of AIDS organizing in Germany by far is *AIDS Hilfe* (AIDS Relief). These local organizations are united in the federal umbrella organization *Deutsche AIDS Hilfe* (DAH, German AIDS Relief). DAH was founded in September 1983 in Berlin as an umbrella organization of then still-to-be-founded local member organizations.

Like its American counterparts, AIDS Relief emerged from the gay movement. Gay activists were the key initiators (e.g., Schilling 2000: 82–3). Despite demobilization prior to the onset of AIDS (Frankenberg 1994; Geene 2000: 229), the mobilizing and organizing potential of gay men was the pivotal condition for the founding of AIDS organizations in Germany, distinguishing gays from other hard-hit groups (Frankenberg 1994: 142–4; see also Schilling 2000). To put it this way, however, would be to ignore more fundamental, discursive conditions that mirror those in the US: as DAH co-founder Rainer Schilling's (2000) retrospective account testifies, AIDS was readily understood by initial AIDS activists as a threat to gay men both in terms of health and, initially of greater importance, in terms of impending discrimination (cf. Cruse 1987: 162–3). A key motive for setting up the first AIDS Relief organizations was to ward off a feared increase in discrimination. To this end an important initial strategy was to disseminate countering information targeted against any attempt to use AIDS as a legitimization of repression against gays (Etgeton 2002: 124; Geene 2000: 230–1; Vielhaber 2002: 134) and to some extent to downplay the disease (Przygoda 1990: 34–6; Reutter 1992: 16). Besides these objectives a constitutive premise was self-help. This also indicates the debt of early AIDS organizing to the gay movement and specifically its grassroots principles. Early AIDS organizing bore an antagonistic or emancipatory orientation. Parts of the gay movement took AIDS as an occasion to overcome its prior splintering (see Geene 2000: 231).

The links between gay movement and burgeoning AIDS organizing are all the more remarkable given that the latter emerged before there was a tangible problem in terms of infection and illness (Geene 2000: 231). In fact, organizers had not as yet realized the dimensions that HIV/AIDS would take on; they assumed that there would be single cases of people in need of care and considered the availability of public funding inconceivable (Przygoda 1990: 37).

In sum, much like in the US, the construction of AIDS as a gay disease was at the basis of emerging AIDS organizing. It is only because of this that AIDS resonated so effectively with pre-existing gay identities. AIDS had originally been constructed mainly in the US contexts as a gay disease and it was those discourses on AIDS that diffused into Germany and were adopted there.[3] German AIDS organizations thus equally emerged along lines of sexual identity. The German case, with AIDS organizing preceding the epidemic, particularly supports this point. This adds weight to the argument that nonprofit organizing is contingent on discursive premises and inherently meaningful.

The power of discourse: the evolution of AIDS policies in Germany

The public-sector reactions to AIDS up to the early 1990s can be divided in three phases (Canaris 1987) that ran closely parallel to those described for the US. This also goes for their links to discursive regimes of HIV/AIDS.

The first phase (c.1982–1984) remained largely within the confines of conventional public health politics. The general passivity of state actors—both politicians and administrative institutions—in this phase has been widely noted (Freeman 1992a: 32; Reutter 1992: 16; see also, for example, Wübker 1988: 47). They left the issue of AIDS mainly to the medical system to deal with, did not consider it a significant public health issue, and thus remained passive (Rühmann 1985: 175, 177). Fundamental to this was the perception at the time that AIDS did not warrant too much concern given that its incidence seemed to be limited to gays. It was not seen as a significant threat to the general population. The Federal Ministry of Health assumed until 1984 that there was no generalized danger of infection and merely alerted the medical professions of the new condition (Canaris 1987: 270; see also Frankenberg 1994: 134; Reutter 1992: 18). Medical experts equally did not see the need for any extraordinary measures. Significantly, it was the assumed "risk-group"/gay nature of the disease that led to this conclusion (Canaris 1987: 270; Frankenberg and Hanebeck 2000: 35; Rühmann 1985: 175). In sum, othering AIDS discourse was fundamental to the initial passivity of German AIDS policy. As long as the majority's AIDS-related fears could be managed through the notion of AIDS as a disease of othered minorities irrelevant to other sections of society, political and public health actors remained passive (Reutter 1992: 19). AIDS Relief thus emerged without much active involvement of dominant political actors.

The state's passivity slowly started to change in late 1984 when the Federal Ministry of Health developed plans for a special law to extend coercive, old public health measures to AIDS (Rühmann 1985: 176–7). The reaction they garnered among political elites marked the advent of a new political approach to AIDS that could take hold in the context of shifting meanings of AIDS. Several regional state governments (most notably Berlin) and medical experts dissented (Canaris 1987: 271–2). Their key concern was that coercive measures would endanger the fledgling autonomous organization of particularly affected groups (mainly gay men) and their willingness to co-operate with the medical system. Instead, it was argued that self-help potentials should be employed.

This burgeoning new public health approach to AIDS politics gained strength and currency during the second phase (1985–1986) when political struggles over AIDS policies intensified. The realization that AIDS would not be curable any time soon heightened the perceived need for prevention. But most crucially AIDS was now seen as a threat to the general population (Canaris 1987: 274).[4] "Once it could be presented as a threat to the 'normal' heterosexual population, and not just for marginalized groups, AIDS became a topic of primary interest" (Frankenberg and Hanebeck 2000: 36). The discursive nature of these changes stands out as the change was not so much based on new epidemiological developments but rather on shifted epidemiological prognoses (Reutter 1992: 5). Political changes were thus initiated by the same transformations of dominant AIDS discourse as in the US—from a disease exclusively of gays and other risk groups to a more generalized view of who could contract HIV. Absolute othering through AIDS discourse was no longer possible and so AIDS-related fears that othering had kept at bay now came to affect large parts of society—a shift in the emotional climate around AIDS. As the rationales in favor of new public health—e.g., the danger of driving affected groups underground—indicate, gays now came to be viewed not only as a threat (as an epidemiological vector) but also as a route to curb the spread of HIV. Dominant AIDS policies responded to the shifting emotional climate of AIDS discourse with containment (Barbalet 1998: 161–2)—again, much like in the US.

In effect, AIDS policies now decidedly turned towards the new public health paradigm with its reliance on information, education and co-operation with civil society organizations. In March 1985 the first meeting took place between members of the civil service, medical and other experts, and representatives of the already existing AIDS Relief organizations. The direct outcome was a division of responsibilities. Public institutions would do prevention work for the general population (see Figure 3.1) while AIDS Relief organizations would act as state partners and carry out prevention work among "special" target groups, such as gays (see Figure 3.2), and later, drug users, women and migrants. AIDS Relief began receiving sizable and swiftly increasing subsidies (see, for example, Freeman 1992a: 35; Miesala-Edel and Schöps-Potthoff 2000: 51). In the process the federal umbrella organization German AIDS Relief became firmly established as the federal state's chief partner for AIDS policy. This was driven by the state's need to have a singular nongovernmental partner or carrier for AIDS policy implementation (Freeman 1992a: 35)—much in line with the fundamental logic of neo-corporatism.

This logic also is evident from the rationales used for legitimizing this approach, which in turn operated on specific constructions of AIDS. For one, old public health was considered impractical in the context of HIV/AIDS (Czada and Friedrich-Czada 1990: 264–5): the construct of a sexually transmitted disease put the focus on HIV contraction in affectively charged situations, not amenable to legal regulation. If carried out by the state, prevention would likely result in alienating already disenfranchised target groups. State institutions also feared damaging their legitimacy if they themselves became involved with the "illegitimate" practices of marginalized groups in an accepting way (Frankenberg 1994: 160; Reutter 1992: 3). Figures 3.1 and 3.2 illustrate the differences in the prevention strategies of public institutions vs. AIDS Relief.

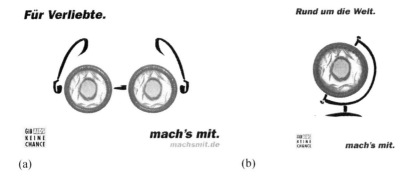

Figure 3.1 Visuals from the campaign of the Federal Center for Health Education, the public agency in charge of doing HIV/AIDS-prevention for the general public, as it evolved from 1993 (Figures 3.1a and 3.1b) to 2007 (Figures 3.1g and 3.1h). Generally, the campaign has been sexually relatively inexplicit using mild innuendos and focusing (literally) on the condom only (*mach's mit* – "Do it with [a condom]"). The first two examples translate "For lovers" and "Around the globe," Figures 3.1c to 3.1e speak for themselves, Figure 3.1f reads "For little angels and little devils." The final two most recent examples (Figures 3.1g and 3.1h) translate "Fits any cucumber!" and "Will safely pop!" (*poppen* being a colloquial expression for having sex).

Source: copyright by Bundeszentrale für gesundheitliche Aufklärung, Köln, Germany. Reproduced with kind permission and support.

AIDS organizations in Germany 47

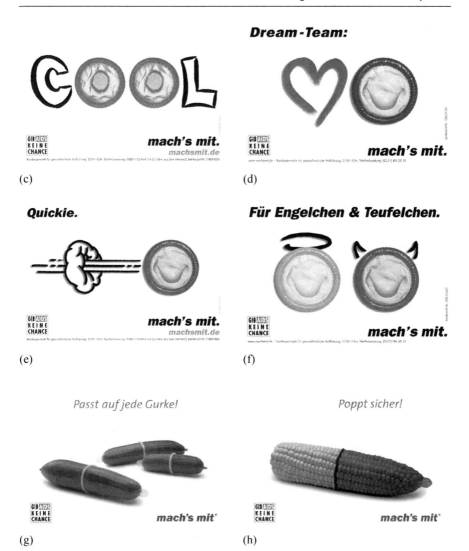

Figure 3.1 Continued

Rosenbrock *et al.* (1999) describe the phase until 1986 as the exceptionalist phase. AIDS was now addressed through innovative rather than conventional public health policies. A number of factors explain this in addition to the ones mentioned thus far (Rosenbrock *et al.* 1999, 2002; Rosenbrock and Schaeffer 2003): AIDS laid bare the powerlessness of medicine and shook the belief in having surpassed the age of infectious diseases; AIDS touched on many symbolically charged meanings, contributing to heated political debates; AIDS policies took shape in the context of great uncertainty as little was known about the

Figure 3.2 Visuals from DAH campaigns. In contrast to the Federal Centre for Health Education, DAH campaigns were in general sexually more explicit and suggestive, eroticizing safer sex and operating close to gay sexual subcultures: Figure 3.2a reads: "Kissing. Hot and safe," Figure 3.2b: "Hot days, hot sand. Always with condom and lube." DAH uses explicit gay vernacular in its campaigns. For many years its central prevention message to gay men, as exemplified in Figure 3.2c, was: "Banging with condoms. No nutting in the mouth. Kissing to your heart's content."

Sources: all images copyright by Deutsche AIDS Hilfe (DAH). Reproduced with kind permission and support. Figure 3.2a: Photography: Ingo Taubhorn. Graphic design: trash line design. Figure 3.2b: Photography: Michael Taubenheim. Graphic design: W. Madura. Figure 3.2c: Photography: Norbert Heuler. Graphic Design: Detlev Pusch.

AIDS organizations in Germany   49

(b)

Figure 3.2 Continued

epidemic in the beginning; finally, there was already considerable doubt about the efficacy and enforceability of old public health measures (as opposed to new public health, see Chapter 2), while the new public health approach was available and had gained support both in Germany and by a global consensus.[5]

The third phase began in November 1986 when open dissent about federal AIDS policies set in. Rejecting the hitherto valid consensus, the Bavarian government started demanding a number of old public health measures.[6] After this

Figure 3.2 Continued

failed to find resonance among the regional state health ministers, Bavaria began implementing those plans on its own. However, only the federal state had the legal mandate to implement most of these plans, so many of these measures were not put into practice. This may warrant describing Bavaria's AIDS policy as merely symbolic for purposes of political competition and mobilization (Czada and Friedrich-Czada 1990: 259). One should not gloss over the fact, however, that the Bavarian approach "was embedded into a moral crusade against 'national decadence' that aimed at 'thinning out' sexually 'degenerate' groups" (Frankenberg 1994: 153).

The Bavarian dissent triggered a widespread public debate about the appropriate political response to AIDS. Proponents of new public health argued pragmatically along the lines outlined earlier—need for co-operation with target groups, practicability issues, etc. This line of argument was endorsed by the federal minister of health and in the end Bavaria remained isolated among the German states. With the minor Bavarian exceptions, new public health became the dominant paradigm of AIDS policies in Germany.

This meant that AIDS organizations became firmly established as political actors in the field. On a federal level, DAH from now on had a solid position as a policy partner and carrier of public AIDS policies, receiving sizable funds. State policies thus played a significant role in establishing AIDS organizations. But public policies also aimed at organizing the field of actors even beyond that, for instance by setting up a federal AIDS Foundation, ministerial working groups and advisory bodies, a parliamentary expert hearings (*Enquête* commission) etc. (Czada and Friedrich-Czada 1990). Locally, sometimes representatives of local public health departments played an active, initiating role in founding AIDS organizations (see also Canaris 1987: 275).

The discursive basis of these policy shifts needs to be highlighted here. While not always spelling it out explicitly, research on German AIDS policy indicates that the state's political passivity ended when AIDS took on a less othering meaning. Frankenberg and Hanebeck (2000: 38) remark: "the basis for the currently widespread solidarity with HIV infected persons was cultivated by AIDS being depicted as an apocalyptic danger for everyone not just for homosexuals." Also Reutter (1992: 4–5) links this shift in policy response to the emergence of scenarios for the epidemiological future that had now become increasingly threatening to the mainstream society: "it was exactly the danger of AIDS being passed on into the heterosexual population that served as a motive for public programs" (1992: 6, my translation). And Przygoda (1990: 48, my translation) notes that AIDS organizations found state support by 1985 "after epidemiological studies proved that AIDS or rather the infection with the HI-virus increasingly spread beyond what had been known up till then as the mainly affected groups." In sum, then, the inclusion of AIDS organizations into public policies was based on a transformation of AIDS discourses that replaced the risk-group paradigm with the notion of generalized risk of infection with marginalized groups as an epidemiological threat. Much like in the US, a shifted emotional climate of fear was the very foundation of this inclusion, triggering a policy change from relative inaction to a pro-active approach based on new public health principles.

Neo-corporatism applies in the German context as well. As in the US, the discursive shifts precipitating the political inclusion of AIDS organizations involved a shift in the emotional climate leading to a realization of interdependence between the state and, in this case, AIDS Relief. The latter represented both an epidemiological threat as well as a route to curbing this threat. This is particularly evidenced by the rationales brought forward in the German debate to legitimize new public health strategies—the fear of driving AIDS-ridden communities underground, the greater proximity of AIDS Relief to those communities and thus their greater expertise and efficiency in prevention, etc. The possibility of independent and potentially coercive state intervention has formed a latent yet quite tangible context for the willingness of gay organizations to become part of emerging state–ASO relations.[7] The political inclusion of AIDS Relief thus unfolded, like in the US, in a climate of mutual fear.

One feature of neo-corporatism, however, is more pronounced in Germany than in the US. Where German AIDS policy evolved as a federally concerted project—involving the regional states under the co-ordinating guidance of the federal state—a national AIDS policy has been found more or less wanting in the US for many years (see Chapter 2). As a result, the political inclusion of ASOs in the US evolved on a local and regional level mainly and entailed a diverse array of independent organizations (Chambré 2006; cf., for example, Lune 2007). In contrast, the German policy process produced a unitary civil society actor. In both the US and Germany, however, ASOs have in principle received funding and are granted political participation in return for their cooperation. Both cases can thus be interpreted in terms of neo-corporatism, if to different degrees and on different administrative levels of the polity. In Germany as in the US, the (different levels of the) state played an active role not only in the formation of AIDS organizations but affected actively the formation of an entire institutional field. This involved setting up institutional actors, modes of routine interaction between them, roles, distribution of power, etc. In the end, this meant establishing legitimate forms of AIDS organizing with specific tasks. This was more pronounced in Germany than in the US, given the explicit division of labor between government agencies and AIDS Relief.

The stakes of AIDS organizing and of its political inclusion

AIDS organizing and its political inclusion is never a neutral endeavor relative to its discursive contexts. It both builds on, and feeds back into, AIDS discourses, at times reinforcing and at times challenging them. In the process the meaning of AIDS, the socio-political position of marginalized groups, their legitimacy, etc. are reconfigured. This finding from the discussion of American AIDS organizations can be extrapolated to the German case.

As mentioned earlier, the Bavarian dissent was embedded into a moralizing project of further marginalizing stigmatized groups. This was a key motive for rejecting the new public health concept and in turn indicates the reverse normative implications of new public health policies: the acknowledgement of AIDS Relief and the communities it represents as valid political actors essentially entailed an official legitimation especially of gays, where before they had been more or less politically excluded.

This inclusion, however, did not come without a price. Neo-corporatist arrangements follow an exchange logic: political inclusion and participation, including fringe benefits such as subsidies, are conditional on the associations' (i.e., their constituent communities') compliance with certain politically desired goals. As for AIDS organizing, its political inclusion was predicated upon preventing the spread of HIV. This logic is visible, for instance, in a statement of the federal minister of health (1985–1988) and key political antipode to the Bavarian project, Rita Süssmuth (cited in Rühmann 1987: 245, original emphasis, my translation):

> As a politician who is opposed to coercive state strategies, one thing is particularly important to me: only if as many people as possible, for whom the test is appropriate, use the *voluntary* programs, can we prove that we chose the right approach

Rühman (1987: 246) found this to be nothing short of encouraging the future victims of repression to prevent their prosecution by adhering to a regime voluntarily that others wold like to enforce by coercion.

As I argued in the previous chapter AIDS organizing feeds back into its discursive contexts in that mobilizing along the lines of collective identities entails an inscription of AIDS—its discursive layers and their emotional climates—onto these collective identities. This pertains also to the German case. It was far from self-evident that AIDS came to be seen as an issue for gay politics. In fact, the gay movement was at first hesitant to pick up the issue, instead "downplaying the threat of AIDS and basically [reacting] to AIDS with the usual set of gay political lines of arguments that emphasize the need to bring up issues of repression and exclusion" (Haunss 2004: 230, my translation; cf. Schilling 2000: 82–3). All in all, AIDS was not considered a central issue by the gay movement.

Much like in the US (cf., for example, Gould 2009), the emergence of AIDS, constructed as a gay disease, was experienced as calling into question gay lifestyles in the wake of gay liberation. This was epitomized by debates between leading activists (Holy 1991: 154–6; Salmen and Eckert 1989: 70–1): Rosa von Praunheim, for instance, publicly called for sexual moderation and behavioral changes in 1984. Matthias Frings, in contrast, urged gays to take a political approach to AIDS and reject any blaming of gays for AIDS—i.e., the emotional climate of guilt in othering AIDS discourse. Martin Dannecker attacked Praunheim directly for betraying his liberationist roots. As Holy (1991: 155–8) argues, AIDS called into question a coherent gay identity as it accentuated the contrast between liberated homosexuality and its political legitimacy. This rift paralyzed the gay movement in its avoidance and rejection of the issue of AIDS. He places the emergence of the first federal gay organization *Bundesverband Homosexualität* (Federal Association Homosexuality), its lack of an own AIDS policy and its oftentimes tense relationship with AIDS Relief in this context. Thus, the gay movement was split, with some activists turning towards AIDS organizing while others pursued gay politics relatively decoupled from AIDS (Haunss 2004: 242; Holy 1991: 156–7). This split can be interpreted in the context of dominant, othering AIDS discourse and its emotional climate of shame and guilt. The debates among German activists indicate that gay liberation and its culture of sexual licentiousness were at stake. Did AIDS call into question gay subculture as a hubris, reverting the presumption of gay pride into guilt and shame, or was it legitimate to try and preserve some of that subculture? Much like in the US, German AIDS organizers and gay activists had to navigate the emotional climate of dominant AIDS discourse.

Essentially, emerging AIDS organizing built on a specific version of AIDS discourse and in effect promoted it—with fundamental implications for gay identity. This is illustrated by DAH activist Rainer Schilling's (2000: 85) account of the difficulties DAH confronted when it chose to emphasize the much higher statistical incidence of HIV among gays in an attempt to counter spiraling fear and hysteria among the general population. Gay activists made the criticism that constructing gay men as a primarily affected group would mean contributing to blaming gay, promiscuous lifestyles for AIDS—a subscription to othering, guilt inducing AIDS discourse. Other activists were concerned that the image of DAH and its local chapters would be tarnished by emphasizing the shaming, stigmatizing link between AIDS and gay men. "This opinion was held mainly by gay men who saw themselves being accepted by society for the first time because of their (charitable) work in the AIDS Hilfe groups" (Schilling 2000: 85; cf. Gould 2009).

Much like in the US with the differential mobilization of gays and ethnic minorities around AIDS, so too in Germany, AIDS organizing involved inscribing the epidemic into collective identities (paradoxically while also acknowledging the risk of HIV infection for everyone). Accepting AIDS as a gay issue—if only relatively so—was precondition to the political inclusion of gay AIDS organizations. This and the implicit political and sexual moderation of gay identities entailed at the same time the elevation of gay politics (in the guise of AIDS organizations) into the ranks of legitimate political actors (cf. also Altman 1988).

The evolution and transformation of AIDS relief

AIDS Relief's political inclusion had fundamental effects on the organization. For one, it precipitated a significant rise in numbers of AIDS Relief organizations, especially through state subsidies (Freeman 1992a: 35; Reutter 1992: 17; Wübker 1988: 48–9).[8] DAH now got firmly established as the federal AIDS organization. Political context and process thus had a formative impact on the organizations. DAH's initial movement orientation—viewing itself as part of a broad array of actors—gave way to the claim of being *the* civil society representative on AIDS issues. At the same time, it shifted focus from addressing AIDS issues quite generally to specific target groups (Geene 2000: 232). In a neo-corporatists fashion it claimed a monopoly of representation within these limits. As part of the emerging division of labor between AIDS Relief ("special" target groups) and the state (general population), this was to some degree imposed on the former (Freeman 1992a: 35).

Political inclusion entailed considerable political legitimation and recognition of AIDS Relief (Geene 2000: 233; Reutter 1992: 17). At the same time—starting around 1985/1986 with the political inclusion (Pieper 1993)—AIDS Relief transformed towards greater professionalism, bureaucratization and increasingly formal and hierarchical structures (Geene 2000: 236; Reutter 1992: 16–17; Theis 1997: 333–4).

German research is much less detailed about this. Reutter (1992: 17; see also Przygoda 1990: 46–7) relates it to the influx of public funding as well as to the broadened range of tasks for AIDS Relief organizations. Indeed, emerging relations with the public sector implied taking on tasks of official public health policies. Pieper (1993) attributes this to a number of factors, such as the professional self-interest of social workers to expand the scope of their work to AIDS. He sees the main reason, however, in how professionalization helped to replace stigma with a new legitimacy. Professionalization contributed to a gradual de-gaying of AIDS Relief. Though organizers were still often gay, gayness was much less emphasized publicly and sometimes even downplayed. Given the dual stigma of disease and non-hegemonic sexuality attached to AIDS work, Pieper (1993: 29) argues, many were glad to have professionals represent the organization publicly, downplaying in public its gay character while retaining it internally. Professionalization received a new impetus with the advent of a new wave of local chapters, starting around 1988. Rather than emerging from constituent communities, these were very often set up by professionals rooted in working with illegal drug users. This added to the de-gaying of AIDS Relief.

Professionalization meant that AIDS Relief organizations moved further away from their initial counter-information approach (Geene 2000: 233) and their grassroots orientation self-help group character. A rhetoric of self-help is still fundamental to its self-understanding (e.g., Bohl 2002). However, self-help has been institutionalized and transformed in the process as shifted labels indicate: initially defining itself as self-help *groups*, AIDS Relief now considers itself self-help *organizations*, i.e., having a professionalized core to organize self-help (cf. the contributions to Deutsche AIDS-Hilfe 2002). Self-help has itself been professionalized. Geene (2000: 234) speaks of the domestication of an underdeveloped political approach. This is also variously noted by DAH representatives, albeit with diverging evaluations. There seems to be a consensus, though, that the initial political orientations have subsided (Bohl 2002: 148–50; Etgeton 2002: 126–8; cf., for example, Hentschel 2002: 63; Vielhaber 2002: 134–5).

Professionalization and inclusion into public policies did not come without friction (see also Chapter 8). Increasing professionalization allowed DAH actors greater self-consciousness vis-à-vis government officials, where these were initially skeptical about self-help (Geene 2000: 235). There were also internal tensions within AIDS Relief. Ritter (1992: 283-4; see also Geene 2000: 235) described how in Hamburg left-leaning, activist gays left the local AIDS Relief chapter in the course of professionalization. De-gaying of AIDS Relief also relates to the emergence of people with HIV/AIDS groups beginning in 1987, who returned precisely to the initial self-help approach and tried to organize independently of institutionalized AIDS Relief (Holy 1991: 158-9).

One key qualification is in place here. AIDS Relief has a specific prevention approach—structural prevention (e.g., Deutsche AIDS-Hilfe 1998)—illustrating to some extent a lasting debt to its gay movement roots. Debates about it began in 1987 when the political choice for new public health had been settled (Etgeton 2000: 73). Structural prevention is premised on the WHO's definition of health not as the absence of disease but as a state of physical, mental and social well-being. Structural prevention is about "improv[ing] the social, political, and cultural contexts in which people live and love so as to enable the individual to better manage his/her own specific risks" (Etgeton 2000: 74). Addressing not only the individual but also the contexts of health behavior, it is explicitly understood as emancipatory, with emancipation of marginalized groups seen as the key route to successful prevention: "activating, supporting and maintaining, to the fullest extent possible, people's self-healing and self-help potential, and promoting their ability to enjoy all the pleasures possible in the meantime" (Etgeton 2000: 76). Self-help forms an integral aspect of structural prevention. However, former DAH executive director Stefan Etgeton's description implicitly reveals that professionalization has left its mark on structural prevention as well. He (2000: 78) notes conflicts between professionals and people with HIV/AIDS who sometimes feel forced into a client role. In this manner, professionalization encroaches on the self-help element of structural prevention transforming self-help into a professional standard and objective—something of a contradiction in terms.

Figures 3.3–3.6 illustrate DAH's structural prevention approach. They show how it aimed at fostering positive gay identities and gay life and how it intervened into gay politics.

The normalization of AIDS

Since the late 1990s the diagnosis of a normalization of AIDS has dominated German (and European) social science research on AIDS. Normalization means "that AIDS advanced from what was socially a barely controllable risk to a manageable disease [...], to just one health and social problem among many, while undergoing at the same time a process of depoliticization" (Rosenbrock *et al.* 1999: 18). This shift is identified—with minor exceptions—throughout the western industrialized world. A number of AIDS unspecific factors, on the one hand explain this: automatic dynamics of issue attention cycles; decreasing sensitivity to

Figure 3.3 Poster fostering gay life in non-urban settings. The caption reads "Greetings from.... We are doing great here."

Source: copyright by Deutsche AIDS Hilfe. Photography: Michael Taubenheim. Graphic design: ComDesign Berlin. Reproduced with kind permission and support.

Figure 3.4 "He is a son, patient, employee, customer. He is gay. He has fewer rights."

Source: copyright by Deutsche AIDS Hilfe. Photography: Ingo Taubhorn. Graphic design: Wolfgang Mudra. Reproduced with kind permission and support.

Figure 3.5 "Laughing, loving, fighting. Together against xenophobia and homophobia."
Source: copyright by Deutsche AIDS Hilfe. Photography: Friedrich Baumhauer. Graphic design: Wolfgang Mudra. Created in collaboration with Schwule Internationale Berlin e.V. Reproduced with kind permission and support.

social problems due to increasing influence of neo-conservatism; decline of volunteerism/activism—as social attention dissipates, gratifications decline and the charisma of the exceptional fades, it becomes more difficult to find motivation for volunteer action; subsequent generations of volunteers are less utopian and altruistic but rather tend to act from a utilitarian motivation (see Schaeffer *et al.* 1992: 19–20).

Apart from this, AIDS specific reasons include (e.g., Rosenbrock *et al.* 1999): much feared epidemiological horror scenarios failed to materialize; the increasing medical progress and concomitant medicalization of AIDS with the medical system becoming the pivotal institution for coping with the epidemic; hitherto weakened in their position, medical doctors regained a position to claim power over how to define and respond to HIV/AIDS and to assert the myth of medical feasibility. This was paralleled by a shrinking readiness of health institutions to show political or financial commitment to AIDS issues (see also Chapters 8 and 9).

Differences—the German case in contrast

While this analysis demonstrates similar mechanisms for German and American ASOs, comparative analysis also points at a number of differences. Most notably, though ASOs may enjoy political inclusion in a range of countries, this

Figure 3.6 "Okay: I am gay. Not only at night, also at day time. I am not afraid. Not of this word in any case. Not of my parents, not of the 'others,' their remarks and jokes, not of gay bashers nor Nazis. I am strong because I am happy, because I have friends that accept me. Until a year ago I thought to accept myself, my being gay, I will never be able to do that. I managed to do it somehow. It was easier than I feared. Now I am a man. A young, self-confident gay who wants to get old, really old."

Source: copyright by Deutsche AIDS Hilfe. Photography: Reinhard Lorenz. Text: Claus Wilhelm Klinker Grafik: Wolfgang Mudra. Reproduced with kind permission and support.

may still vary in degree and quality. For instance, comparing the UK and Germany, Freeman (1992a, 1992b) points to a considerably lower and less stable degree of political participation in Britain: the relationship between DAH and the German state took on the form of a partnership and a social contract defining respective functional competences and securing sustained funding. The Terrence Higgins Trust, the British equivalent, in turn only had the status of a subcontractor where the state exploited the services of a relatively weak AIDS organization. Freeman (1992b, 1992a) attributes this to the centralizing thrust of the British polity that used AIDS organizations to fill in the gaps until the statutory health agencies (mainly the National Health Service) were ready to respond to the epidemic. German federalism not only provided AIDS organizations more access points to political decision making but also meant that the federal state could employ AIDS organizations to get a foothold into health policy—otherwise the domain of the regional governments.

Indeed, as Panchaud (1995; see also Panchaud and Cattacin 1997) has shown in her comparison of 12 European countries, political inclusion of AIDS organizations was ubiquitous but there were different patterns of distinct state–nonprofit relations: (i) the neo-conservative management of the epidemic puts primacy on public actors with a relatively[9] low integration of private ones into decision making or policy co-ordination; the latter tend to fill in the gaps left by official policies. With (ii) technocratic management public actors still play a central role, but nonprofits are considered partners in realizing specific and narrowly defined activities albeit under strong control by public agencies. Finally, (iii) the societal management of the epidemic aims at synergies between public and private actors through mixed planning centers. Essentially, this typology points at different degrees of political inclusion.

There is no research available that directly compares the political inclusion of German and American ASOs, but there is some scattered evidence to suggest that the former enjoyed greater influence or autonomy than the latter. One notable difference is that AIDS service organizing in Germany took on the form of a unified actor—the fact that AIDS Relief is the by far predominant form of AIDS organizing with a federated umbrella organization as its spearhead vis-à-vis the federal state. In contrast, ASOs in the US are formally far more diversified. This is already indicative of a more powerful position vis-à-vis public agencies of German ASOs relative to their American counterparts.

What is more, to the extent that their activities were financed with federal monies, the work of American ASOs has been significantly curbed by the infamous Helms amendment. The law, named after its sponsor Senator Jesse Helms, prohibited federal funding for any activities that could be seen as promoting homosexuality (Hunter 1996). More generally a range of vocal religious or conservative advocates effectively opposed explicit prevention messages (Baldwin 2005: 135):

> On the whole, early educational programs in America were deemed to have failed their objective by overly emphasizing the unattainable goal of abstinence while neglecting the practicalities of safe sex. Not until the late 1980s, and especially during the Clinton administration, were more aggressive campaigns for condoms possible. Others have similarly pointed out how government oversight and restrictive social climates prevented explicit prevention campaigns.
>
> (See also Bayer and Kirp 1994: 56–9; Lune 2007: 26–7)

In comparison, German ASOs have enjoyed relatively more autonomy. For one, this is indicated by the explicit division of labor between public health institutions (general public) and AIDS Relief ("special" target groups). There was no equivalent to the Helms amendment. In effect, AIDS Relief managed to employ prevention strategies that were close to the life-worlds they addressed using the (explicit) vernacular of target groups, especially gays (Frankenberg 1994: 160). Figures 3.7 and 3.8 illustrate this, as does Figure 3.2. This autonomy is perhaps

Figure 3.7 DAH visual addressing the gay leather/fetish scene, in the style of Tom of Finland, with explicit reference to kinky sexual practices. The caption reads: "Let's go. Sensitively, responsibly." *Einfühlsam* ("sensitively") is an innuendo here, meaning literally feeling into.

Source: copyright by Deutsche AIDS Hilfe. Illustration: Hansheinrich Salmon. Reproduced with kind permission and support.

Figure 3.8 Excerpt from a DAH brochure entitled "Better Blowing. Tips and infos for a lot of fun and little risk," which provides explicit, how-to tips for oral sex between gay men and has several photographs of gay men having oral sex.

Source: copyright by Deutsche AIDS Hilfe. Concept: Michael Klinkebiel, Dr. Dirk Sander. Text: Michael Klinkebiel. Photography: Norbert Benike. Layout: Carmen Janiesch. Reproduced with kind permission and support.

best evidenced by AIDS Relief's dominant approach of structural prevention described earlier. This aims exactly at tackling structural and cultural barriers to health-conscious behavior, such as homophobic stigmatization. As part of that, for instance, some of German AIDS Relief's public campaigns have primarily aimed at fostering a positive sense of gay identity (see also Figures 3.3–3.6). Especially in smaller to mid-sized cities, local chapters and their social events (e.g., weekly open bar evenings or Sunday brunches) function as important elements of the local gay scene.

These differences also play out in drug policy where AIDS Relief pursued a harm reduction approach—focusing more on preventing HIV-infection rather than abstinence. This involved a conflict about the provision of clean needles to drug users. AIDS Relief was relatively successful in this, resulting in a decriminalization of needle exchange programs; by contrast, such programs have faced much greater resistance in the US (Baldwin 2005: 142–52; cf. also Pant 2000: 195).

In sum, this points at important differences in the configuration of state–ASO relationships varying along the dimension of the latter's autonomy from, and influence on, public institutions. Crucially, as Panchaud's (1995) research has pointed out, this is more a matter of degree as ASOs have been an important element in all the national AIDS policies she studied. While she does not provide an explanation for such differences, the argument can be made that they relate to different national patterns of state–nonprofit relations that are to some extent independent of AIDS politics (Salamon and Anheier 1996).

Conclusion

In sum then, the development of AIDS service organizations in Germany has largely followed the same pattern as in the US. The key features, mechanisms and developmental trajectories of the model proposed in Chapter 2 can be applied to the German case as well. Specifically, this goes for the links of AIDS discourse and its emotional climates with AIDS organizing ranging from the beginnings of AIDS Relief, to its political inclusion and the resulting transformation towards professionalized agencies. This comparative perspective thus bolsters the critique of dominant nonprofit theorizing. Nonprofits emerge, are structured, and evolve as embedded into discourses and their emotional implications. In contrast to the automatism of state/market failure theories, they are fundamentally contingent on how organizers navigate dominant meanings and emotional climates. Finally, a comparative perspective highlights the variability of the political inclusion of nonprofit organizations, following existing patterns of state–nonprofit relations.

Notes

1 AIDS arguably never lost its discursive link with gays entirely, even though this link has been diluted to something of a connotation.
2 There were even some institutional (governmental, organizational) contacts and exchanges (Aue 1999; Frankenberg and Hanebeck 2000: 35).
3 Unfortunately, there is no research about AIDS organizing by other groups, but see Chapter 9.
4 This discursive shift was premised on a prior linking of the disease with intravenous drug users and prostitutes, that is groups with much more fluid borders who could thus function as an "epidemiological bridge" into mainstream society (Freeman 1992a: 31, 1992b: 54; see Jones 1992: 441).
5 This consensus led in 1986 to the so-called Ottawa Charta (WHO), which codified principles of new public health.
6 These included, for example: compulsory testing for "primarily affected groups"; the legal requirement for people with HIV/AIDS to inform sex partners and medical personnel about their serostatus; banning them from breast feeding or donating blood, sperm or any organs, and from working as prostitutes, etc.
7 Frankenberg and Hanebeck (2000: 39) make this relatively explicit:

> The guiding principle was to give education and information precedence over the traditional epidemiological control. This included measures authorized by the Federal Law on Communicable Diseases, which served as a backup and were to be used only in the case of "incorrigible" individuals who recklessly put others at risk.

Compare also activist Rosa von Praunheim's 1984 statement in favor of sexual moderation and behavioral changes (cited in Salmen and Eckert 1989: 70, my emphasis, my translation): "*If we don't want the state to tell us once more how we are to live and to fuck*, then gays need to do something themselves [...] we need to change our behavior: first talk—then fuck." See also Holy (1991: 156), who talks of the need to present a prevention concept in order to ward off state intervention.
8 By 1986 the number of local AIDS Relief organizations had multiplied by ten to a total of 40 and kept growing after that.
9 "Relatively" needs to be emphasized here. Panchaud (1995: 13) considers, for instance, a public funding rate of 30–60 percent of the total budget of nonprofits as rather low.

References

Altman, Dennis. 1988. "Legitimation through Disaster: AIDS and the Gay Movement." Pp. 301–15 in *AIDS: The Burdens of History*, edited by E. Fee and D. M. Fox. Berkeley, Los Angeles, London: University of California Press.
Altman, Dennis. 1998. "Globalization and the 'AIDS-Industry'." *Contemporary Politics* 4(3): 233.
Altman, Dennis. 1999. "Globalization, Political Economy, and HIV/AIDS." *Theory and Society* 28(4): 559–84.
Aue, Michael. 1999. "Wie alles anfing." Pp. 17–28 in *Zwischen Selbstbezug und solidarischem Engagement*, edited by T. Biniasz, D. Hetzel, K. Lemmen, G. Mattke and K.-U. Merkenich. Berlin: Deutsche AIDS-Hilfe.
Baldwin, Peter. 2005. *Disease and Democracy: The Industrialized World Faces AIDS*. Berkeley, Los Angeles, London: University of California Press.
Barbalet, Jack M. 1998. *Emotion, Social Theory, and Social Structure: A Macrosociological*

Approach. Cambridge, New York, Melbourne, Madrid, Cape Town, Singapore, Sao Paulo: Cambridge University Press.
Bayer, Ronald and David Kirp. 1994. "USA: Im Zentrum des Sturms." Pp. 23–73 in *Strategien gegen AIDS. Ein internationaler Politikvergleich. Ergebnisse sozialwissenschaftlicher Aids-Forschung*, edited by D. Kirp and R. Bayer. Berlin: Edition Sigma.
Bohl, Michael. 2002. "Ist die Positivenarbeit der AIDS-Hilfe eigentlich noch Zeitgemäß?" Pp. 146–52 in *AIDS Selbst Hilfe*. Berlin: Deutsche AIDS-Hilfe.
Canaris, Ute. 1987. "Gesundheitspolitische Aspekte im Zusammenhang mit AIDS." Pp. 266–303 in *Leben mit AIDS—mit AIDS leben*, edited by J. Korporal and H. Malouschek. Hamburg: EB-Verlag Rissen.
Chambré, Susan M. 2006. *Fighting for Our Lives: New York's AIDS Community and the Politics of Disease*. New Brunswick, New Jersey, London: Rutgers University Press.
Cruse, Karl-Georg. 1987. "Deutsche AIDS-Hilfe. Unsere Aufgaben und Ziele." Pp. 162–9 in *Aids als Risiko. Über der Umgang mit einer Krankheit*, edited by V. Sigusch. Hamburg: Konkret Literatur Verlag.
Czada, Roland and Heidi Friedrich-Czada. 1990. "Aids als politisches Konfliktfeld und Verwaltungsproblem." Pp. 257–73 in *Aids-Prävention*, edited by R. Rosenbrock. Berlin: Edition Sigma.
Deutsche AIDS-Hilfe, ed. 1998. *Strukturelle Prävention: Ansichten zum Konzept der Deutschen AIDS-Hilfe*. Berlin: Deutsche AIDS-Hilfe.
Deutsche AIDS-Hilfe, ed. 2002. *AIDS Selbst Hilfe*. Berlin: Deutsche AIDS-Hilfe.
Etgeton, Stefan. 2000. "Structural Prevention: The Basis for a Critical Approach to Health Promotion." Pp. 71–81 in *Partnership and Pragmatism: The German Response to AIDS Prevention and Care*, edited by R. Rosenbrock and M. T. Wright. London: Routledge.
Etgeton, Stefan. 2002. "Professionalisierung ohne Profilverlust." Pp. 123–31 in *AIDS Selbst Hilfe*. Berlin: Deutsche AIDS-Hilfe.
Frankenberg, Günter. 1994. "Deutschland: Der verlegene Triumph des Pragmatismus." Pp. 134–72 in *Strategien gegen AIDS. Ein internationaler Politikvergleich*, edited by D. Kirp and R. Bayer. Berlin: Edition Sigma.
Frankenberg, Günter and Alexander Hanebeck. 2000. "From Hysteria to Banality: An Overview of the Political Response to Aids in Germany." Pp. 35–47 in *Partnership and Pragmatism: The German Response to AIDS Prevention and Care*, edited by R. Rosenbrock and M. T. Wright. London: Routledge.
Freeman, Richard. 1992a. "Governing the Voluntary Sector Response to AIDS: A Comparative Study of the UK and Germany." *Voluntas: International Journal of Voluntary and Nonprofit Organizations* 3(1): 29–47.
Freeman, Richard. 1992b. "The Politics of AIDS in Britain and Germany." Pp. 53–67 in *AIDS: Rights, Risk, and Reason*, edited by P. Aggleton, P. Davies and G. Hart. London: Routledge.
Geene, Raimund. 2000. *AIDS-Politik. Ein neues Krankheitsbild zwischen Medizin, Politik und Gesundheitsförderung*. Frankfurt am Main: Mabuse-Verlag.
Gould, Deborah. 2009. *Moving Politics: Emotion and ACT UP's Fight against AIDS*. Chicago: University of Chicago Press.
Haunss, Sebastian. 2004. *Identität in Bewegung. Prozesse kollektiver Identität bei den Autonomen und in der Schwulenbewegung*. Wiesbaden: Verlag für Sozialwissenschaften.
Hentschel, Axel. 2002. "Selbsthilfeförderung in der akzeptierenden Drogenarbeit." Pp. 45–84 in *AIDS Selbst Hilfe*. Berlin: Deutsche AIDS-Hilfe.

Holy, Michael. 1991. "Historischer Abriss der zweiten deutschen Schwulenbewegung 1969–1989." Pp. 138–60 in *Neue soziale Bewegungen in der Bundesrepublik Deutschland*, edited by R. Roth and D. Rucht. Bonn: Bundeszentrale für politische Bildung.

Hunter, Nan D. 1996. "Censorship and Identity in the Age of AIDS." Pp. 39–53 in *In Changing Times: Gay Men and Lesbians Encounter HIV/AIDS*, edited by M. P. Levine, P. N. Nardi and J. H. Gagnon. Chicago, London: Chicago University Press.

Jones, James W. 1992. "Discourses on and of AIDS in West Germany, 1986–90." *Journal of the History of Sexuality* 2(3): 439–68.

Karnik, Niranjan. 2001. "Locating HIV/AIDS and India: Cautionary Notes on the Globalization of Categories." *Science Technology Human Values* 26(3): 322–48.

Kenis, Patrick and Bernd Marin. 1997. "Managing AIDS: Analysing the Organizational Response to HIV/AIDS in European Countries." Pp. 1–25 in *Managing AIDS: Organizational Responses in Six European Countries*, edited by P. Kenis and B. Marin. Aldershot: Avebury.

Kirp, David and Ronald Bayer, eds. 1994. *Strategien gegen AIDS. Ein internationaler Politikvergleich*. Berlin: Edition Sigma.

Kruse, Kuno. 1987. "AIDS in den Medien." Pp. 304–18 in *Leben mit AIDS—mit AIDS leben*, edited by J. Korporal and H. Maluschek. Hamburg: EB-Verlag Rissen.

Lune, Howard. 2007. *Urban Action Networks HIV/AIDS and Community Organizing in New York City*. Lanham: Rowman & Littlefield.

Miesala-Edel, Dorle and Martina Schöps-Potthoff. 2000. "The Role of the German Federal Government in Fighting the Epidemic." Pp. 48–60 in *Partnership and Pragmatism: The German Response to AIDS Prevention and Care*, edited by R. Rosenbrock and M. T. Wright. London: Routledge.

Panchaud, Christine. 1995. "Welfare States Facing HIV/AIDS: Organizational Responses in Western Europe (1981–91)." *Swiss Political Science Review* 1(4): 65–94.

Panchaud, Christine and Sandro Cattacin. 1997. "The Contribution of Non-Profit Organisations to the Management of HIV/AIDS: A Comparative Study." *Voluntas: International Journal of Voluntary and Nonprofit Organizations* 8(3): 213–34.

Pant, Anand. 2000. "Die HIV-Epidemie unter I.v.-Drogenbenutzern: Verlauf, Primärprävention und drogenpolitische Reaktion." Pp. 184–210 in *Glück gehabt? Zwei Jahrzehnte AIDS in Deutschland*, edited by U. Marcus. Berlin, Wien: Blackwell Wissenschafts-Verlag.

Pieper, Kajo. 1993. "Die AIDS-Hilfe—Ein Historischer Abriß." Pp. 25–32 in *10 Jahre Deutsche AIDS-Hilfe. Geschichten und Geschichte*. Berlin: Deutsche AIDS-Hilfe.

Przygoda, Jutta. 1990. *Konservative AIDS-Politik und AIDS-Selbsthilfe—Ein strukturelles Spannungsverhältnis?* Diploma-Thesis, Freie Universität Berlin, Berlin.

Pulver, Marco. 1999. *Tribut der Seuche oder: Seuchenmythen als Quelle sozialer Kalibrierung. Eine Rekonstruktion des AIDS-Diskurses vor dem Hintergrund von Studien zur Historizität des Seuchendispositivs*. Frankfurt am Main, Berlin, Bern, New York, Paris, Wien: Peter Lang Verlag.

Reutter, Werner. 1992. *AIDS, Politik und Demokratie. Ein Vergleich Aids-politischer Maßnahmen in Deutschland und Frankreich*. Berlin: Wissenschaftszentrum Berlin für Sozialforschung.

Ritter, Claudia. 1992. "Auf der Flucht vor Aids. Sozialstruktur und Bewältigungsstrategien." Pp. 267–89 in *Zwischen Bewußtsein und Sein. Die Vermittlung "objektiver" Lebensbedingungen und "subjektiver" Lebensweisen*, edited by S. Hradil. Opladen: Leske + Budrich.

Rosenbrock, Rolf, Doris Schaeffer, Françoise Dubois-Arber, Martin Moers, Patrice Pinell and Michel Setbon. 1999. *The AIDS Policy Cycle in Western Europe: From Exceptionalism to Normalization*. Berlin: Wissenschaftszentrum Berlin für Sozialwissenschaften.

Rosenbrock, Rolf, Doris Schaeffer, Françoise Dubois-Arber, Martin Moers, Patrice Pinell and Michel Setbon. 2002. "Die Normalisierung von Aids in Westeuropa. Der Politikzyklus am Beispiel einer Infektionskrankheit." Pp. 11–68 in *Die Normalisierung von AIDS. Politik—Prävention—Krankenversorgung*, edited by R. Rosenbrock and D. Schaeffer. Berlin: Edition Sigma.

Rosenbrock, Rolf and Doris Schaeffer. 2003. "AIDS—Vom Ausnahmezustand zur Normalität." Pp. 9–18 in *AIDS im Wandel der Zeiten. Teil 1*, edited by Deutsche AIDS-Hilfe. Berlin: Deutsche AIDS-Hilfe.

Rosenbrock, Rolf, Doris Schaeffer and Martin Moers. 2000. "The Normalisation of AIDS in Germany." Pp. 231–48 in *Partnership and Pragmatism: The German Response to AIDS Prevention and Care*, edited by R. Rosenbrock and M. T. Wright. London, New York: Routledge.

Rühmann, Frank. 1985. *AIDS. Eine Krankheit und ihre Folgen*. Frankfurt am Main, New York: Edition Qumran im Campus Verlag.

Rühmann, Frank. 1987. "Wege aus dem Zwang? Zur Aids-Politik der Bundesregierung." Pp. 240–6 in *Aids als Risiko. Über der Umgang mit einer Krankheit*, edited by V. Sigusch. Hamburg: Konkret Literatur Verlag.

Salamon, Lester M. and Helmut K. Anheier. 1996. "Social Origins of Civil Society. Explaining the Nonprofit Sector Cross-Nationally." *Voluntas. International Journal of Voluntary and Nonprofit Organizations* 9(3): 213–48.

Salmen, Andreas and Albert Eckert. 1989. *20 Jahre bundesdeutsche Schwulenbewegung 1969–1989*. Köln: Bundesverband Homosexualität.

Schaeffer, Doris, Martin Moers and Rolf Rosenbrock. 1992. "Aids-Krankenversorgung zwischen Modellstatus und Übergang in die Regelversorgung." Pp. 11–25 in *Aids-Krankenversorgung*, edited by D. Schaeffer, M. Moers and R. Rosenbrock. Berlin: Edition Sigma.

Schilling, Rainer. 2000. "The German Aids Self-Help Movement: The History and Ongoing Role of Aids-Hilfe." Pp. 82–90 in *Partnership and Pragmatism: The German Response to AIDS Prevention and Care*, edited by R. Rosenbrock and M. T. Wright. London: Routledge.

Theis, Wolfgang. 1997. "AIDS—oder die teuer erkaufte Professionalisierung der Schwulenbewegung." Pp. 327–35 in *Goodye to Berlin? 100 Jahre Schwulenbewegung*, edited by Schwules Museum and Akademie der Künste Berlin. Berlin: Verlag Rosa Winkel.

Vielhaber, Bernd. 2002. "Therapieaktivisten in Deutschland—Eine vom aussterben bedrohte Spezies." Pp. 132–9 in *AIDS Selbst Hilfe*. Berlin: Deutsche AIDS-Hilfe.

Weilandt, C., W. Heckmann, M. Kraus, J. Lambrecht and C. Pervilhac. 2001. *HIV Prevention in Europe: A Review of Policy Practice in 25 Countries*. Berlin: Edition Sigma.

Weingart, Brigitte. 2002. *Ansteckende Wörter. Repräsentationen von AIDS*. Frankfurt am Main: Suhrkamp.

Wießner, Peter. 2003. "AIDS als Moderner Mythos." Pp. 19–71 in *AIDS im Wandel der Zeiten. Teil 1*, edited by Deutsche AIDS Hilfe. Berlin: Deutsche AIDS Hilfe.

Wübker, Anke. 1988. *Struktur und Bedeutung der AIDS-Hilfsorganisationen in der Bundesrepublik Deutschland*. Berlin: Deutsche AIDS-Hilfe.

Chapter 4

Making sense of neo-corporatism and neo-institutionalism

The previous two chapters have analyzed AIDS organizing mainly from a macro- and meso-perspective, highlighting the role of the state and professionalization as embedded into dominant AIDS discourse and its emotional climate. AIDS service organizations emerged from this analysis as a vehicle for extending hegemonic power into constitutive communities. This analysis has, if sometimes implicitly, relied on elements of discourse analysis, neo-corporatism, the sociology of emotions and neo-institutionalism. This opened a number of inroads into a new perspective on nonprofits that moves past the shortcomings of third sector theorizing. Contrasting the functionalist and state-centered bent of this theorizing, nonprofits emerge as constituted, structured—in short contingent upon institutionalized meanings, emotional climates and the power dynamics that emotion-laden discourses engender.

Yet these perspectives leave a crucial dimension unaddressed. How do individual organizers relate to these processes and dynamics; how do they exert agency in them? After all, the previous chapters showed that nonprofits are not mere passive recipients of dominant discourses but have degrees of agency themselves. Organizers navigate the emotional climate of dominant AIDS discourse. But how exactly do they relate to emotion laden discourses? This will be a central question of the empirical case studies in Chapters 6–9. In this present chapter I will develop an organization theory that allows us to focus on individual organizers and how they relate to power structures and emotion laden discourses. I will argue that both neo-corporatism and neo-institutionalism are of little help in addressing the lacking micro-foundation of third sector theorizing. Karl Weick's sensemaking approach provides a useful alternative here. His theory will allow analysis of single AIDS organizations, and their dissolution processes, from the vantage point of individual actors while taking into account the meaningful nature of nonprofit organizing. Chapter 5 will address the role of emotion in this.

Neo-corporatism—principle considerations

Using neo-corporatism to analyze AIDS organizations in the US and Germany may seem a heterodox choice. Neo-corporatism describes a specific system of interest intermediation where the state grants strong, centralized associations regular participation in policy making, that is, a monopoly in interest representation in exchange for moderating its political claims (Czada 1998: 365; Schmitter 1974: 93–4, see also 1982: 65). Much research has focused on the capital–labor conflict from a macro-perspective: negotiations of macro-social/economic programs between large umbrella organizations—unions, employers—and, when relevant, the state (Cawson 1985a: 1; Lehmbruch 1979a, 1979b; see also Molina and Rhodes 2002). This may seem ill-suited for AIDS organizations. However, the theory has been extended to the meso- and micro-level (e.g., Cawson 1985b) with a particular focus on bilateral constellations of a more limited thematic scope, where single interest associations are granted participation in the policy process (Cawson 1985a; Heinze and Voelzkow 1999). This also meant greater emphasis on the state commissioning collective self-government by social groups (Streeck 1994: 17). This was exactly the logic behind the political inclusion of ASOs.

Second, the US is generally not characterized as a neo-corporatist polity and Germany only to some extent. However, more recent third sector theories (Salamon and Anheier 1996) in fact analyze the third sector in Germany as neo-corporatist. The US, in turn, come out of this research as a liberal nonprofit regime, with lower state funding for a nevertheless relatively large nonprofit sector. This corresponds to the greater political inclusion of German ASOs (Chapter 3). At the same time, this should not lead to underestimating the role of the state for the American nonprofit sector. Prominent research rather points at the pivotal significance of the state for the American nonprofit sector (Skocpol 1999, 2004; Smith and Lipsky 1993), hence dubbed the shadow state (Wolch 1990). This sometimes even shares key assumptions with neo-corporatism (e.g., Salamon 1987).[1] It is for these reasons that neo-corporatism is useful for analyzing AIDS organizations in both countries (and for bringing some possible differences into view). After all, as the previous two chapters illustrate, neo-corporatism provides rather pertinent explanatory perspectives in both cases and helps to highlight relevant power processes.

The rationalist premises of neo-corporatism

In some ways, however, neo-corporatism also diverges from the general perspective on AIDS organizations used here. Overall, this has to do with neo-corporatism's rationalist bent.

Interdependence

For one, interdependence—the pivotal condition for neo-corporatism to emerge—seems an objectively constituted condition made up of "hard" factors such as: states' desire to extend the reach of interventions; benefits from using associations' expertise, avoiding involvement with illegitimate issues (e.g., drugs and sex), taming civil society actors, and avoiding the burdens of direct intervention. Associations may gain material benefits, political influence and status, organizational stabilization, while avoiding "too much" autonomous state intervention.

However, interdependency is rather of a constructed, discursive-emotional nature. Analysis of AIDS organization has underscored this point. Political inclusion of AIDS organizations rested on pivotal discursive transformations and on changes in the emotional climate.[2] Shifting collective fears and ways of dealing with them were constitutive of perceptions of interdependence. To make neo-corporatism more discursive we can draw on claim making and social problems theory (Groenemeyer 2010; Schneider 1985; e.g., Spector and Kitsuse 1973, 1977). This research focuses on rhetorical strategies of constructing issues as social problems that necessitate political intervention. Specifically, this includes constructions of the issue's nature, causes and consequences, and thereby prefigures solutions, responsibilities and, more generally, ways of relating to it. It also supports the notion, proposed in the previous chapters, that nonprofits have discourses about their cause inscribed into them and carry them into the life spheres of constituent communities (see, for example, Groenemeyer 2010). However, neo-corporatism has a much stronger focus on the process of political inclusion of associations and its immanent power dynamics. More than claim making theory, it is a theory of organizations. We thus need a discourse- and emotion-sensitive version of neo-corporatism to understand the political inclusion of AIDS organization. After all, political inclusion was not due to the claim making of disenfranchised groups but due to discursive shifts largely not of their making.

Private interest government: a rational formation of interests and identities?

The notion of private interest government (Streeck and Schmitter 1985) was particularly useful to bring power processes in the field of AIDS organizing into focus. However, on closer look it leaves an incomplete picture as it insufficiently theorizes the micro-level of rank-and-file members.

Other than pluralism, neo-corporatism intriguingly views associations as active producers of interests and identities of their members and constituencies by way of organizational form (Streeck 1994: 10)[3] or through staff and functionaries and their power in setting internal rules and in formally structuring the organization ("politics of formal organization," Schmitter and Streeck 1981: 122–3). A key mechanism is seen in the allocation of selective incentives by functionaries (goods, status, services, etc.) made possible and buttressed by the state through the provision of resources, regulations to foster or even mandate membership, entrusting the association with public functions and privileged political influence (Schmitter 1984: 22; see also Streeck 1994: 15). Pivotal, however, is what Schmitter (1984: 16) calls the "whip in the window"—the legitimate possibility to have recourse to state authority in order to enforce consent. The wish to avoid the whip thus shapes collective interest and identity formation in the organizations (see, for example, Cawson 1985a: 6). Chapters 2 and 3 showed how persisting legal possibilities of coercive public health measures were a formative context for AIDS organizations and their constituent communities.

Organizational leaders and elites figure centrally for the formation of identities and interests. They are conceived as essentially rational, self-interested actors who balance an orientation towards serving members/constituencies (*logic of membership*) with an orientation towards the state (*logic of influence*). This includes among other things influencing members by setting selective incentives. Neo-corporatist associations—i.e., the interests and identities they embody—are formed by how leaders reconcile these two logics (Schmitter and Streeck 1981).

In the end, however, neo-corporatist theorizing falls short of its ambition to link associations with the formation of interests and identities. While it provides some insight into this issue, it fails to explain the substance of interests and identities. Neo-corporatist theorizing ultimately considers interests and identities as mere aggregates of pre-existing preferences, which in turn remain external to the organizational process—a contradiction to neo-corporatists' rejection of pluralist premises. It views the formation of interests and identities as produced by internal selective and other incentives (whip in the window). Interests and identities thus become a matter of rational choice. We can thus only understand it via recourse to already existing preferences—or, rather, interests and identities—whose origin, however, remains unclear much in line with rational choice theory. Ultimately, therefore, neo-corporatism fails to capture the formation of interests and identities as meaningful constructs.

Consonant with this, individual interests tacitly figure as a residual category in neo-corporatism, an interference to be controlled. The notion of a logic of membership is much less developed than the logic of influence and falls short of granting rank-and-file interests a constitutive role. While members' interests cannot be completely ignored, they appear as more or less manipulable by organizational elites. Empirical findings point instead at the bottom-up formation of organizational goals (Flam 1990). Overall, neo-corporatism lacks a sufficient micro-foundation (see also Flanagan 1999; Nedelmann and Meier 1979: 101–2). While it is aware of the rank-and-file it emphasizes a top-down-regulation of members' interests.

This translates into theoretical problems with respect to social change. A static picture predominates (Nedelmann and Meier 1979), where neo-corporatist arrangements exist simply because they are functional in meeting fundamental imperatives of capitalist economies for their reproduction (e.g., Schmitter 1974: 107–8). As Molina and Rhodes (2002) argue, it is for this functionalist bias that much theorizing in this field is blinded to what is actually a dynamic nature of neo-corporatist constellations. These faithful critics of neo-corporatism call for a more process-oriented view that takes issues of micro-foundation—actors' shifting goals, resources, actions, and interpretations—into sharper focus. From this perspective then, neo-corporatist constellations need to be analyzed as embedded into conflicts and discourses as they evolve over time. This adds further support to a wedding of neo-corporatism with a discourse focus, as advanced in Chapters 2 and 3. However, this does not resolve the issue of a sufficient micro-foundation.

Neo-institutionalism

Neo-institutionalism comes closer to embedding organizations in social meaning systems. Like neo-corporatism, it links organizations and the state as well as professionals, but widens the theoretical scope by considering the role of cultural factors. This way it presents an expanded theory of organizational elites that neo-corporatism largely conceives in rationalist terms. However, much like neo-corporatism, neo-institutionalism misses an adequate conception of individual action. As I will show, an over-socialized image prevails, entailing a static view unable to capture the ongoing, dynamic and meaningful grappling of individual actors with discourses, emotional climates and power processes.

The central idea of neo-institutionalism in organization theory is that the structures of organizations reflect social institutions, i.e., systems of meanings and concomitant patterns of action, which are made up of symbolic elements and buttressed by regulatory processes (Scott 1994: 56). As symbolic systems, institutions guide action by establishing a shared, valid, yet socially constructed understanding of reality. Social action is thus co-ordinated by institutionalized meaning systems rather than by norms, sanctions or incentives. More fundamentally, institutions constitute preferences and actors defining specific rationalities for different social spheres (see also DiMaggio and Powell 1991a: 7–11; Friedland and Alford 1991). Organizational form is thus not what is necessitated by objective rationality, but rather reflects what is institutionalized, that is socially constructed as rational. Nor do legal regulations suffice to explain organizations as these too, upon a closer examination, turn out to require interpretation and these interpretations have to become hegemonic within a field to have a coercive effect. Therefore, organizations and their environments remain in a relationship of mutual causality (Edelman and Suchman 1997; see also Scott 2001).

Key assumptions of neo-institutionalism

Meyer and Rowan (1991) were the first to argue that legitimacy, rather than "hard" technical or efficiency requirements, is pivotal for organizational formation and survival. To attain legitimacy, they argue, organizations reflect in their structures what is institutionalized in their environments as legitimate, that is taken for granted, socially constructed ways of organizing. However, they do so only outwardly, so as to present themselves as legitimate. They decouple the core of their activities, leaving these relatively untouched by institutional influences. The rational character of organizational structures is thus a myth as it is socially constructed.

Organizations are also embedded into organizational fields, that is an environment of other organizations formed by increased internal interaction, structures of dominance and coalitions, increased internal exchange of information, a mutual awareness of each other and a sense of commonality (DiMaggio and Powell 1991b). Organizations are structured into fields by social institutions, especially state and professions but also competition. Three kinds of forces within a field will tend to structure organizations into increasing resemblance (isomorphism; see DiMaggio and Powell 1991b): *coercive* isomorphism through state regulation, other powerful organizations, or cultural expectations; *mimetic* isomorphism through emulating other organizations deemed legitimate or successful; *normative* isomorphism chiefly through members of professions whose training equips them with normative ideas about proper ways of organizing. Professions have as such a certain autonomy over defining these, which, crucially for the present purposes, is ultimately granted and upheld by the state (DiMaggio and Powell 1991b).

The concepts of legitimacy and organizational fields help elucidate pivotal dimensions of AIDS organizing (see Chapters 2 and 3). Professionalization was in part a quest for legitimacy. The field concept introduced an important level of power structures pertinent to AIDS organizations. More fundamentally, the cultural-constructive conception of legitimacy expands theoretical sensitivity to discursive power processes, where neo-corporatism was limited to more tangible power plays. However, professionalization of AIDS organization was empirically often conflictual and to some extent contingent. This aspect cannot be captured with the described neo-institutionalist theories. The reason for this is a missing micro-foundation and an over-socialized actor-model (Wilkens *et al.* 2003: 221; Zucker 1987a): organizations appear as rather passive recipients of institutionalized knowledge. The notion of decoupling leaves actual social relations and processes in the organization untheorized and irrelevant (Zucker 1987a: 455). Concomitantly, neither social change, individual choice among multiple social realities, nor how organizational actors react to institutional stipulations can be fully understood from this perspective (see also Scott 2001: 151; Zucker 1987a: 451, 454–5).

This is where the promoters of a micro-strand of neo-institutionalism propose that institutions also emerge from within organizations. The evolution of an organization thus amounts to the increasing institutionalization of organizational structures transforming individual actions into routines (Zucker 1987b: 34). Repeated interactions slowly turn into institutionalized, i.e., subjectively pregiven and objective, patterns. This is a dynamic process and institutionalized patterns must be sustained over time given endemic tendencies for change (Zucker 1991). Retention of institutions depends on coherent social networks and strong interlinkages between institutions, which bestow legitimacy on each other (Zucker 1987b). These arguments make the theory more dynamic. Organizations now figure as a continuous interactive process alternating between stability and change. However, while this is an important step towards a theoretical incorporation of individual action in organizations, it still falls short of adequately conceptualizing individual action. Though individual actors figure as producers of patterns of action as a basis of institutionalization there is no conception of how they act to produce those patterns and how exactly they would diverge from them if conditions were favorable for it (cf. also Barley and Tolbert 1997: 96). Key to how institutions guide social action is their taken-for-grantedness. It is for this very quality that their prescriptions appear as literally without alternatives (e.g., DiMaggio and Powell 1991a: 10–11), as objective (Zucker 1991), thus rendering anything else unthinkable. Institutions not only constrain but also enable social action: they constitute actors, interests and options for meaningful action (e.g., DiMaggio and Powell 1991a: 7; Friedland and Alford 1991; March and Olson 1996; Scott 1991: 238–9, 1994). This enables a pervasive form of social control, operating through the construction of reality rather than incentives. However, from this perspective social action can only be conceived as institutionally guided by pre-existing institutions. There is no conception for how institutionally constituted/guided actors can creatively feed back into an institutional order—in sum, we are confronted with an over-socialized view of social action.

Neo-institutionalism and social change

The neo-institutionalist conception of actors becomes acutely problematic in relation to social change. Social change, conflict and innovation, have remained marginal to neo-institutionalist theorizing (Barley and Tolbert 1997: 95; Clemens and Cook 1999: 442). Some have addressed the issue, but their propositions turn out to be problematic on closer inspection as they often have recourse to strategic-rationalist approaches (Oliver 1991; e.g., Suchman 1995). This, however, contradicts neo-instituionalist attempts to overcome such premises.

Basic perspectives

Zucker's (1991) argument is fundamental here: institutionalization varies in degree and is a process. It includes the potential for de-institutionalization given the fundamental entropy in social systems (Zucker 1987b). This entropy is due to: personal characteristics of actors; specific situations may make deviations necessary; self-interests of individuals, their use of power and coalition formation; finally, possible gaps and contradictions between institutions on the micro vs. macro level. Another important argument points to the potentially contradictory or vague institutional requirements and multiple but contradictory institutional environments (Friedland and Alford 1991; Scott 2001: 189). This may afford actors a degree of autonomy (e.g., Clemens and Cook 1999; Jepperson

1991: 152–3). Specifically this would allow them to make strategic decisions about which actors/environments to relate to (Scott 2001: 76, 171). With such recourse to rationalist conceptions of social action, i.e., strategic decisions about pertinent environments, however, neo-institutionalists fail to prove their own constructivist premises about the institutional constitution of actors, interests and domain-specific rationalities (Walgenbach 2003: 351). Another recurring idea is that of exogenous shocks or disruptions that may impact and change institutional orders. The examples used often have a certain ad hoc plausibility, such as political crises (Powell 1991: 200) or economic turmoil, new technologies, management-innovations, etc. (Scott 2001: 187). However, it remains unclear what exactly constitutes the nature of any given event as a shock to or a disruption of an institutional order.

Exemplary theorizing

Few studies focus squarely on conditions for institutional change. The following four examples show (but see also Quack 2006) how the failure to base neo-institutionalism in an adequate conception of individual action becomes problematic.

Oliver (1992) lists a broad range of factors for deinstitutionalization. *Political factors* include failure of the organization to produce desired outcomes, internal dissent, external pressures for innovation or shifting external dependencies. *Functional factors* involve changes in the instrumental value of an institution, for instance in economic or symbolic (prestige, legitimacy) terms. If the goals of an organization become more efficient, institutional myths are likely to become deinstitutionalized. Increased competitive pressures and new information that is incompatible with existing institutional practice are also in this category. Finally, *social factors* cover internal fragmentation, personnel fluctuation, increased internal diversity, historical discontinuity, poor organizational socialization, increased interlinkages with other organizations and state pressures. Though having great heuristic potential, this does not overcome the lack of a microfoundation as the underlying processes and their outcomes cannot be explained within this framework. Most of the factors Oliver discusses can be understood only in connection with contingent processes of interpretation and sensemaking. For instance, how does an organization come to perceive its production of benefits as problematic? When does it view itself as obsolete or in danger of failure? What makes certain incoming information so dissonant that it can disrupt established institutional patterns and so on?

Greenwood and Hinings (1996) correctly argue that organizations are not passive recipients of institutional stipulations but mediate institutional effects through their internal dynamics (cf. Scott 2001: 151). To understand internal dynamics they argue that functional differentiation in organizations creates subgroups with different, possibly competing interests, depending on market contexts. This may result in dissatisfaction of some groups relative to others, which would translate into pressures for change, depending on patterns of value commitment: all subgroups may be against changes (status quo commitment); or may be indifferent (indifferent commitment); subgroups may favor different patterns (competitive commitment); finally, all groups may be opposed to the established pattern (reformative commitment). These patterns of allegiance to social institutions would vary with the following factors: the organization's position in the field (central vs. peripheral); degree of internal functional differentiation; the organization's market success; finally, the degree of inconsistency of institutional requirements. To prevail with its desire for change, a group must possess sufficient power, in turn depending on market forces—a resource dependence argument—as well as on institutional factors (strong allegiance to dominant institutionalized patterns in central vs. weak allegiance in peripheral organizations). In short, they rely mostly on resource-dependence arguments and hence fall short of living up to neo-institutional, constructivist premises.

Clemens and Cook (1999) add to the above the idea of a policy-feedback cycle: institutions not only constitute their own actors but can in principle also delineate identities of challengers. Institutional in/stability thus depends on the scope and effectiveness of how institutions regulate and support social order and conversely allow or preclude dissent and deviation. A "politics of effective institution-building" (Clemens and Cook 1999: 457) includes incentives and action opportunities for stakeholders but limits opportunities for new actors and new issues. Discursive strategies create analogies to strongly institutionalized patterns, construct alternatives as risky or unthinkable, or cognitively decouple certain issues or specific interpretation of experience. This comes down to a restatement of neo-institutional arguments to explain social order (contagion of legitimacy, taken-for-grantedness). Where the reach of the thus theorized social order ends, actors gain liberties to promote social change. However, to understand this change-initiating action the authors end up having recourse to rational action (incentives and opportunities).

This argument resembles a variant of institutionalist theorizing which has change—or, rather, evolution—at its heart. This is rule system theory or actor system theory (e.g., Burns 2006, 2008; Burns and Dietz 1992; Burns and Flam 1987). What is more, it also devotes much greater consideration to the individual actor (Burns and Engdahl 1998a, 1998b). Arguments as to the sources of institutional change resemble those of neo-institutional organization theory, including, for instance: ambiguity, multiplicity and contradictions of institutional rules; imperfections in the transmission (e.g., inter-generational) or everyday application of rules; intentional innovations in the face of situational exigencies; etc. (e.g., Burns and Dietz 1992; Burns and Engdahl 1998a: 72). These conditions make for a constant degree of innovation which, however, must become institutionalized, that is selected, to become dominant. Innovation thus figures as a constant and a mere priori condition that is not fully explained in itself. Rather, the focus is on conditions for innovations to become selected, replicated and diffused. This is understood in mostly institutional, rather than agentic, terms as structured by institutional constraints, resource allocation, powerful elites, dynamics of social structure (e.g., in-migration), and, finally, by conditions of the material environment of human action (Burns and Dietz 1992). The effect of such selections is understood in rationalist terms: elites prescribe and enforce, socialize and sanction, control the recruitment of leaders, control career patterns, etc. (e.g., Burns 2006: 429–30). Institutionalization is thus the outcome of a strategic power process, or, rather, rational-strategic action of elites (Burns 2006: 415, see also 2008: 61). To the extent that rule system theory thus deviates from neo-institutionalism's emphasis on legitimacy and taken-for-grantedness, the theory simply eschews the problem of how actors and their rationales can be constituted by *taken-for-granted* institutions and are at the same time in a position to change what is taken for granted by them. What is more, individual actors do not play an especially active role in this view of institutionalization, despite some statements to the contrary. In the process of institutionalization individual actors figure as either recipients of rule systems or as actors whose innovating deviance is merely axiomatic. It is no coincidence that rule system theory develops its more elaborated arguments about individual actors starting with collectivities (Burns and Engdahl 1998a, 1998b): in line with neo-institutionalism, actors and agency are constituted through institutions which provide a meaningful basis for social action (Burns and Engdahl 1998a: 73). In short, institutions constitute social meaning. This is on a first level a collective reality of collective actors and a shared conception of the collective. It is on the basis of this collective level that individual social actors are constituted, resulting from "collective naming, classifying, judging, reflection, and discourse applied to individual members or participants in the collective" (Burns and Engdahl 1998b: 166). Socialization into collectives is thus (a constraining and enabling) precondition to individual agency and there is a detailed argument for how institutions affect, and indeed constitute, individual actors. Interestingly, the theory also acknowledges that actors are active and creative as they process incoming information (Burns and Engdahl 1998b: 171–3): experiencing (inner or external) change would initiate processes of reflectivity. Actors try to integrate changes into pre-existing understandings. Socially acquired cognitive frameworks thus structure experience. Change, however, may also produce instances that actors find to be at odds with preconceptions and expectations. In this case "particular mechanisms or processes are activated to resolve this: re-framing, selective focusing, re-interpretation, and re-definition processes as well as other mechanisms to reduce ambiguity or dissonance and to stabilize cognitions and images" (1998b: 173). At this point it is not entirely clear if this will lead to an adaptation of how changes are experienced in order to fit them better into socially acquired categories of understanding or if this will actually lead to altering the latter. Certainly, rule system theory makes no detailed link between individual reflectivity and the emergence of newly institutionalized rules—as argued above, the process of institutionalization is largely understood as the outcome of strategic action of a limited set of actors and individual deviation merely a constant.

These arguments, nevertheless, point to another theory which focuses on how environmental change leads actors to create meaning by both relying on pre-existing meaning and feeding back into those meaning systems. I want to argue that Weick's (1985, 1995) sensemaking approach can help us address the problem of a dynamic image of organizations that are reproduced or changed through the meaningful interactions of their members. Unlike the other theories discussed in this section, this approach provides a keenly constructionist perspective on individual action without taking recourse to notions of rational action.

The sensemaking approach

Closer investigation reveals a number of convergences between neo-institutionalism and sensemaking and there has been an, albeit hesitant, rapprochement between the two: Scott (2001), for instance, repeatedly refers to Weick's approach. Jennings and Greenwood (2003) relate both theories, although in the end in an opposing way. Weick (1995; Weick et al. 2005: 417) himself sees his approach as a micro-foundation for neo-institutionalism which is partially backed by some neo-institutionalists (Porac and Shapira 2001: 210). Weick shares a constructivist perspective (e.g., Berger and Luckmann 1996) but emphasizes the creative part of social construction.

Sensemaking: the process of organizing

Only gradually acknowledged in neo-institutionalism, environmental ambiguity is precisely the point of departure for Weick. As reality is per se meaningless and allows for a multitude of potential meanings—a fundamentally ambiguous and amorphous stream of input—actors need to impose meaning on it. Sensemaking understands organizations as an ongoing process of creating a meaningful environment by reducing the ambiguity and complexity of "raw" reality (rather than viewing organizations as determined by their environments). Weick (1985) conceptualizes this through a circular process containing four steps.

Ecological change and enactment

The sensemaking cycle begins with environmental change—the first step. Discontinuities and unexpected events interrupt routine action. In contrast to neo-institutionalism, however, sensemaking asks how the disruptive or divergent nature of events is constituted, opening itself to individual agency. Discrete events must first be constituted as distinct units from the amorphous stream of events (Weick et al. 2005: 411). This bracketing is only one aspect of enactment—the second step. As organizations turn produced meanings into action, they feed back into their environment and may in principle create further changes which in turn necessitate more sensemaking. Enactment not only contributes to emerging sensemaking but is in turn informed by schemata derived from past experience/sensemaking within a recursive dynamic (Weick 1985: 221–6): past and ongoing sensemaking mutually influence each other.

Selection

In the next step, bracketed, yet cognitively still unconnected, elements are put into a meaningful relation to each other. Selection answers the question of what is happening here. While bracketing prefigures selection to some extent, past experience, again, provides templates for this. This means that classifications, interpretations, causal assumptions, etc. will be selected which allow connecting newly enacted environments with old ones. There is thus a tendency to further buttress older meanings and try to match changed environments with older meanings. This is the source of organizational routine and inertia. However, this dynamic view of routines is not deterministic. The notion of an ongoing, dynamic grappling with changing environments includes the possibility of changes in sensemaking—a fundamental contrast to neo-institutionalism. Conditions for changes in routines thus move into focus.

Retention

The last step is, simply put, the memory of an organization. Retention means that products of successful sensemaking—enacted environments—are stored and kept available for future sensemaking. Again, previously stored meanings influence this process (see Weick 1985: 299–301 for more details). Retained meanings inform both enactment/bracketing and selection.

Seven characteristics and some sources of sensemaking

Weick (1995: 2) describes seven properties of sensemaking. Much like neo-institutionalism he emphasizes the role of *identity* and its socially constructed nature. Sensemaking thus starts with the sensemaker as identity forms a central lens for experience. At the same time, sensemaking is always a *social* process. Individuals always form meanings in interaction, which need not mean, however, that meanings be shared across an organization. Third, sensemaking is *retrospective*. Meanings can only emerge as actors step out of the amorphous stream of events and impose a temporal structure on it. *Enactment* rejects any simplistic notion of environment as a determining force while avoiding the assumption of complete autonomy. To a significant extent actors produce their environment. It appears real to them, while at the same time being a product of their of sensemaking. This is a central convergence with institutionalism as the focus is equally on institutionalization of social constructions (Weick 1995: 36). But other than in neo-institutionalism the underlying *process* of institutionalization remains an integral part of theory past the emergence of institutions. This also relates to a view of sensemaking as an *ongoing* process. Sensemaking is focused on and through *cues*. Extracted in the course of bracketing, they are the point of departure for more complex constructs of meaning. Finally, sensemaking aims at *plausibility*, rather than accuracy. In sum (Weick 1995: 55):

> Once people begin to act (enactment), they generate tangible outcomes (cues) in some context (social) and this helps them discover (retrospect) what is occurring (ongoing), what needs to be explained (plausibility), and what should be done next (identity enhancement).

Having no beginning, sensemaking does not start from scratch within an entirely meaningless space, but is rather prefigured by pre-existing collective meaning systems. These "vocabularies" form the substance of sensemaking or rather "minimal sensible structure[s]" (Weick 1995: 109). Weick discusses a number of such vocabularies, that I will only briefly and selectively[4] summarize here. For each of them he is at great pains to show that they always involve significant ambiguity.

Ideologies—world views that bind people together—form a link to institutional theorizing as ideologies may be produced and supplied by professions, organizational fields, (trans)national cultures, etc. However, contrasting a neo-institutionalist fallacy, they are neither homogenous nor compelling and actors adopt them selectively and creatively rather than passively (Weick 1995: 112–13). Another link to neo-institutionalism and its emphasis on professionalism, *paradigms*—implicit assumptions of what makes up reality and how—are equally much less unequivocal than often assumed, especially when it comes to their concrete content. *Stories* relate to the notion that narrativity is a central aspect of individual experience. They are constructed in search of causal explanations for experience and represent past experience.

Conclusion

Much like neo-institutionalism, Weick's theory is concerned with routines and the taken for granted. It is also keenly attuned to the effects of overarching meaning systems (vocabularies). However, unlike neo-institutionalism, their influence is not seen as deterministic. Institutionalized knowledge is both a basis and a product organizational action. In theory, this would be acknowledged by neo-institutionalists, but in practice the productive part remains axiomatic to them. Where individual agency is considered, neo-institutionalism abandons its constructivists premises and takes recourse to notions of rational-instrumental action. Weick's theory, in contrast, puts this productive action, that is sensemaking, center stage and can thus conceive of actors who are simultaneously guided by institutionalized knowledge as they act to reproduce or change that knowledge—keeping with a constructivist premise. Persistence and change come into analytical focus—an issue largely ignored by neo-institutionalists (see Scott 2001: 122). In sum, then, arguably "sensemaking is the feedstock of institutionalization" (Weick 1995: 36) and provides an adequate theory of action that neo-institutionalism lacks. From a sensemaking perspective we can begin to focus on conditions for maintaining patterns of meaning in organizations and for their destabilization.

Power, meso- and macro-structures

The sensemaking approach has been criticized as being not adequately sensitive to issues of power (see Helms Mills 2003: 43, 153). Indeed, both neo-corporatism and neo-institutionalism seem to have much more refined analytical tools to capture processes and structures of power. However, power is not entirely absent from sensemaking, as Weick *et al.* (2005: 418) emphasize. Weick's characterization of sensemaking as "social" may indeed only hint at it (Helms Mills 2003: 152–3). The sensemaking of some actors in organizations will likely have much greater chances of becoming dominant and valid than that of others. In a more recent statement Weick *et al.* (2005: 418) specify that from a sensemaking persective power operates

> through things like control over cues, who talks to whom, proffered identities, criteria for plausible stories, actions permitted and disallowed, and histories and retrospect that are singled out. To shape hearts and minds is to influence at least seven dimensions of sensemaking: the social relations that are encouraged and discouraged, the identities that are valued or derogated, the retrospective meanings that are accepted or discredited, the cues that are highlighted or suppressed, the updating that is encouraged or discouraged, the standard of accuracy or plausibility to which conjectures are held, and the approval of proactive or reactive action as the preferred mode of coping.

To be sure, this is a decidedly micro-social perspective on power processes. It seems difficult to integrate this with power-structures on the meso- and macro-level, where powerful actors may use resources such as money, information, formal rule setting or jurisdiction, status, etc. to constrain or enable actions by others. Sensemaking theory says little about the operations and formation of such larger power structures. There is no theory for how institutionalization on the micro-level of single organizations might feed back into overarching institutional structures. A point of departure would be to conceive of powerful actors in terms of sensemaking as well. As we have seen in the previous chapters, even though the fostering of specific forms of AIDS organizing by the state operated also through the allocation of resources, this was deeply embedded into collective sensemaking of, or rather discourses about, AIDS. Nevertheless, this remains unresolved and reflects also in the persistent bifurcation of neo-institutional theorizing into a macro- and a micro-strand.

However, even in situations where power takes on the shape of direct orders or the allocation of resources, sensemaking allows us to focus on how actors make sense of and relate to instances of power, comply with them, act in defiance and resistance, etc. In other words some bases of authority's legitimacy, that is of authority's effects on the subordinate, come into view. From this perspective, sensemaking becomes particularly suitable for the analysis of AIDS organizations and for how organizational actors deal with the lines of power that constitute AIDS organizing.

After all, pertinent forms of power are very much in the discursive realm. How actors in AIDS service organizations are constituted by such forms of power dominant in the field of AIDS work, how their action is guided by them, how it entails specific constructions of organizational reality involving varying degrees of politicization, how they relate to ecological changes towards adverse power constellations will be the focus of the empirical part of this study. Before I can focus on these issues, however, the next chapter will outline methodological issues of researching sensemaking and its links to emotions empirically.

Notes

1 Both focus on interdependence between state and nonprofits and the utilization of nonprofits/associations through the state in order to implement social policies (cf., for example, Streeck 1994: 16–18; Streeck and Kenworthy 2003: 449–53).
2 Neo-corporatist theorizing only hints at discursive dimensions when talking about actors' perceptions (Lehmbruch 1983: 412–13, e.g., 1984: 67; Nedelmann and Meier 1979).
3 For instance, large unified or industry-wide unions (vs. small, specialized or regional/local ones) will lean towards overarching solidarity across different groups of workers and pursue non-particularistic interests (Streeck 1979; Streeck *et al.* 1981).
4 Weick (1995) discusses three more that I omit here: *third-order controls* via taken-for-granted assumptions and definitions; *theories of action* are organizational definitions of causal links perceived in the environment; *traditions*, as beliefs about the past, need to be perpetuated in, and are thus very much a product of, the present.

References

Barley, Stephen R. and Pamela S. Tolbert. 1997. "Institutionalization and Structuration: Studying the Links between Action and Institution." *Organization Studies* 18(1): 93–117.

Berger, Peter L. and Thomas Luckmann. 1996. *The Social Construction of Reality: A Treatise in the Sociology of Knowledge*. London, New York, Ringwood, Toronto, Auckland: Penguin Books.

Burns, Tom R. 2006. "The Sociology of Complex Systems: An Overview of Actor-System-Dynamics Theory." *World Futures: The Journal of General Evolution* 62(6): 411–40.

Burns, Tom R. 2008. "Rule System Theory: An Overview." Pp. 57–84 in *Rule Systems Theory: Applications and Explorations*, edited by H. Flam and C. Marcus. Frankfurt am Main, Berlin, Bern, Bruxelles, New York, Oxford, Wien: Peter Lang Verlag.

Burns, Tom R. and Thomas Dietz. 1992. "Cultural Evolution: Social Rule Systems, Selection and Human Agency." *International Sociology* 7(3): 259–83.

Burns, Tom R. and Erik Engdahl. 1998a. "The Social Construction of Consciousness: Part 1. Collective Consciousness and Its Socio-Cultural Foundations." *Journal of Consciousness Studies* 5(1): 67–85.

Burns, Tom R. and Erik Engdahl. 1998b. "The Social Construction of Consciousness: Part 2. Individual Selves, Self-Awareness, and Reflectivity." *Journal of Consciousness Studies* 5(2): 166–84.

Burns, Tom R. and Helena Flam. 1987. *The Shaping of Social Organization: Social Rule System Theory with Applications*. London, Beverly Hills, Newbury Park, New Delhi: SAGE.

Cawson, Alan. 1985a. "Introduction. Varieties of Corporatism: The Importance of the Meso-Level of Interest Intermediation." Pp. 1–21 in *Organized Interests and the State: Studies in Meso-Coporatism*, edited by A. Cawson. London, Beverly Hills, New Delhi: SAGE.

Cawson, Alan, ed. 1985b. *Organized Interests and the State: Studies in Meso-Corporatism*. London, Beverly Hills, New Delhi: SAGE.

Clemens, Elisabeth S. and James M. Cook. 1999. "Politics and Institutionalism: Explaining Durability and Change." *Annual Review of Sociology* 25: 441–66.

Czada, Roland. 1998. "Korporatismus/Neo-Korporatismus." Pp. 365–70 in *Wörterbuch Staat und Politik*, edited by D. Nohlen. Bonn: Bundeszentrale für politische Bildung.

DiMaggio, Paul J. and Walter W. Powell. 1991a. "Introduction." Pp. 1–38 in *The New Institutionalism in Organizational Analysis*, edited by P. J. DiMaggio and W. W. Powell. Chicago, London: Chicago University Press.

DiMaggio, Paul J. and Walter W. Powell. 1991b. "The Iron Cage Revisited: Institutional Isomorphism and Collective Rationality in Organizational Fields." Pp. 63–82 in *The New Institutionalism in Organizational Analysis*, edited by P. J. DiMaggio and W. W. Powell. Chicago, London: Chicago University Press.

Edelman, Lauren B. and Mark C. Suchman. 1997. "The Legal Environment of Organizations." *Annual Review of Sociology* 23: 479–515.

Flam, Helena. 1990. *Corporate Actors: Definition, Genesis, and Interaction*. Köln: Max-Planck-Institut für Gesellschaftsforschung, Discussion Paper 90/11.

Flanagan, Robert J. 1999. "Macroeconomic Performance and Collective Bargaining: An International Perspective." *Journal of Economic Literature* 37(3): 1150–75.

Friedland, Roger and Robert R. Alford. 1991. "Bringing Society Back In: Symbols, Practices, and Institutional Contradictions." Pp. 232–63 in *The New Institutionalism in Organizational Analysis*, edited by P. J. DiMaggio and W. W. Powell. Chicago, London: Chicago University Press.

Greenwood, Royston and C. R. Hinings. 1996. "Understanding Radical Organizational Change: Bringing together the Old and the New Institutionalism." *Academy of Management Review* 21(4): 1022–54.

Groenemeyer, Axel. 2010. "Doing Social Problems—Doing Social Control." Pp. 13–56 in *Doing Social Problems*, edited by A. Groenemeyer. Wiesbaden: VS Verlag für Sozialwissenschaften.

Heinze, Rolf G. and Helmut Voelzkow. 1999. "Verbände und 'Neokorporatismus'." Pp. 227–39 in *Kommunalpolitik. Politisches Handeln in den Gemeinden*, edited by H. Wollmann and R. Roth. Opladen: Leske + Budrich.

Helms Mills, Jean. 2003. *Making Sense of Organizational Change*. London, New York: Routledge.

Jennings, P. Devereaux and Royston Greenwood. 2003. "Constructing the Iron Cage: Institutional Theory and Enactment." Pp. 195–207 in *Debating Organization: Point and Counterpoint in Organization Studies*, edited by R. Westwood and S. Clegg. Malden, MA: Blackwell Publishers.

Jepperson, Ronald L. 1991. "Institutions, Institutional Effects, and Institutionalism." Pp. 143–63 in *The New Institutionalism in Organizational Analysis*, edited by P. J. DiMaggio and W. W. Powell. Chicago, London: Chicago University Press.

Lehmbruch, Gerhard. 1979a. "Consociational Democracy, Class Conflict, and the New Corporatism." Pp. 53–61 in *Trends toward Corporatist Intermediation*, edited by P. C. Schmitter and G. Lehmbruch. Beverly Hills, London: SAGE.

Lehmbruch, Gerhard. 1979b. "Liberal Corporatism and Party Government." Pp. 147–83 in *Trends toward Corporatist Intermediation*, edited by P. C. Schmitter and G. Lehmbruch. Beverly Hills, London: SAGE.

Lehmbruch, Gerhard. 1983. "Neokorporatismus in Westeuropa: Hauptprobleme im internationalen Vergleich." *Journal für Sozialforschung* 23(4): 407–20.

Lehmbruch, Gerhard. 1984. "Concertation and the Structure of Corporatist Networks." Pp. 60–80 in *Order and Conflict in Contemporary Capitalism*, edited by J. H. Goldthorpe. Oxford: Clarendon Press.

March, James G. and Johan P. Olson. 1996. "Institutional Perspectives on Political Institutions." *Governance: An International Journal of Policy and Administration* 9(3): 247–64.

Meyer, John W. and Brian Rowan. 1991. "Institutional Organizations: Formal Structure as Myth and Ceremony." Pp. 41–62 in *The New Institutionalism in Organizational Analysis*, edited by P. J. DiMaggio and W. W. Powell. Chicago, London: Chicago University Press.

Molina, Oscar and Martin Rhodes. 2002. "Corporatism: The Past, Present, and Future of a Concept." *Annual Review of Political Science* 5: 305–31.

Nedelmann, Brigitta and Kurt G. Meier. 1979. "Theories of Contemporary Corporatism: Static or Dynamic?" Pp. 95–118 in *Trends toward Corporatist Intermediation*, edited by P. C. Schmitter and G. Lehmbruch. Beverly Hills, London: SAGE.

Oliver, Christine. 1991. "Strategic Responses to Institutional Pressures." *Academy of Management Review* 16(1): 145–79.

Oliver, Christine. 1992. "The Antecedents of Deinstitutionalization." *Organization Studies* 13(4): 563–88.

Porac, Joseph and Zur Shapira. 2001. "On Mind, Environment, and Simon's Scissors of Rational Behavior." *Journal of Management and Governance* 5(3–4): 206–12.

Powell, Walter W. 1991. "Expanding the Scope of Institutional Analysis." Pp. 185–203 in *The New Institutionalism in Organizational Analysis*, edited by P. J. DiMaggio and W. W. Powell. Chicago, London: Chicago University Press.

Quack, Sigrid. 2006. "Institutioneller Wandel. Institutionalisierung und De-Institutionalisierung." Pp. 172–84 in *Einführung in den Neo-Institutionalismus*, edited by K. Senge and K.-U. Hellmann. Wiesbaden: VS Verlag für Sozialwissenschaften.

Salamon, Lester M. 1987. "Partners in Public Service: The Scope and Theory of Government-Nonprofit Relations." Pp. 99–117 in *The Nonprofit Sector: A Research Handbook*, edited by W. W. Powell. New Haven: Yale University Press.

Salamon, Lester M. and Helmut K. Anheier. 1996. "Social Origins of Civil Society: Explaining the Nonprofit Sector Cross-Nationally." *Voluntas. International Journal of Voluntary and Nonprofit Organizations* 9(3): 213–48.

Schmitter, Philippe C. 1974. "Still the Century of Corporatism?" *Review of Politics* 36(1): 85–131.
Schmitter, Philippe C. 1982. "Modes of Interest Intermediation and Models of Societal Change in Western Europe." Pp. 63–94 in *Trends toward Corporatist Intermediation*, edited by G. Lehmbruch and P. C. Schmitter. London: SAGE.
Schmitter, Philippe C. 1984. *Neo-Corporatism and the State*. Florence: European University Institute, Working Paper 106.
Schmitter, Philippe C. and Wolfgang Streeck. 1981. *The Organization of Business Interest: A Research Design to Study the Associative Action of Business in the Advanced Industrial Societies of Western Europe*. Berlin: Wissenschaftszentrum Berlin für Sozialwissenschaften. Discussion Paper 81–13.
Schneider, Joseph W. 1985. "Social Problems Theory: The Constructionist View." *Annual Review of Sociology* 11: 209–29.
Scott, W. Richard. 1991. "Unpacking Institutional Arguments." Pp. 164–82 in *The New Institutionalism in Organizational Analysis*, edited by P. J. DiMaggio and W. W. Powell. Chicago, London: Chicago University Press.
Scott, W. Richard. 1994. "Institutions and Organizations: Toward a Theoretical Synthesis." Pp. 55–80 in *Institutional Environments and Organizations: Structural Complexity and Individualism*, edited by W. R. Scott and J. W. Meyer. Thousand Oaks, London, New Delhi: SAGE.
Scott, W. Richard. 2001. *Institutions and Organizations*. Thousand Oaks, London, New Delhi: SAGE.
Skocpol, Theda. 1999. "How Americans Became Civic." Pp. 27–80 in *Civic Engagement in American Democracy*, edited by T. Skocpol and M. P. Fiorina. Washington: Brookings Instition Press and Russell Sage Foundation.
Skocpol, Theda. 2004. *Diminished Democracy: From Membership to Management in American Civic Life*. Norman: University of Oklahoma Press.
Smith, Steven Rathgeb and Michael Lipsky. 1993. *Nonprofits for Hire: The Welfare State in the Age of Contracting*. Cambridge, MA, London: Harvard University Press.
Spector, Malcolm and John I. Kitsuse. 1973. "Social Problems: A Re-Formulation." *Social Problems* 21(2): 145–59.
Spector, Malcolm and John I. Kitsuse. 1977. *Constructing Social Problems*. Menlo Park: Cummings.
Streeck, Wolfgang. 1979. "Gewerkschaftsorganisation und industrielle Beziehungen. Einige Stabilitätsprobleme industriegewerkschaftlicher Interessenvertretung und ihre Lösung im westdeutschen System der industriellen Beziehungen." Pp. 206–26 in *Sozialer Wandel in Westeuropa: Verhandlungen des 19. Deutschen Soziologentages*, edited by J. Matthes. Frankfurt am Main, New York: Campus.
Streeck, Wolfgang. 1994. "Einleitung des Herausgebers. Staat und Verbände: Neue Fragen. Neue Antworten?" Pp. 7–34 in *Staat und Verbände*. Opladen: Westdeutscher Verlag.
Streeck, Wolfgang and Lane Kenworthy. 2003. "Theories and Practices of Neo-Corporatism." Pp. 441–60 in *A Handbook of Political Sociology: States, Civil Society and Globalization*, edited by T. Janoski, R. R. Alford, A. M. Hicks and M. Schwarz. New York: Cambridge University Press.
Streeck, Wolfgang and Philippe C. Schmitter. 1985. "Community, Market, State—and Associations? The Prospective Contribution of Interest Governance to Social Order." Pp. 1–29 in *Private Interest Government: Beyond Market and State*, edited by P. C. Schmitter and W. Streeck. Beverly Hills: SAGE.

Streeck, Wolfgang, Peter Seglow and Pat Wallace. 1981. "Competition and Monopoly in Interest Representation: A Comparative Analysis of Trade Union Structure in the Railway Industries of Great Britain and West Germany." *Organization Studies* 2(4): 307–30.
Suchman, Mark C. 1995. "Managing Legitimacy: Strategic and Institutional Approaches." *Academy of Management Review* 20(3): 571–610.
Walgenbach, Peter. 2003. "Institutionalistische Ansätze in der Organisationstheorie." Pp. 319–53 in *Organisationstheorien*, edited by A. Kieser. Stuttgart: Verlag W. Kohlhammer.
Weick, Karl E. 1985. *Der Prozeß des Organisierens*. Frankfurt am Main: Suhrkamp.
Weick, Karl E. 1995. *Sensemaking in Organizations*. Thousand Oaks, London, New Delhi: SAGE.
Weick, Karl E., Kathleen M. Sutcliff and David Obstfeld. 2005. "Organizing and the Process of Sensemaking." *Organization Science* 16(4): 409–21.
Wilkens, Uta, Reinhart Lang and Ingo Winkler. 2003. "Institutionensoziologische Ansätze." Pp. 189–242 in *Moderne Organisationstheorien 2. Strukturorientierte Ansätze*, edited by E. Weik and R. Lang. Wiesbaden: Gabler.
Wolch, Jennifer R. 1990. *The Shadow State: Government and Voluntary Sector in Transition*. New York: Foundation Center.
Zucker, Lynne G. 1987a. "Institutional Theories of Organization." *Annual Review of Sociology* 13: 443–64.
Zucker, Lynne G. 1987b. "Where do Institutional Patterns Come from? Organizations as Actors in Social Systems." Pp. 23–48 in *Institutional Patterns and Organizations: Culture and Environment*, edited by L. G. Zucker. Cambridge, MA: Ballinger.
Zucker, Lynne G. 1991. "The Role of Institutionalization in Cultural Persistence." Pp. 83–107 in *The New Institutionalism in Organizational Analysis*, edited by P. J. DiMaggio and W. W. Powell. Chicago, London: Chicago University Press.

Chapter 5

Sensemaking, narrative analysis and emotions[1]

How can sensemaking be studied empirically? Specifically, how can we apply it to empirical research into dissolved AIDS organizations? I want to argue here that narrative analysis provides useful tools for this. To make this point, this chapter first presents a summary of key principles of narrative analysis to then describe convergences with sensemaking theory.

Both sensemaking and existing approaches to narrative analysis are more or less mute on emotions (but see, for example, Flam 1998; Gammerl 2009). In the second part I will therefore develop a narrative conception of emotions and explore how this can help us trace emotions in narrative interview texts. Given the innovative nature of crafting tools for the analysis of emotions through qualitative empirical methods, I will afford myself some license to develop and introduce this methodology broadly. This provides a foundation for exploring the role of emotions in sensemaking in the third part.

Narrative methodology and analysis

The fundamental theoretical premise of narrative analysis is that human experience has a crucial narrative dimension.[2] It is organized along a temporal, sequential order of "first this, then that", "befores and afters" (Schütze 1987: 15; similarly Weick 1995: 127). The idea is that people have specific "narrative" knowledge—the knowledge of how things have come about, a kind of knowledge that has not been abstracted and that is thus only accessible in its narrative form. Based on this knowledge, how things have come about can only be recounted as a story rather than in theoretical, reflected terms (which would build on a different kind of experiential knowledge).

Narrative analysis essentially dissects the narrative structure of the interview text (e.g., Schütze 1983, 1987; for the following, see also Labov and Waletzky 1967; Lucius-Hoene and Deppermann 2004). Stories are made up of a series of discrete narrative segments. These describe phases or events, for instance: graduation from high school, deciding what to do after that, finding a university, etc. These segments have an inner structure. Their beginnings and endings are marked in various ways. This includes linguistic markers, such as a shift in focus or segment-summarizing abstracts at the beginning: "[*shift in focus*:] and then [*abstract*:] I had to decide what I wanted to do after high school..." A preamble indicates the overall meaning of the segment: e.g., "something horrible happened." An orientation indicates temporal, spatial and other situational contexts and relevant actors. The core of a segment—the so-called complication—is the narrative sentences. These sentences actually narrate what happens. That something happens, that is a change in time, is the constitutive feature of narrative. In this respect, narration of events contrasts with two other textual modes, which are typically present in the interview text as well: description (evoking a static picture) and argumentation (evaluative or theoretical-explanatory comments). The narrative parts may be interjected with detailing remarks about the backgrounds of what happened. The segment may be closed by a resolution and coda that summarize the result and meaning of what happened. At the segment end there can also be prosodic markers such as a falling intonation or pauses.

A key analytical principle pertains to sequentiality (e.g., Schütze 1983: 283): the meaning of any part of text can only be understood in its textual context. This goes not only for the micro-structure of segments but equally for how segments are structured into a sequence: which events follow each other, how are meanings of events based on previous ones, etc. (for a summary, see Lucius-Hoene and Deppermann 2004). There may be suprasegmental contexts, main and side-lines of the narrative.

The temporal structure of the narrative may be compressed, expanded or parallel to the original experience. There may be temporal leaps and gaps as well as interruptions in the narrative. Narratives can have a linear structure, where events follow successively on each other or narrators interrupt the flow of the story to look back into the preceding past or make indications of what is to come. A narrative may also be repetitive or iterative.

In sum, there is a broad array of specific analytical perspectives in narrative analysis ranging from the structure of single segments to an overarching focus on the entire narrative or larger parts of it. A common denominator of these diverse specific aspects, however, is to identify the different narrative elements of a story and look at the significance of these elements within the story in relation to each other—how is meaning constituted as the different narrative elements interrelate. Crucially, narrative analysis allows us to see both which aspects of experience matter to the narrator and how they matter. This is obviously only a very cursory overview, but it will allow me to show in principle how narrative analysis can help us research sensemaking and emotions.

Convergences: sensemaking and narrative analysis

With this in mind we can outline a number of fundamental convergences with sensemaking theory. Narrative analysis and sensemaking theory share a number of fundamental premises. Both understand social experience as an ongoing process (Schütze 1987: 14–16; Weick 1985, 1995). In fact Schütze (1987: 37) devised the narrative interview to capture the process quality of social life. Neither narrative analysis nor sensemaking are realist: they are interested in subjective experience rather than in what "really" happened (cf. Schütze 1987: 20). For narrative analysis, this involves the premise, akin to Weick's notion of enactment, that social and biographical processes are interdependently intertwined and constitute each other (Schütze 1987: 42). There is equally a shared focus on identity, as sensemaking "begin[s] with a sensemaker" (Weick 1995: 18) and narrative analysis assumes that the essence of narrating is to express changes, however subtle, in the—individual and collective—identity of the narrator (Schütze 1987: 27, 42). Finally, Weick accords a central role to narrativity in organization when he endorses the idea that people "think narratively rather than argumentatively or paradigmatically" arguing that "most organizational realities are based on narration" (1995: 127).

More importantly, convergences extend beyond principal premises. In fact, narrative analysis opens perspectives on sensemaking in real-time as it were (Holtgrewe 2002: 74). A closer look can substantiate this claim. Essentially, narrative analysis comes down to identifying the different elements of a narrative and how they relate to each other as they constitute a story or, rather, meaning. In other words, we can see which things matter centrally for actors in their continuous stream of experience, down to the categories and words used to construct them as such. In short, we get a glimpse of the bracketing element of the sensemaking process. Second, narrative analysis looks at how discrete narrative elements (core narrative sentences, background conditions, resolutions, detailing elaborations, etc.) and sequences of segments are connected to each other, that is how they constitute a meaningful narrative through the specific ways of being interrelated. It brings into focus what is happening in the actors' subjective experience—the principle aspect of selection in sensemaking. Finally, sequentiality is a key principle of narrative analysis. The meaning of any part or element of the narrative can only be understood in the narrative context. In other words, we can see how any given instance is being matched into the previous stream of experience or introduces deviations from patterns of sensemaking. Narrative analysis thus reflects the recursive nature of the sensemaking process where retention informs selection and both of them impinge on enactment.

Emotions and narrative analysis

One premise of this study is the emotional nature of nonprofit organizing. Yet neither sensemaking nor narrative methodology seem to easily lend themselves to an analytical focus on emotions. In the following I want to address first how narrative analysis can be extended to capture the emotional dimension of experience before I draw conclusions on the role of emotions in sensemaking theory.

The increase in popularity of emotion research in the social sciences has had surprisingly little impact so far on methodological debates. How sociology and other social sciences can study emotions empirically in systematic ways has been the focus of relatively little attention and has only recently taken on momentum (Flam and Kleres 2015). Notable exceptions to this include a line of research that has developed sets of linguistic markers for certain specific emotions, such as shame and anger (e.g., Scheff 1988; Retzinger 1991) or more generally positive and negative self-feelings (Bloch 1996). Interestingly, this addresses covert instances of emotions—a key methodological problem (Bloch 1996). However, these frameworks are limited to specific emotions. Tamar Zilber (1998) advanced a more inclusive framework when she listed some linguistic markers of emotionality per se. However, this remains partial and is not embedded into a sociological conception of emotions nor into a more general methodological frame. Qualitative methodology books are largely mute on the matter. If they do mention emotions it concerns, for example, the role of emotions during interviewing or within the narrative process, but without an analytical access to emotions as manifested in interview text (e.g., Lucius-Hoene and Deppermann 2004; Gilbert 2000; Kleinman and Copp 1993; Lee-Treweek and Linkogle 2000).

This chapter thus deals with a very concrete problem: how can we systematically analyze emotional experience through qualitative methods? In particular, how can we do this if interviewees regularly fail to spell out their emotions explicitly? I want to argue that we can fruitfully extend the principles of narrative analysis to the systematic empirical analysis of emotions. This involves a specific view on emotions—the notion of emotions' narrative nature. This will allow me to argue how narrative analysis can be the basis for emotion analysis. Finally, employing mainly linguistic (and some cognate) research will help elaborate narrative analysis as an empirical technique for the study of emotions.

The narrativity of emotions

The premise of narrative analysis is the assertion that human experience has a crucial narrative dimension. If we acknowledge at the same time emotions' fundamental relevance to social life, this begs the question whether narrativity extends to emotions as well. And if so, how exactly do emotion and narrative bear on each other: is there a storied quality to emotions? To consider this issue, we need to depart from certain dominant notions and adopt a novel understanding of emotions—the idea that the nature of emotions is narrative and conversely that narratives are emotional.

The notion of narrative emotions has not enjoyed much attention in the social sciences. In the sociology of emotions we may perhaps come across the idea that *certain* emotions have a narrative quality, such as love (see Illouz 1997; Illouz and Wilf 2009: 125; Sternberg 1996). This limited concept of emotions' narrativity contrasts with the more basic concept I will employ here. In other academic disciplines there has been more talk about narrative emotions, particularly in philosophy (e.g., De Sousa 1980, 1990; Deslandes 2004a, 2004b; Goldie 2000; Nussbaum 1988, 2003; Turski 1991) and to a lesser extent in psychology, albeit with varying meanings of the term.

The storied nature of emotions

Despite some theoretical differences, we can identify a recurring idea—the notion that emotions are embedded in narratives and are in fact socially learned through narratives. De Sousa, for instance, argued that "we are made familiar with the vocabulary of emotion by association with *paradigm scenarios*" (1980: 142, original emphasis). These paradigm scenarios connect objects, which they help identify, with emotional responses that they prescribe as normal (De Sousa 1990: 182). Similary Nussbaum (1988: 226) views emotions—how to feel, our emotional repertoire—as taught to us by society through paradigm stories:

> it seems right to say [...] not only that a certain sort of story shows or represents emotion but also that emotion itself is the acceptance of, the assent to live according to, a certain kind of story. Stories, in short, contain and reach forms of feeling, forms of life.

Finally, Goldie describes emotions as complex, episodic and structured. An emotion "is structured in that it constitutes part of a narrative—roughly, an unfolding sequence of actions and events, thoughts and feelings—in which the emotion itself is embedded" (Goldie 2000: 13).

The crucial idea to be taken from this is that the narrative elements of a story together configure emotional experience. The *gestalt* of actors, events, conditions, thoughts, feelings, etc. constitutes an emotion. From the constructivist perspective of narrative analysis we can add the emphasis that subjective representations of these elements, their significance, are highly contingent.

Emotions and temporality

A constitutive feature of narratives is temporality. Narrativity is defined by a change in time. Paradigm scenarios can in this sense be understood as narratives. The way De Sousa (1980, 1990) or Nussbaum (1988) define paradigm scenarios or stories, however, they resemble more concise narrative segments rather than elaborate and in practice typically very complex narratives. Yet the principle of sequentiality in narrative analysis emphasizes the embeddedness of each segment or narrative element into the ongoing stream of the narrative. Temporality thus figures in a much more overarching way. In her later work on emotions Nussbaum (2003: 178–9, 236) elaborates on the issue of temporality. She argues that any specific instance of emotionality cannot be fully understood unless there is some consideration of its history. This would tie well with the premises of narrative analysis. However, her notion of this history seems to be indebted to psychology, it is the history of any emotion in childhood and infancy. This is more of a developmental perspective than a narrative one. She does argue, however, "that the cognitive content of emotions arrives embedded in a complex narrative history, without mentioning which one frequently cannot give an account of the full specificity of the emotion itself" (2003: 179). From the perspective of narrative analysis, we need not subscribe to the psycho-developmental aspect of Nussbaum's argument to appreciate this latter point (cf. also Archer 2000: 29 and her conceptualization of "Me" as an emotional memory bank). This is buttressed by Jack Katz' theorizing: emotions are "a double commentary on social interactions," that is not only on the present interaction but also a "comment on the overall stories that they are constructing as they shape a path through their life" (1999: 324). Emotional moments are part of a two-fold sensemaking project (Katz 1999: 324–5): they involve the micro-story of the present situation, but this story is embedded in, and gains (emotional) significance through, larger narrative contexts. Katz (1999: 327) concludes that "all socially situated emotions are dualistic narrative projects." From this perspective then, the narrative past is indispensable for understanding any present instance of emotionality.

The emotional nature of narratives

The above remarks on the narrativity of emotions, it seems, could support a purely cognitive conception of emotions as narrative, as they appear to be constituted by cognitive, narrative elements (the *gestalt* of actors, events, conditions, etc.) and indeed Nussbaum's theory is purely and admittedly cognitive. Emotions, in her (1988, 2003) view, are intricately linked to beliefs or judgments about the world, which, she argues, are indeed sufficient for the emotion: "if I do not get angry, then I do not really truly accept or believe that I have been wronged" (Nussbaum 1988: 232). The beliefs in question are cognitive categories about what is valuable and important (1988: 232–3, 2003). From this perspective, then, narratives can be seen as the causes of emotions. There is, however, a fundamental problem with this view. Applying a linguistic-constructivist perspective, it seems tautological to argue that I *get* angry because I believe (cognitively) that I have been wronged. The very construction and perception of having been wronged *is* at the core of feeling angry rather than *causing* the emotion of anger. It is tantamount to an emotional construct. This has to do with a more fundamental problem: despite aiming at a cognitive theory of emotions, Nussbaum's argument implicitly and involuntarily points at the more pervasive role of emotions and feelings when she qualifies the specific kinds of beliefs pertinent to her argument as crucially involving subjective valuation and attribution of importance. Arguably, at this point emotions sneak back into her argument: they are critical in constituting salience (De Sousa 1990: xv) and the very concepts of value and importance are inextricably emotional (cf. also Archer 2000: 196).

Philosophical tendencies to over-intellectualize emotions are criticized on a general level by Goldie (2000). Against this, he proposes a specific notion of the intentionality of emotions, i.e., their directedness towards an object. He warns against the mistake of capturing this intentionality in terms of beliefs and/or desires, as both could be feelingless. Instead, he proposes the notion of *feeling towards*: "*thinking of* with feeling so that your emotional feelings are directed towards the object of your thought" (Goldie 2000: 19, original emphasis). There is a perceptual quality to this kind of thinking of (Goldie 2000: 19–20):

> Feeling towards, as it is thinking of with feeling, is a sort of thinking of. One can come to think of something as being a particular way; certain features become salient. And thinking of is related to seeing an aspect.

This perspective resonates with arguments about an interlacing of reason, thought and emotion. From a sociological perspective, already Hochschild (1983) talks about emotions as clues and thus as a precondition to perception and ultimately to forms of rationality. Barbalet (1998) makes a sweeping argument for the interlacing of rationality and emotion. Katz (1999: 332) criticizes the view that "emotions are in tension with reason, self-reflection, or thought […]. Emotions are ways of turning back on the self, ways of reflexively amplifying and giving added resonance to the transcendent meanings of situated action." In his view, emotions are a form of perception in that persons do not apprehend the implications of a situation cognitively but rather in a sensual appreciation: "One commonly *feels* situations" (Katz 1999: 332, original emphasis). He terms these latent or incipient emotions. Coming from a quite different vantage point Schwarz-Friesel (2007: 112) concludes from her discussion of psychological theorizing that emotions and cognition are not separate, isolated and autonomous phenomena, but rather different aspects of one and the same phenomenon, that is the human mind.

From this perspective, emotionality is intimately intertwined with what can be described as the cognitive dimension of narrative. Narratives thus not only present us with the cognitive dimension of emotions, but with emotionality itself as it is an inextricable part of the narrative. This idea can be further developed, relying on Sarbin's (1989, 2001) theory. He argues against the essentialist, reifying idea that emotions are "quasi-objects, sometimes cranial, sometimes visceral" (see also Archer 2000: 196–7; Goldie 2000: 13, 2001: 217), which is immanent in much other writing on emotions and narrativity. Instead, he argues for studying emotional life rather than discrete emotions, which he views as mere names of narrative plots. Emotions then appear as narrative emplotments (Sarbin 1989). Rather than asking what emotions are, Sarbin (1989: 188) advises us to focus instead on the specifics of situations, such as the actors involved, the setting, the actual actions, etc. These aspects form the integral elements of an emotion narrative. In a similar vein, Turski (1991) argues against a purely intra-psychological account of emotions. He departs from a separation of meaning and emotion to conclude: "what gets identified in emotion formation is emphatically neither a simple feeling nor an abstract proposition about the world but a *form of activity*, a sense of engagement with that world" (1991: 378, original emphasis). He goes on to define emotions as temporally and dramatically structured. The plot of the prototypical social dramas underlying emotions "at once defines the agent's role, feelings and reactions characteristic of the emotion as just that way of existing—as just that way […] of being directed to something in the world" (1991: 378).

From this perspective, then, narratives provide us with more than merely the cognitive antecedents of emotions. They grant us access to human experience as it is inextricably meaningful and emotional at the same time. The very nature of emotional experience can be conceptualized as essentially narrative in nature (rather than mediated by narratives) and vice versa: narratives essentially are emotionally structured. Emotions emerge from this as narrative configurations, scenarios or *gestalt*. Rather than existing as discrete, isolated, reifyable things, they exist in the very sets of narrative elements that make up a specific instance of emotional experience, that is a specific configuration of actors, objects, conditions, actions, events, etc. While these elements may be represented in thought, a merely cognitive rendition of these elements would ignore the fact that they are constitutive, integral elements of emotional experience. This concept of narrative emotions thus blurs the distinction between thought and emotion and renders them two sides of the same coin, that is human experience.

Towards narrative emotion analysis

A methodology of narrative emotion analysis can fruitfully build on this conception of emotion. To develop the notion of narrative emotions in methodological terms, it proves very instructive to draw on existing research in other academic fields. In particular, linguistic research about emotions provides a wealth of analytical tools to approach the emotional content of texts (Fiehler 1990; Jahr 2000; e.g., Schwarz-Friesel 2007). Together, this body of research shows how texts—as in a way cognitive representations of experience—are inseparably emotional. This research thus further buttresses the idea that emotionality is an inextricable element of narrative.

In line with the arguments from the previous section, linguistic research identifies more often than not markers of emotionality per se rather than describing linguistic profiles of certain emotions. This is because emotions are not explicable without recourse to other dimensions such as meaning and context (Jahr 2000; Ochs and Schieffelin 1989: 15). What linguistic analysis can thus provide us with are the analytical tools that allow dissecting and interpreting a text's emotionality.

The principal perspective

An albeit small and scattered body of research in linguistics and cognate fields has focused on how we convey emotions narratively. The basic idea is that narratives present us with the antecedents of emotional experiences. Emotion narratives have been theorized this way as mere rationalizations, as legitimizing accounts (Fischer and Jansz 1995; cf. Rymes 1995): the modern, western subject is culturally supposed to be rational/unemotional and any display of emotions will thus threaten one's image. Socially stipulated feeling rules (Hochschild 1983), however, have legitimizations inscribed into them. These legitimizing accounts can then be used to make sense of and rationalize an emotional episode and thus to restore one's image as a rational actor. Thus, emotions and emotion narratives operate on essentially separate levels. This would be very much in line with a more cognitive notion of narrative emotions.

Contrasting this view, the notion of narrative emotions developed above suggests a more realist take on this. If emotions *are* narratives, emotional experience is then rather *constituted* by the situational circumstances, events and conditions *as they matter* for the emoting subject. To analyze emotions narratively we thus need to ask who acts how to whom and what happens (Sarbin 1989: 188). This is the principal approach to narrative analysis of emotions. This is to say that antecedents are made up of narrative elements. Anger episodes, for instance, involve elements that together form a scene of faulty, unfair behavior by others (Fischer and Jansz 1995: 73).

However, analysis should go beyond these narrative elements as antecedents are already configured by the very words used to constitute subjective reality. Compare for instance the following vignettes:

Sue/ granny Sue/ granny/ grandmother/ the old tart ...

... passed away/ was called by the Lord/ bit the dust/ kicked the bucket.

All of these vignettes imply a different emotional stance towards one and the same referential event. Crucially, quite different, even opposing emotions can be expressed by changing only one or two words, while keeping the referential content of the phrase the same.

The salient point is that by analyzing narrative components and their relations within the story, narrative analysis looks at the antecedents of emotional experience. It shows us which elements make up subjective experience and how they relate to each other, for instance, which are the core events, how are they rendered, how do they relate to which backgrounds, how does an entire episode matter, etc. Narrative analysis can thus serve as a principal approach to empirical emotion analysis.

Structure

From here a number of more specific aspects can be considered. One such aspect concerns the narrative structure. Hudson *et al.* (1992), for instance, compared the structure of three different kinds of emotion narratives and found specific variations in their structures depending on the focal emotion: happiness episodes showed little dramatic action; madness narratives had rising action, a climax and then falling action; scared narratives showed dramatic action rising to a climax but lacking falling action after that. They also developed a distinction of different narrative forms: moment-in-time stories recreate a specific mood lacking a climax; chronologies connect elements temporally but not causally without climax or mood recreation (emotions are described rather than evoked); plotted stories are causally structured and include a climax. Hudson *et al.* (1992) demonstrated how the three emotions under consideration correlated with these three narrative types: happiness—moment-in-time stories/chronologies; scared and mad narratives—plotted stories. As this research shows, both the dramatic structure as well as the specific mode of linking the narrative elements are expressive of emotional experience.

The concept of dramatic structure can be further explicated by recourse to narrative analysis concepts such as the temporal structure of the narrative: which parts are narrated in real-time, slow motion or are speeded up. Another aspect of temporal structure is to be found in the order of events as narrated, that is what happens when in the narrative and how these events are temporally and causally connected. What is the degree of detail? Repetitions may have a dramatic effect as well.

Imagine for instance how a sense of being overwhelmed may be expressed by a staccato-like structure of the overwhelming instances that thus seem to fall down on the experiencer. Compare this to a minutely detailed, slowly progressing story. Or think how shock may be expressed by narrating a number of soothing and pleasant instances, presented with much narrative embellishment and no hint at impending doom—the negative event will appear with shocking suddenness. Compare this to a structure where the eventual negative event appears as a possibility from the outset and there is a description of how things gradually built up to it—perhaps a story of defeat, disappointed hopes or escalating fear? Consider also how a hope narrative might be structured, for instance by narrating numerous negative and discouraging instances, but by interspersing them with references to information that could justify hope.

Another aspect of structure has to do with the constructions of oppositions/comparisons. These have been described, on a syntactical level, as forms of emotional expressions (Fiehler 1990: 238; Jahr 2000: 97–8; Schwarz-Friesel 2007: 190–5). However, they feature not only syntactically (see next section) but also in the narrative structure sometimes simply by way of juxtaposition. In fact they can often be found in narratives (e.g., Glinka 2003). Think for instance how a narrative about anger invoking unfairness may not so much directly address and express this unfairness as such but simply narrate the unfair situation and interweave this with another story line about another actor emphasizing certain parallels between both story lines which lead, however, in the second case to contrary, better outcomes. A hope narrative might involve comparative flashbacks to similar situations in the past where the outcomes were eventually positive. It might also involve comparative references to other actors seen in a similar situation. Such comparison with others may not only induce hope but also envy that may in turn translate into anger but also admiration (Neckel 1999; Simmel 1992: 318–19).

Agency

Another aspect concerns the narrative construction of agency (e.g., Schütze 1981)—"*who* is doing what to *whom*" (Bamberg 1997: 317, my emphasis). Research has shown how emotion narratives have agency configured in specific ways (Bamberg 1997). Anger narratives, for instance, may operate with an agentic other, with self as an object. Shameful situations may be narrated by diluting the agency of the self. Helplessness may involve a non-agentive experiencer as indicated by such grammatical features as modal auxiliaries, hypothetical past/future constructs, "try" predicates and negation (Capps and Ochs 1995: 419). The empirical part of this study includes many instances where interviewees were not outraged by certain political conditions. Lacking some kind of political analysis they found no-one to ascribe agency to.

The key issue here is that self can be rendered as an object to others' actions or as agentic itself (Bamberg 1997). As Bamberg (1997) further shows, agency can be emphasized or de-emphasized by referring to the agent in a very concrete, individualizing vs. a rather vague way. It can be added to these findings that an agentic other can be vague to the point of anonymity, where the narrator may attribute agency, for instance, to an unspecified or ambivalent "they." The passive voice may have that effect too (e.g., Capps and Bonanno 2000). A causative agent may be entirely missing and things just seem to happen. Grammatically this may take the form of ellipsis (Capps and Bonanno 2000: 5). Rymes (1995) argues that agency is mitigated narratively in cases where the agent's action is narrated as inevitable, a matter of necessity or duty. Specifically this may involve verbs of necessity (e.g., "had to"; Capps and Bonanno 2000: 5). Similarly, Pomerantz (1978) points out that the attribution of blame depends on antecedent events. Rymes also points to grammatical limiters of agency, like "just" or discursive markers like "so": "so I's jus' bangin' his head" (1995: 506). Prosodic features may equally modulate agency, like intonation and hesitancy. Finally, Capps and Bonanno (2000) add to this list: the use of generic, impersonal forms of self-reference ("you just got to do that in this situation"), hypothetical past constructions (implying that a given result was not inevitable, followed by hypothetical acts/conditions that would have entailed a different outcome), and nominalization of emotions ("feelings of anger started up again").

Agency is not simply attributed in narratives, but actors are being constructed at the same time. Specifically, this refers to contingent constructions of identities in the narrative—a pivotal basis for emotional experience. Consider, for instance, how solidarity (e.g., Goodman 2009) or compassion (e.g., Sznaider 1998) operate on the basis of constructs of difference and identification. In a similar vein it has also been argued (Flam and Kleres 2008) that the scientific construction of research subjects as agentic vs. passive entails different feeling rules: dominant theorizing in the German social sciences, for instance, casts neo-Nazis in the role of victims of modernization while migrants are blamed themselves for the social problems they are facing. This helps invoke different specific feelings towards these subjects of scientific inquiry, such as some degree of empathy and sympathy for neo-Nazis and indifference or antipathy for migrants.

Other linguistic manifestations of emotions

I have argued above that antecedents of emotionality are most fundamentally configured by the very words used to represent them. Implicitly, this points to the fact that emotions are not only constituted narratively but also on the level of words and sentences. The following section will present some selected possibilities for emotions to be constituted lexically and syntactically, while a full treatment of these aspects is beyond the scope of this study. Considering these issues will show how intricately emotionality and meaning are intertwined when viewed linguistically. This will provide further evidence of the blurry distinction between meaning and emotion that I have proposed under the label of narrative emotions.

The lexical level: words

Turning to the lexical dimension—or, more plainly, words—(see the overviews in Jahr 2000: 86–93; Schwarz-Friesel 2007: 144–54), we can distinguish so-called emotion words, which refer *descriptively* to emotional states. Languages have lexemes to refer to a given emotion category. For instance fear, concern, fright, dread, etc. refer to the emotion category FEAR (Schwarz-Friesel 2007: 144). But there are also emotion *expressing* words such as: "Yuck!", "Gross!", "Finally!" or "Darling!" These do not explicitly reference emotions, but they provide direct information about emotional impressions and attitudes qua their semantic content. Specifically they may involve the use of diminutives and augmentatives (e.g., hottie, doggie, uber/super-accurate), evaluative pre-/suffixes (e.g., peacenik, fashionista, underachiever, hypersensitive), connotations (e.g., whining), modal words/particles[3] (e.g., finally, unfortunately, of course), etc. To this we could add interjections, such as: well, oh my, gee, heck, ah, uhm, ouch, etc. Beyond such direct emotional expressions words predicate events or situational circumstances that can imply emotional experience (e.g., "Grandma just died."; "The rain really hit us hard.").

The syntactical level: sentences

Emotions may also be expressed at the level of entire sentences (Jahr 2000: 93–4; Schwarz-Friesel 2007: 173–209). This includes: direct references to emotions—"I am scared"; double propositions, where a neutral sentence is embedded in an emotive one, such as "I'm afraid that ..."; optative sentences, expressing a wish, as in "If only I could ..."; exclamations ("What a day!"); hyperbole ("the worst day of my life"); intensifying, repetitive genitive constructs ("the book of books"); questions and rhetorical questions; finally, comparisons as in "I felt about my wife's illness like I felt as a soldier during the war." The latter can be seen as part of a larger group of emotion expressions, that is figurative language. Here we also find metonymy and metaphors, which are a particularly suitable way of expressing emotions (Kövecses 2003). As Gibbs *et al.* (2002) argue, metaphors allow for the expression of emotional states that are otherwise inexpressible. They also allow for a more vivid expression of emotions creating a sense of intimacy between speaker and addressee. For this reason, literal expression may be inadequate or insufficient to convey emotional states in their complexity. Other forms of figurative language include the use of irony specifically involving sarcasm, rhetorical questions, satire, hyperbole, understatement and overstatement (Gibbs *et al.* 2002: 140–6). Emotionality is conveyed by "irony's ability to mock, attack, and ridicule, provoking embarrassment, humiliation, even anger" (Gibbs *et al.* 2002: 142).

Prosody

A final level of analysis that is particularly relevant to spoken texts, such as interviews, is prosody—i.e., the rhythm, stress and intonation of speech—and other para-verbal aspects. Again, this is in itself a complex issue and I can only present some selected aspects of it here (but see, for example, Bachorowski and Owren 2008; Frick 1985; Kehrein 2002; Tischer 1993). As Fiehler (1990: 170) summarizes, this involves characteristics of the *voice*: loudness, pitch, vocal mode (e.g., trembling, coarse, cold or amused voice); *emphasis*: specific intonation curves, special emphases, modulation of accentuation, expressively stretched words ("noooo!"); *speech speed*; aspects of *vocal style*: e.g., staccato, separation of syllables ("shame-less!," "puh-lease!"), extremely correct pronunciation; and finally aspects of *verbal planning*, such as hesitation, aborted sentences, re-formulation/repairs, stuttering. Despite many attempts to identify prosodic profiles of emotions, empirical results are not entirely conclusive. At best, empirical research can identify prosodic correlates of certain emotional states (for overviews, see, for example, Frick 1985; Tischer 1993: 110–13). For instance anger may be expressed by increased pitch, increased loudness, fast rate of speech and a specific prosodic contour (intonation curve of average pitch that is characteristically interrupted by jumps on stressed syllables) (Frick 1985). Bloch (1996) found that a melodious, singing tone of voice, rapid speech and audible inhaling were associated with positive self-feelings. In contrast, whispering, self-interruption and stammering marked the expression of negative self-feelings. In her study, there were also a number of ambiguous markers. Laughter, for instance, was at times associated with embarrassment and at times an expression of joy. Again, this points to the need to understand the emotional significance of discrete linguistic elements within their context. Interestingly, Bloch (1996: 335) also found that prosodic features may parallel the narrative structure of interview texts. For instance, there may be a pattern where prosodic markers of negative self-feeling are followed by sequences with prosodic markers of positive self-feeling, which structures the narrative into a story of relief.

A note on realism in narrative interviewing

The analytical tools described in this chapter open a perspective on the emotionality of (narrative interview) texts per se. So far, this has left a crucial question unaddressed: how much can we learn about the actual, past social, emotional life from such texts? This is in fact a problem that pertains to all forms of interviewing, but has sparked particular debate in the context of narrative analysis (Küsters 2009: 36). However, as a closer examination will show, while making certain methodological claims, this approach has the analytical potential to expose any cracks in the narrative text. What is more, this aspect of narrative analysis proves to be a particularly fruitful lens in respect to emotions.

Aiming at reanimating sedimented streams of past experience through the technique of narrative interviewing, Schütze (1976: 197) assumed that there is a principle homology between ad hoc narratives and original processes of experience. This is not to say that narratives provide information about what *actually* happened, but rather that the structure of the narrative interview text will parallel, and be expressive of, the structure of the original subjective experience (Bohnsack 1997: 205; Wohlrab-Sahr 2000: 155). Schütze framed this within a theory of the narrative process (Kallmeyer and Schütze 1977): the dynamic of spontaneous face-to-face narration forces the narrator to include the necessary and sufficient aspects in order to constitute a plausible, coherent and complete story. Only the strictly narrative elements of the text will run parallel to the structure of the original experience (cf. Katz 1999: 8–9, who draws on Howard Becker for a similar argument), while description and argumentation can be much more expressive of present contexts. This does not mean that narrators will just overcome any barriers to recounting the past. It does mean, however, that any such barriers will most likely become visible: narrators often mark their post hoc perspective more or less explicitly (as indicated, for example, by such expressions as: oddly, surely, maybe, that had to happen, etc., Schütze 1976: 178–9). Barriers may be expressed symptomatically, for instance through leaps, hesitations, pauses and silences, efforts at leaving the narrator role and having the interviewer comment/react, through ostensible vagueness, or through changes in the textual mode (argumentation/description rather than narration), etc. (Schütze 1976: 198, 1987: 44, 97). Finally and importantly, analysis involves comparisons between the strictly narrative elements of the text and its descriptive and argumentative parts (Schütze 1983): a careful consideration where both dimensions do or do not converge and what functions instances of argumentation and description have at a specific point in the narrative (e.g., orientation, interpretation, legitimation, avoidance, repression) provides a particularly useful lens for interpretation. After all, this goes specifically for the narrator's emotions since any moves of narrative evasion will likely occur at emotionally charged, problematic junctures in the narrative (Nelson and Horowitz 2001; Schütze 1987).

This may be briefly illustrated by Schütze's (1992b, 1992a) analysis of an interview with a former German World War II soldier. Although the soldier was not committed to Nazi ideology, and was to some extent unsympathetic, he nevertheless complied with the regime as he willingly participated in the war. This could be expected to have caused guilt in him, especially as he came to be more and more exposed to the atrocities of genocide, war and prosecution. And yet—in seeming contradiction to the homology postulate—when he directly narrates his war experience there seems to be no reference to guilt or guilt-inducing circumstances. This void, however, can be taken as a datum for analysis rather than as an instance of forgetfulness—all the more so as he does indicate, at later points of the narrative, awareness at the time of what was going on. He almost completely fails to narrate encounters with victims of the regime in the war "chapter" of his story. In making some closing commentaries on that segment he only briefly alludes to the disappearance of Jews (e.g., by mentioning abandoned synagogues, Jews having been driven away) and swiftly moves away from the topic in a crucially argumentative-theoretical textual mode. Much later, however, when his wife had a stroke many years after the war, he refers to, and elaborates in great detail on, his war experience for making the present feeling of powerlessness plausible. One of these illustrative episodes is about an encounter with Jewish slave workers in the Russian winter landscape raising the agonizing question whether to attempt to help them or not and whether that would be possible at all. Seemingly unable to feel guilty at the time, memories later came alive again and with them the ability to mourn. This is not just a lapse of memory. Theorizing compliance with a totalitarian regime, Schütze (1992a, 1992b) interprets this as a then dominant—institutionally backed and interactionally sustained—mode of fading out atrocities that would otherwise be shocking. It is in this way that the structure of the narrative does in the end reflect past (emotional) experience.

Non-conscious emotions

Having described a number of textual features that convey emotionality, it has become clear that narrative interviewing and analysis provides excellent access to emotions. Specifically, this builds on the notion of the narrative nature of emotions and reveals how many dimensions of narrative analysis are indeed indicative of emotions. What is more, emotion analysis cannot and should not stop at the narrative level, but must include other linguistic markers of emotions as well.

As this analytical framework shows, emotions are inextricably interwoven with the meaning dimension of texts to the point where the distinction between cognition and emotion becomes blurry. I have suggested that both may be better understood as two sides of the same thing, that is human experience, which can be described analytically in terms of emotions and meaning. The linguistic research I have presented here, emphasizing the interlacing of meaning and emotion, gives further substance to this claim.

The perspective of narrative emotion analysis then helps us overcome a specific methodical problem: the issue of emotions' low visibility or rather of non-conscious emotions. This issue may not be readily accepted by some emotion researchers. However, several theorists have elaborated on this notion: Scheff (1988) talked about covert shame but based this in his specific theorizing of this one emotion. Barbalet (1998, 2009) theorized non- or unconscious emotions from a general vantage point. Katz (1999: 332) equally argued against necessarily conscious experience of emotions. Nussbaum (2003: 71–2) also acknowledged the (albeit exceptional) possibility of non-conscious emotions. More recently, Theodosius (2012) provided a nuanced account of non-conscious emotions.

The notion of non-conscious emotions is in line with a fundamental premise of narrative analysis: that is the assumption that actors know more about their experience than they can present in abstracted terms when asked directly. As I outlined at the beginning, they have narrative knowledge, the knowledge of how things have come about, which is only accessible in its narrative form. Under the concept of narrative emotions, this premise can be extended to emotions as well. From this perspective then, non-conscious emotions emerge as much more pervasive than Nussbaum would have it. Indeed it can thus be assumed to be the dominant mode of emotional experience (cf. Archer 2000: 197).

Sensemaking and emotions

Much like with narrative methodology, emotions have been largely marginal to sensemaking theory. Weick (1995: 45–9) provides only a rudimentary argument on emotions. Emotions would thus emerge if ongoing courses of action are interrupted by something unexpected: "It is precisely because ongoing flows are subject to interruption that sensemaking is infused with feeling" (Weick 1995: 45). Resultant emotional arousal indicates such interruptions to the actor and would then trigger new sensemaking as it leads actors to wonder what is going on. When this new sensemaking is completed, however, emotions seem to disappear again: "Emotion is what happens between the time that an organized sequence is interrupted and the time at which the interruption is removed, or a substitute response is found that allows the sequence to be completed" (Weick 1995: 46). Emotions thus figure in Weick's (1995) approach as merely—positive or negative—emotionality or, rather, "arousal." Qualitative differences of emotions are not considered. They function as it were as energy only. This may be because emotions end up as both fundamental and yet external to the sensemaking process: the momentary trigger of sensemaking that remains irrelevant beyond that point of triggering. Emotion and reason stay separated in that emotion guide or, rather, stimulate reason (for a critique of this separation, see Barbalet 1998). It is in part for these reasons that the sensemaking approach has been criticized for falling short of advancing something of a theory of organizational emotions (Magala 1997: 323–4), a point recently endorsed by Weick *et al.* (2005: 418–9). An alternative view would rather see emotions as an integral part of ongoing sensemaking processes.

The proposed framework for narrative emotion analysis helps us take a step forward in this direction. If emotions are narrative—with meaning and emotions intertwined in the storied nature of social experience—and if narrativity is central to organizational sensemaking, it follows then that emotions are of central and continuous significance to sensemaking in their full diversity and specificity. The production of an organizational reality is then as much about the making of emotions as it is about making sense.

But how can we integrate emotions into the recursive logic of the sensemaking argument? Weick hints at this, arguing that the emotions engender mood congruent sensemaking: "People remember events that have the same emotional tone as what they currently feel" (1995: 49). Again, this keeps emotion and reason separated and emotions would thus have a logic that is largely independent from the meaning generated in the sensemaking process. Based on a narrative view of emotions, an alternative argument maintains that the constitution of a meaningful reality also entails an emotional stance towards that reality. The formative significance of retained reality constructs for present instances of sensemaking also means that the past helps to constitute present emotions. What is more, this also means that emotions are enacted into the environment.

These ideas connect with recent theorizing of the reflexive self engaged in inner dialogue (Archer 2000, 2010; Wiley 1994, 2006, 2010). This research has proposed that the present self "I" is engaged in inner dialogue with the "me"— representing the past—and the "you"—potential futures selves. While for Wiley emotions remain marginal (cf., for example, 2006: 6, 7, 17), Archer (2000) conceptualizes the "me" as a memory bank of past emotional experiences. Emotions function here as commentaries on the (physical, practical, social) concerns of the individual. The balance between different and typically irreconcilable concerns is constantly re-negotiated between I and you with reference to past experience (me), trying to find a compromise that the self feels it can live with. This balance—the personal identity that arises from it—subsequently becomes a source of concerns itself as it functions as a basis for emotional commentary on future occurrences. These may in turn reinforce or alter pre-existing balances.

This balancing makes for a fundamental source of ambivalence. However, this is not the only source of ambivalence. Wiley and Archer theorize the self only in its moral or social contexts, but not as situated in the power structures of society (Flam 2010): this fails to capture the social causes of emotions and limits an understanding of the conditions allowing or preventing an inner dialogue. Socially dominant views of certain kinds of selves (e.g., based in racism or sexism) may be internalized and thus silence the self's inner voice. "Humiliation, disappointment and sadness kill their self-esteem, making voice unlikely" (Flam 2010: 189). This is the silenced self.

For a different view of the self Flam (2010) draws on Cooley's looking-glass self and the Jewish concept of voice. A self-image develops from how we see others seeing us and how this relates to the aspirations of the "I." Others' power over the self can also stem from their signifying voice which functions through orders, naming, degrading, denying, etc. Others' positive voice can lead to a constructive dialogue with the self's voice, while a negative, dominating voice of others results in the self losing its voice and the ability to understand what is happening. In both accounts of internalization "the idea is that what others see and how they think of and feel about us does matter. As the main elements in any interaction/communicative action, their thoughts and emotions about us co-constitute us" (Flam 2010: 190–1).

However, even in the case of strong domination the inner voice of a self-seeing self—the way that the self sees itself—as another determinant of one's self-image may be silenced but never quite ceases. Socialization and domination are never total and other social forces (e.g., counter-discourses of subcultures or social movements) can effect an amplification of dormant outlaw emotions. In this way the fundamental ambivalence of the self—feeling, for example, ashamed and angered at the same time—can be tilted and—another contingency—channeled into self-reflexivity and social criticism. In sum, the self emerges from

> (i) the mirroring eyes/signifying-outer voice as the carriers of hatred and contempt, (ii) the self-seeing-self/inner voice as the locus of anger and indignation at one's degradation by the other, and, finally, (iii) a self-image which is an uneasy tension between these two: containing deep shame and anger.
>
> (Flam 2010: 193)

But there is another, more subtle way of distorting the inner voice. Where Archer (2000) treats all emotions as authentic commentaries on our concerns, Flam (2010: 194–8) draws our attention also to processes of the construction of emotions and especially to Hochschild's (1979, 1983) argument that emotions are socially prescribed by way of feeling rules. From this perspective, a self comes into view whose inner voice is engaged in self-deception, self-delusion, self-blame, self-denial, obsessions or scapegoating—the short-circuited self. Hochschild emphasized that feeling rules and framing rules are mutually implied: "when an individual changes an ideological stance, he or she drops old rules and assumes new ones for reacting to situations, cognitively and emotively" (1979: 567). This tallies well with the methodological argument advanced above that the meaningful elements making up subjective reality simultaneously constitute emotional stances towards that reality. The crucial point is that this links actors in more subtle ways to power structures as they are manipulated to see and feel things in a certain way. As Flam (2010) reminds us, this goes in particular for organizations. From this perspective then, emotions are already inscribed in the vocabularies of sensemaking. This adds another source of ambiguity. The short-circuited self "oscillates between possible cognitive frames and emotions corresponding to these frames" (Flam 2010: 199).

Notes

1 An earlier version of parts of this chapter was published as Kleres (2011).
2 This is not to exclude other forms of experience and action, such as routines and habits or flow experience (Bloch 2000). which narrative analysis cannot capture (e.g., Schütze 1976, 1987).
3 Words and particles that reflect the mood and attitude of the speaker, they change the mood of the verb.

References

Archer, Margaret S. 2000. *Being Human: The Problem of Agency*. Cambridge, New York: Cambridge University Press.
Archer, Margaret S., ed. 2010. *Conversations about Reflexivity*. London, New York: Routledge.
Bachorowski, Jo-Anne and Michael J. Owren. 2008. "Vocal Expression of Emotion." Pp. 196–210 in *Handbook of Emotions*, edited by M. Lewis, J. M. Haviland-Jones and L. F. Barrett. New York, London: The Guilford Press.
Bamberg, Michael. 1997. "Language, Concepts and Emotions: The Role of Language in the Construction of Emotions." *Language Sciences* 19(4): 309–40.
Barbalet, Jack M. 1998. *Emotion, Social Theory, and Social Structure: A Macrosociological Approach*. Cambridge, New York, Melbourne, Madrid, Cape Town, Singapore, Sao Paulo: Cambridge University Press.
Barbalet, Jack M. 2009. "Consciousness, Emotions, and Science." Pp. 39–71 in *Theorizing Emotions: Sociological Explorations and Applications*, edited by D. R. Hopkins, J. Kleres, H. Flam and H. Kuzmics. Frankfurt am Main, New York: Campus.
Bloch, Charlotte. 1996. "Emotions and Discourse." *Text* 16(3): 323–41.
Bloch, Charlotte. 2000. "Flow: Beyond Fluidity and Rigidity." *Human Studies* 23(1): 43–61.
Bohnsack, Ralf. 1997. "Dokumentarische Methode." Pp. 191–212 in *Sozialwissenschaftliche Hermeneutik*, edited by R. Hitzler and A. Honer. Opladen: UTB/ Leske + Budrich.
Capps, Lisa and George Bonanno. 2000. "Narrating Bereavement: Thematic and Grammatical Predictors of Adjustment to Loss." *Discourse Processes* 30(1): 1–25.
Capps, Lisa and Elinor Ochs. 1995. "Out of Place: Narrative Insights into Agoraphobia." *Discourse Processes* 19: 407–39.
De Sousa, Ronald. 1980. "The Rationality of Emotions." Pp. 127–51 in *Explaining Emotions*, edited by A. O. Rorty. Berkeley, Los Angeles, London: University of California Press.
De Sousa, Ronald. 1990. *The Rationality of Emotion*. Cambridge: MIT Press.
Deslandes, Jeanne. 2004a. "A Philosophy of Emoting." *Journal of Narrative Theory* 34: 335–72.
Deslandes, Jeanne. 2004b. *Narrative Emotion*. PhD thesis, European Graduate School. Retrieved September 16, 2009 (www.egs.edu/pdfs/jeanne-deslandes-narrative-emotion.pdf).
Fiehler, Reinhard. 1990. *Kommunikation und Emotion. Theoretische und empirische Untersuchungen zur Rolle von Emotionen in der verbalen Interaktion*. Berlin, New York: Walter de Gruyter.
Fischer, Agneta H. and Jeroen Jansz. 1995. "Reconciling Emotions with Western Personhood." *Journal for the Theory of Social Behaviour* 25(1): 59–80.

Flam, Helena. 1998. *Mosaic of Fear*. Boulder: East European Monographs.
Flam, Helena. 2010. "Emotion, and the Silenced and Short-Circuited Self." Pp. 187–205 in *Conversations about Reflexivity*, edited by M. S. Archer. London, New York: Routledge.
Flam, Helena and Jochen Kleres. 2008. "Ungleichheit und Vorurteil. Deutsche SozialwissenschaftlerInnen als ProduzentInnen von Gefühlsregeln." *Österreichische Zeitschrift für Soziologie* 33(2): 63–81.
Flam, Helena and Jochen Kleres, eds. 2015. *Methods of Exploring Emotions*. London, New York: Routledge.
Frick, Robert W. 1985. "Communicating Emotion: The Role of Prosodic Features." *Psychological Bulletin* 97(3): 412–29.
Gammerl, Benno. 2009. "Erinnerte Liebe. Was Kann eine Oral History zur Geschichte der Gefühle und der Homosexualitäten beitragen?" *Geschichte und Gesellschaft. Zeitschrift für Historische Sozialwissenschaft* 35(2): 314–45.
Gibbs, Raymond W., John S. Leggitt and Elizabeth A. Turner. 2002. "What's Special about Figurative Language in Emotional Communication?" Pp. 125–49 in *The Verbal Communication of Emotions: Interdisciplinary Perspectives*, edited by S. R. Fussell. Mahwah, NJ, London: Lawrence Erlbaum Associates.
Gilbert, Kathleen R. 2000. *The Emotional Nature of Qualitative Research*. Boca Raton: CRC Press.
Glinka, Hans-Jürgen. 2003. *Das Narrative Interview. Eine Einführung für Sozialpädagogen*. Weinheim, München: Juventa.
Goldie, Peter. 2000. *The Emotions: A Philosophical Exploration*. Oxford: Clarendon Press.
Goodman, James. 2009. "Refugee Solidarity: Between National Shame and Global Outrage." Pp. 269–89 in *Theorizing Emotions: Sociological Explorations and Applications*, edited by D. R. Hopkins, J. Kleres, H. Flam and H. Kuzmics. Frankfurt am Main, New York: Campus.
Hochschild, Arlie R. 1979. "Emotion Work, Feeling Rules, and Social Structure." *American Journal of Sociology* 85(3): 551–75.
Hochschild, Arlie R. 1983. *The Managed Heart: Commercialization of Human Feeling*. Berkeley: University of California Press.
Holtgrewe, Ursula. 2002. "Narratives Interview." Pp. 71–102 in *Methoden der Organisationsforschung. Ein Handbuch*, edited by S. Kühl and P. Strodtholz. Reinbek bei Hamburg: Rowohlt Taschenbuch Verlag.
Hudson, Judith A., Janet Gebelt, Jeanette Haviland and Christine Bentivegna. 1992. "Emotion and Narrative Structure in Young Children's Personal Accounts." *Journal of Narrative and Life History* 2(2): 129–50.
Illouz, Eva. 1997. *Consuming the Romantic Utopia: Love and the Cultural Contradictions of Capitalism*. Berkeley, Los Angeles, London: University of California Press.
Illouz, Eva and Eitan Wilf. 2009. "Hearts or Wombs? A Cultural Critique of Radical Feminist Critiques of Love." Pp. 121–41 in *Theorizing Emotions: Sociological Explorations and Applications*, edited by D. R. Hopkins, J. Kleres, H. Flam and H. Kuzmics. Frankfurt am Main, New York: Campus.
Jahr, Silke. 2000. *Emotionen und Emotionsstrukturen in Sachtexten*. Berlin, New York: de Gruyter.
Kallmeyer, Werner and Fritz Schütze. 1977. "Zur Konstitution von Kommunikationsschemata der Sachverhaltsdarstellung." Pp. 159–274 in *Gesprächsanalysen*, edited by D. Wegner. Hamburg: Buske.

Katz, Jack. 1999. *How Emotions Work*. Chicago: Chicago University Press.
Kehrein, Roland. 2002. *Prosodie und Emotionen*. Tübingen: Niemeyer.
Kleinman, Sherryl and Martha A. Copp. 1993. *Emotions and Fieldwork*. Washington: SAGE.
Kleres, Jochen. 2011. "Emotions and Narrative Analysis: A Methodological Approach." *Journal for the Theory of Social Behaviour* 41(2): 182–202.
Kövecses, Zoltán. 2003. *Metaphor and Emotion: Language, Culture, and Body in Human Feeling*. Cambridge University Press.
Küsters, Ivonne. 2009. *Narrative Interviews*. Wiesbaden: VS Verlag für Sozialwissenschaften.
Labov, William and Joshua Waletzky. 1967. "Narrative Analysis: Oral Versions of Personal Experience." Pp. 12–44 in *Essays on the Verbal and Visual Arts*, edited by J. Helms. Seattle: University of Washington Press.
Lee-Treweek, Geraldine and Stephanie Linkogle, eds. 2000. *Danger in the Field: Risk and Ethics in Social Research*. London, New York: Routledge.
Lucius-Hoene, Gabriele and Arnulf Deppermann. 2004. *Rekonstruktion narrativer Identität. Ein Arbeitsbuch zur Analyse narrativer Interviews*. Wiesbaden: VS Verlag für Sozialwissenschaften.
Magala, Slawomir J. 1997. "The Making and Unmaking of Sense." *Organization Studies* 18(2): 317–38.
Neckel, Sieghard. 1999. "Blanker Neid, blinde Wut? Sozialstruktur und Kollektive Gefühle." *Leviathan* 27(2): 145–65.
Nelson, Kristin and Leonard Horowitz. 2001. "Narrative Structure in Recounted Sad Memories." *Discourse Processes* 31(3): 307–24.
Nussbaum, Martha C. 1988. "Narrative Emotions: Beckett's Genealogy of Love." *Ethics* 98(2): 225–54.
Nussbaum, Martha C. 2003. *Upheavals of Thought: The Intelligence of Emotions*. Cambridge, New York, Melbourne, Madrid, Cape Town: Cambridge University Press.
Ochs, Elinor and Bambi Schieffelin. 1989. "Language Has a Heart." *Text* 9(1): 7–25.
Pomerantz, Anita. 1978. "Attributions of Responsibility: Blamings." *Sociology* 12(1): 115–20.
Retzinger, Suzanne M. 1991. *Violent Emotions: Shame and Rage in Marital Quarrels*. Newbury Park, London, New Delhi: SAGE.
Rymes, Betsy. 1995. "The Construction of Moral Agency in the Narratives of High-School Drop-Outs." *Discourse and Society* 6(4): 495–516.
Sarbin, Theodore R. 1989. "Emotions as Narrative Emplotments." Pp. 185–201 in *Entering the Circle: Hermeneutic Investigation in Psychology*, edited by M. J. Packer and R. B. Addison. Albany: State University of New York Press.
Sarbin, Theodore R. 2001. "Embodiment and the Narrative Structure of Emotional Life." *Narrative Inquiry* 11(1): 217–25.
Scheff, Thomas J. 1988. "Shame and Conformity: The Deference-Emotion System." *American Sociological Review* 53(3): 395–406.
Schütze, Fritz. 1976. "Zur Hervorlockung und Analyse thematisch relevanter Geschichten im Rahmen soziologischer Feldforschung—dargestellt an einem Projekt zur Erforschung von kommunalen Machtstrukturen." Pp. 159–260 in *Kommunikative Sozialforschung*, vol. 159, edited by Arbeitsgruppe Bielefelder Soziologen. München: Fink.
Schütze, Fritz. 1981. "Prozeßstrukturen des Lebenslaufs." Pp. 67–156 in *Biografie in handlungswissenschaftlicher Perspektive*, edited by J. Matthes and M. Stosberg. Nürnberg: Verlag der Nürnberger Forschungsvereinigung e.V.

Schütze, Fritz. 1983. "Biographieforschung und narratives Interview." *Neue Praxis* 13(3): 283–93.
Schütze, Fritz. 1987. *Das narrative Interview in Interaktionsfeldstudien I.* Hagen: Fernuniversität.
Schütze, Fritz. 1992a. "Pressure and Guilt: War Experiences of a Young German Soldier and Their Biographical Implications (Part 1)." *International Sociology* 7(2): 187–208.
Schütze, Fritz. 1992b. "Pressure and Guilt: War Experiences of a Young German Soldier and Their Biographical Implications (Part 2)." *International Sociology* 7(3): 347–67.
Schwarz-Friesel, Monika. 2007. *Sprache und Emotion.* Tübingen, Basel: A. Francke (UTB).
Simmel, Georg. 1992. *Soziologie. Untersuchungen über die Formen der Vergesellschaftung.* Frankfurt am Main: Suhrkamp.
Sternberg, Robert J. 1996. "Love Stories." *Personal Relationships* 3(1): 59–79.
Sznaider, Natan. 1998. "The Sociology of Compassion: A Study in the Sociology of Morals." *Cultural Values* 2(1): 117–39.
Theodosius, Catherine. 2012. " 'Feeling a Feeling' in Emotion Management." Pp. 63–85 in *Emotions Matter: A Relational Approach to Emotions,* edited by D. Spencer, K. Walby and A. Hunt. Toronto: University of Toronto Press.
Tischer, Bernd. 1993. *Die Vokale Kommunikation von Gefühlen.* Weinheim: Beltz, PsychologieVerlagsUnion.
Turski, George. 1991. "Experience and Expression: The Moral Linguistic Constitution of Emotions." *Journal for the Theory of Social Behaviour* 21(4): 373–92.
Weick, Karl E. 1985. *Der Prozeß des Organisierens.* Frankfurt am Main: Suhrkamp.
Weick, Karl E. 1995. *Sensemaking in Organizations.* Thousand Oaks, London, New Delhi: SAGE.
Weick, Karl E., Kathleen M. Sutcliff and David Obstfeld. 2005. "Organizing and the Process of Sensemaking." *Organization Science* 16(4): 409–21.
Wiley, Norbert. 1994. *The Semiotic Self.* Chicago: University of Chicago Press.
Wiley, Norbert. 2006. "Pragmatism and the Dialogical Self." *International Journal for Dialogical Science* 1(1): 5–21.
Wiley, Norbert. 2010. "Inner Speech and Agency." Pp. 17–38 in *Conversations About Reflexivity,* edited by M. S. Archer. London, New York: Routledge.
Wohlrab-Sahr, Monika. 2000. "Biographieforschung jenseits des Konstruktivismus?" Pp. 151–62 in *Ortsbestimmungen der Soziologie: Wie die kommende Generation Gesellschaftswissenschaften betreiben will,* edited by U. Beck and A. Kieserling. Baden: NOMOS Verlagsgesellschaft.
Zilber, Tamar. 1998. "Using Linguistic Features of the Narrative to Recognize and Assess Its Emotional Content." Pp. 154–64 in *Narrative Research: Reading, Analysis, and Interpretation,* edited by A. Lieblich, R. Tuval-Mashiach and T. Zilber. Thousand Oaks, London, New Delhi: SAGE.

Chapter 6

Activists, volunteers and small town adversities

AIDS Relief D-Town consisted of a handful of non-professional members based in D-Town, a small town in a relatively rural, predominantly Catholic region. Paul was the founder of and driving force behind it. He started out in the next bigger city where he had been involved in self-help initiatives. This brought him into contact with Barbara, a physician working for the public health department of D-Town. She had the idea to create an independent local AIDS organization. Exploring the need for this on-site exposed Paul to a local climate of ignorance and hostility and to the extreme fears of locals living with HIV/AIDS. This led him to set up what was initially called Working Group AIDS together with Barbara and Petra, a local woman with HIV/AIDS. The experience of hostility continued. For instance, it proved impossible to receive any support (e.g., use of premises) from established institutions. They nevertheless managed to operate from Paul's private apartment.

A persistent problem was that Paul—a trained health care worker and HIV positive himself—felt the co-organizers made him do the bulk of work. Eventually this led Paul to break away from that initial group and he re-established the organization as an informal self-help group of people with HIV/AIDS. Later, continued experience of institutional discrimination led him to seek the group's inclusion in the federation of AIDS Relief organizations (see Chapter 3), where he hoped to find powerful reinforcement. He thus formally re-constituted the group as AIDS Relief D-Town. The problems of an imbalanced work load, however, persisted.

In addition, I interviewed Sandra and Claudia. Sandra was still a high-school student when she joined. She had been involved in a student volunteer group that raised money for AIDS causes by selling red ribbons. This brought her into contact with Paul who recruited her for AIDS Relief D-Town and its board. Claudia met Paul and learned about the problems in AIDS Relief D-Town when he was a regular customer in her taxi. She offered to help out and joined the organization's board. Both Sandra and Claudia stayed on until the organization disbanded.

Paul grew increasingly exhausted from work overload and declining health. At the same time he felt unable to quit and attempted suicide twice. Only when his health problems made it physically impossible to continue did he quit. The remaining members found they could not continue without Paul and soon decided to disband the organization. Analysis will show how this seemingly self-evident decision—the remaining members' sense of inevitability to disband—rested on contingent social conditions, the intricate interplay of differential meanings and emotions. These differences came down to the different modes of civic action of the three interviewees—activism vs. volunteerism.

Paul's activism: moral shocks in a climate of adversity

The local climate of hostility was pivotal in precipitating Paul's organizing activities in D-Town. His emotional reactions to it formed a crucial and compelling motive for his activism even as his exhaustion grew. Initially, however, AIDS organizing in D-Town had no particular urgency. This changed as he became increasingly confronted with hostility, leading to feelings of puzzlement, astonishment and disbelief. First his partner—a D-Towner—threatened to break up with him if he created the organization. Later he tried to meet Petra, a local living with HIV, who agreed to meet him at different cafés several times but never seemed to show up. When they finally met it turned out she had been at the cafés but first wanted to be sure he was not with the police. To Paul this was a "confrontation with the fears of people with HIV/AIDS" and only added to his consternation, as if he had delved into an alien, unfathomable world. Bewildered, Paul still lacked an understanding of the situation in D-Town. This changed when Paul contacted established local welfare organizations, looking for premises he could use:[1]

> and then i started together with [barbara] (--) and then we tried via the city; via CAritas; via [another big agency]; (-) via everybody to get premises [I: uhum] (---) and then we got to listen: : to the oddest (---) reasons (---) [I: yes] (–) why not [I: yes] u: hm from: (–) but he [clients] also touches banisters (1.0) or he: (-) he washes his face in the bathroom (---) or [I: mhm] (1.0) he uses the john for GODS! sake you'd have to replace the entire JOHN but those were the things derision that we were confronted with; [BARbara] and I were like thunderstruck [I: yes] we thought that MUST! not be what did we get ourselves INTO!

Disbelief and shock, as in the last sentence, now mingled with moral outrage. This bestowed meaning on puzzling experiences and led him to straightforward consequences:

> a: nd (-) THEN I said [barbara] i simply start with it (---) i cannot wait; [I: uhum] i have the feeling there are a lot of people here; [I: mhm] who at least want some decent counseling; [I: mhm] but who dare not even go to the

public HEALTH! department; [I: mhm] cause she always said she gets hardly any calls (-) i thought that is quite l: : : Ogical to me [I: mhm] [...] i wouldn't call the public health department on the countryside (--) right (1.0) a: : n: : d (---) DID then from MY apartment did a counseling phone line a [I: yes] via my private phone did counseling

Paul did not stop at witnessing firsthand the dire situation of locals with HIV/AIDS but linked this to institutional conditions, and it is this link which compelled him to take action. At the basis of his organizing efforts was the emotion of solidarity.

Political solidarity

I use the term "solidarity" in a very specific sense, namely as what some have called political solidarity (Scholz 2010), and conceptualize it as an emotion (Kleres 2015). As an emotion, it involves two mutually constitutive elements. One of these is empathy with suffering others, yet with a significant twist that sets it apart from other empathetic emotions. Other than compassion or pity, solidarity establishes a community with suffering others not as distressed individuals but conceptually with their multitude (Arendt 2006: 88).[2] I want to argue that this is not coincidental but results from a second emotional dimension: in relating to the multitude of suffering others, it relates in antagonism to the external source of that suffering. Antagonism, however, is constituted through emotions, hence solidarity's affinity with such emotions as anger, outrage or resentment, which indicate a breach of moral standards, values, norms, etc. The important point here is that categorical empathy and antagonism to the cause of suffering mutually constitute each other. This is akin to Simmel's (1992a: 288–9, 360) theory on the link between group cohesion and external antagonism, which he understood very much as emotional. Given its antagonistic element solidarity inspires a disposition to counter the cause of distress itself or, if this is impossible, its effects.

The above excerpts express precisely this kind of solidarity. There is a shocked apprehension of the social climate around HIV/AIDS and it leads Paul to relate to locals living with HIV/AIDS on a general basis. The emotional quality in this is particularly evident from how Paul felt compelled to move on and start the organization.

How can we explain Paul's solidarity? Some of his exclamations in the excerpts above seem to suggest a "moral shock" (Jasper 1998). However, beyond its ad hoc plausibility, this concept does little to help us understand what constitutes something as morally shocking (and what the outcome would be). From a narrative perspective the bases of Paul's solidarity are to be found in his prior experience. Indeed, as his overall point of departure in the interview, Paul briefly indicated a history of engagement in self-help structures in the next bigger city and as an HIV positive activist. Self-help contains a feeling rule of solidarity, given a certain anti-institutional bent—the idea that in the face of adversities people ought to take matters into their own hands and help each other.

Ultimately, Paul's resentment related to the emotional climate of AIDS discourse (see Chapters 2 and 3). He had witnessed first hand the fear (and, arguably, the shame) instilled in locals with HIV/AIDS ultimately by these discourses. He also experienced how representatives of dominant institutions operated on the same premises of othering AIDS discourse, understanding AIDS as something alien to them and their region ("caritas told us yes we are catholic here there is no aids"). Paul's organizing efforts took on the character of countering these local conditions as he set out to challenge dominant institutional power structures based as they were in dominant AIDS discourses. This is true also in another respect.

Bureaucratization

Paul's feelings of solidarity mattered not only with regards to the local climate of ostracism but formed the basis for his ongoing sensemaking. Crucially, it translated into a recurring motive for his activism: a critical stance towards established, bureaucratized AIDS organizations, which he constructed as an infringement on the solidaristic community. This, and its link to solidarity, emerged already at the beginning when Paul talked about exploring the local need for an AIDS organization, emphasizing a communal element.

> i didn't fancy doing bureaucracy at all i have always liked working with people with hiv/aids [...] so the contact with people was important to me

The same motive also gave an initial impulse to set up the organization in D-Town: Paul had been volunteering with an AIDS organization in the next bigger city when a newly hired director stipulated that all (existing) volunteers/ activists had to complete formal training before they were allowed even to talk to a person with HIV/AIDS. Paul's objection that he is HIV positive himself was met with disbelief referring to his healthy looks: "But you seem rather rotund for an H.I.V.'er." He reacted with outraged reassertion ("what organization is that") and left to set up the organization in D-Town.

The episode is about direct, hierarchical power—a key aspect of professionalization. More fundamentally, it is about a denial of his agency and identity as HIV positive. What is more, through its implicit othering, it was essentially a denial of solidarity that Paul had taken for granted. In these ways, it subverted his sensemaking and its emotional bases. Effectively, this cast fundamental self-doubt on Paul and left him with a feeling of absurdity[3] literally unable to fathom and make sense of what was going on ("am I stupid now"). In his outrage, Paul reasserted his agency and with it the principles and values of self-help and solidarity he held dear but which were absurdly blunted here.

This intricately related to dominant AIDS discourse. Professionalization of AIDS work has been linked to the increasing weight of a medicalizing paradigm of AIDS discourse (see Chapter 2). By rendering AIDS—including its social ramifications—in scientific terms, it transformed AIDS work into something of a technicality requiring expertise and skill, putting professionals center stage and volunteers into an auxiliary position. And although seemingly more neutral, this left the othering, that is shaming, aspects of AIDS discourse intact (see Chapter 2 and, especially, Gamson 1989). Essentially, Paul experienced not only the disempowerment through professionalization but also how it operated on the basis of, and conveyed, an othering discursive regime. On a basic level, this is what his outrage also related to, as new rules for volunteers were premised on the notion that people with HIV/AIDS are fundamentally and in complicated ways different—are others to the normal—and therefore require special skills and expertise for any interaction with them. Essentially, this premise makes professionalization incompatible with Paul's feelings of solidarity.

The critical stance towards bureaucratization continued later on. Harsh personal discrimination in a hospital made him seek affiliation with a powerful organization to back him up. Joining the AIDS Relief federation promised that, but, it turned out, instead chiefly entailed unexpected burdens for him which he found quite difficult to shoulder: administrative work; steep membership fees; and mandatory attendance at central meetings. Paul found himself alone with these burdens. His objecting reference to his (partly HIV-related) mounting health problems, however, was blunted with ignorance for his entire situation and denial of his agency: "why then are you leading an aids relief chapter". While he maintained hope for the better for some time his frustration with AIDS Relief peaked during a central meeting, where he found attendants haggling about how an executive director's salary could be covered by subsidies meant for specific projects. This enraged Paul so much that he threw a temper tantrum and left the room, effectively breaking with AIDS Relief:

> i went outside then i was so pissed right [one of the other attendants] brought me back in and then i really exploded and then i said you are all such assholes and then i chucked everything down at them and it was clear to me i was not to to reappear there

His experience of bureaucratized AIDS Relief comes down to a sharp discrepancy between his hope for solidarity vs. the lack of support, additional burdens and the denial of his agency. Significantly, the episode was interspersed with references to the pressing issues of his work in D-Town, followed by a staccato-like listing of people he did care work for and their mounting problems. It is against this backdrop that Paul's experience of bureaucratized organizations took shape and meaning: issues other than what was most pressing and central to Paul turned out to be paramount there. It was a denial of solidarity. His moral–emotional engagement with the local social realities of AIDS proved incommensurable with the emotional register of professionalized AIDS work,[4] which operated as a technicality on the basis of the medicalized paradigm of AIDS discourse.

Communal counter-organizing and its discontents

In this context where other AIDS organizations failed to act in solidarity, given a climate of stigma and ostracism, Paul's AIDS organizing took on the quality of a counter project of organizing in solidarity, which, however, remained precarious throughout. His peers in D-Town tended to delegate much of the work to Paul, and specifically the work of dealing with people with HIV/AIDS:

> NO that was very very strange (-) [barbara] and [petra] said then (-) well you are the [health care worker] you just do that with the people with aids [...] then i said but i must MYSELF first find information on this

Finding specialist literature unhelpful, he asked himself how he would like to have it as a client: being treated normally, i.e., just like someone who is not HIV positive. Essentially, this normalizing meant a reversion of othering. It implied the solidaristic ideal of interpersonal relations on equal footing, in contrast to the implicit othering he witnessed at professionalized AIDS organizations. However, internal dynamics in AIDS Relief D-Town—the unbalanced work load—ran counter to this. Similar issues turned up not much later:

> a: nd (--) there was the big question: (-) what do we do when a person with aids comes in; then i said but what should we do [I: mhm] we just talk to him normally ["vernünftig"] [...] you are a [health care worker] you are h.i.v.-POSITIVE [I: mhm] and and also [petra] pushed it all toWARDS me, right the, i thought (--) well like i said i CAN not do all of that [... phone counseling, administration, buddying ...] and what MORE are you expecting from me, and plus, i said, i am POSITIVE myself [I: yes] (---) don't you underSTAND that [I: yes] <<naive tone of voice>oh yeah: : (1.0) well can't you do that or don't you want to> [I: uhum] then i said i want to hear something decent from you that (--) you want to participate with me;

Paul's peers felt helpless, intimidated and fearful about facing actual people with HIV/AIDS ("big question")—emotions relating to the othering in dominant AIDS discourse. This effectively curbed any feeling of solidarity in Paul's peers. Paul's failed efforts at pushing his peers to enact normalcy illustrate the power of this discoursive-emotional regime. Paul was again left with a baffling and suffocating feeling of absurdity in relation to this situation. He had turned to average people—rather than established organizations—in search of a community of solidarity, and yet these same people both participated and proved insusceptible to this idea. He was left with most of the burden of work at AIDS Relief D-Town.

Eventually Paul broke with his peers over this issue and reconstituted the group as a pure self-help group of people with HIV/AIDS. However, hope for the better proved to be futile. A sense of community failed to materialize for lack of commitment. At the same time he had to cope with stifling discrimination by a hospital and his employer.[5] Institutional support from two AIDS organizations in neighboring cities failed, adding to his sense of abandonment. His first attempt to commit suicide was in this context of comprehensive abandonment. But stigmatizing treatment in the mental hospital after his suicide attempt rekindled Paul's sense of stubborn re-assertion and led him to the conclusion that he needed a powerful organization—AIDS Relief—to back him up. However, this only entailed additional burdens and the hope for support proved illusory (see previous section).

Paul's retreat

After his first suicide attempt, he reconstituted the organization as AIDS Relief D-Town only to find his hopes for finding solidarity and support in AIDS Relief eventually frustrated. At the same time his co-organizers continued to fail to fully commit themselves. He desperately struggled but was barely able to shoulder what he described as an overwhelming series of burdens. This led to his second suicide attempt. Following this, the final section of Paul's narrative recounted a cascade of experiences that amounted to the repetitive recurrence of the same, absurd problems. He confided his situation to a doctor only to find his serostatus questioned again. The doctor, upon repeating the test, failed to be of adequate support. Outraged about rude and inadequate treatment at a hospital, Paul sought support from a professionalized AIDS organization in an adjacent city, but this equally failed. Finally, he reported how disclosing his problems to a friend resulted in the friend questioning whether Paul actually had HIV (given his healthy-looking appearance). In other words, as he sought help from various institutions and individuals, the support failed to acknowledge his issues and effectively denied solidarity to him. This feeling of absurdity once more became explicit in his conclusion:

> so also the interactions among people [I: mhm] that is just something that up till today i still don't [understand] and i experience this over and over [I: mhm] right if i am too stupid? and i now keep out of such matters as much as possible

As Paul kept facing the same absurdities, unlike before, a new mode of response emerged:

> and then i thought why are you doing this actually you are just so stupid

At this point Paul had turned in vain to a broad range of actors, individual and institutional, in order to find a basis for AIDS organizing grounded in solidarity and, at this point, felt he had exhausted these options. Rather than reacting with outraged resistance as he had done before Paul started doubting his activism, quit AIDS Relief D-Town and moved to the next bigger city. His struggle between feelings of solidarity and absurdity collapsed into an agonizing, bitter and disenchanted conclusion touching on key dimensions of his activist experience (institutions, AIDS organizations, community) while wrestling with his continuously strong feelings of solidarity which he now constructs as clients' shackles:

> <<weeping>oh god i am relieved that i (am here) now […] that would have become my grave [I: mhm] that would have, my, that would have become my grave (in) [d-town] > <<still with a sobbing tone of voice>but i was able to help some [I: mhm] and i felt they were very grateful [I: mhm] but everything around that was shit that was only shit [I: mhm] from the people with hiv/aids to the institutions from aids relief everything shit everything, they have, they have never learned to interact with people with hiv/aids [I: mhm] i don't know, they have, they have not, that ka [I: mhm] i don't know they have cashed in mi millions they have cashed in millions and [inaud.] people with aids, where did it end up [I: mhm] they they have gotten themselves positions, they have furniture, aids relief chapters, furniture, they and i have had to pay everything out of my own pocket i had to finance everything myself> [I: mhm] and I had the feeling, i had, i couldn't chuck it down, i couldn't simply chuck it down [I: yes] i have always said stop it, [paul] stop, it kills you but i couldn't chuck it down and then i was actually somehow this may sound silly but i was somehow glad that i [got] [disabled] […] be forced that way to simply stop [I: yes] and this they accepted, [I: mhm] with nothing else could i come, could i loosen loosen the shackles, those shackles of the relatives, could i loosen the shackles of the people with hiv/aids

Activism

Paul's civic action challenged dominant power structures in a number of ways. This ranged from the local, ostracizing social climate, to professionalized AIDS organizations, to the lack of commitment of his co-organizers. Implicitly, this was also a challenge to dominant AIDS discourses that were fundamental to these power structures. In this sense, Paul's activism was ultimately embedded into cultural conditions of AIDS organizing. Key to this were his feelings of solidarity including a keen sense of resentment, which constituted an alternative and frequently antagonistic emotional register to the emotional climate established by dominant AIDS discourse and its various concrete implications.

The power of this cultural context was particularly evident from the feelings of absurdity that eventually led to the breakdown of Paul's organizing. This discursive power draws on establishing meanings of, and feelings about, AIDS as taken for granted and bestows the same quality on any concrete social action based on it. Absurdity is constituted by the simultaneous *validity* of incommensurable meanings and feelings—in this case Paul's keen sense of solidarity and the powerfully asserted concrete manifestations of dominant AIDS discourse. Paul managed to resolve absurdities only momentarily and pragmatically—e.g., moving to D-Town when his old organization professionalized, reconstituting as AIDS Relief, etc. But the very absurdities he tried to evade caught up with him again—a Don Quixote-like spiral that eventually undermined his ability to make sense of it all and led to his demise and retreat from AIDS work altogether: "that is just something that up till today i still don't (understand)".

Volunteerism: Sandra and Claudia

Let me now turn to some of Paul's co-organizers, Sandra and Claudia. Despite working in the same organization, their stories differ significantly, omitting certain things while attaching different meanings to others (cf. Weick and Roberts 1993). These differences in sensemaking bring the difference between activism and volunteerism as different modes of civic action into relief. The sensemaking perspective also highlights the ongoing effort of retaining such modes throughout the process of organizing and the emotion management involved in this. Alternative realities—and with them alternative emotional stances—often lurk just beneath the surface and must be carefully managed.

Getting involved

Some of these differences are already evident from how Sandra and Claudia describe how they got involved with AIDS Relief D-Town. In sharp contrast to Paul, explicit references to the adverse climate in D-Town or HIV/AIDS issues in general were largely absent throughout their narratives. Sandra started out from a high-school student group that sold red ribbons in public spaces in order to raise money. Through this she met Paul:

> and somehow i don't know i got uhm (-) the idea to look for nearby aids relief chapters [I: yes] which could provide us with better material that we could sell and where we could directly donate the money [I: yes] 'cause it is nice if we can support something regional and then, i just was that, i ended up at [paul's] [I: mhm] and he was super nice and i think the next day i immediately drove there [...] and he gave me then an enormous card box with aids ribbons quite pretty ones that we could then sell pretty well

Curiously missing here is any reference to a problematic reality of AIDS that Sandra wanted to address with her work. Other than the quality and saleability of ribbons, and to "support something regional," the reasons for contacting AIDS Relief D-Town seemed unclear to her ("somehow i don't know").

As her narrative proceeds, it was rather for interpersonal dynamics beyond her control that she "[got] drawn" into (!) AIDS Relief D-Town: Paul's captivating nature and insistence ("wouldn't let me leave anymore"). This passivity culminates in her "sudden" election as a board member, marked by a sense of overwhelming powerlessness:

> and uhm i don't know how [inaud.] suddenly [inaud.] that was i think at a birthday party of [paul] (i just thought) i just [go] there, simply to be <<laughing>nice> [I: mhm] and then i was elected on the board and that was actually where i all of a sudden fell into it [I: mhm] into that board (--) and uhm (1.0) DID WANT to be a part of it of course. so it all DID go very very FAST

There is a curious sense of impersonal social obligation forcing her into the new position without her intention: just not wanting to say no; "of course" (!) she wanted to be part of it as she later added; and a lack of agency. This impersonal quality can be interpreted as a subscription to an abstract normative ideal of doing good—the ideal of the caring citizen or, rather, the volunteerist ideal.

This passive, non-urgent mode continued after this as her role came to include supporting co-organizers and information work. Her evaluative conclusion to this work was paradigmatic for her: "i found that pretty nice ['schön']." A self-referential evaluation, again without reference to an addressed social problem, it is an expression of pride about living up to the normative ideal of doing good as an end in itself.

In a similar fashion, it was the relation to Paul, rather than HIV/AIDS issues, that had Claudia join the organization. Paul was a regular customer of hers and so she learned about the lack of wo/manpower at AIDS Relief D-Town. Eventually, she offered Paul to help out, joined the organization, and soon became a board member, dealing with financial matters mostly. Repeatedly, she characterized her joining as "unspectacular" or as "stumbling into it" indicating its lack of significant meaning. Without reference to urging HIV/AIDS issues, her intention simply was to help Paul maintain the organization. This was in fact a baseline for her volunteer work. Having Paul work with clients, Claudia and the others did mostly administrative and some information work.

This had to do with Claudia's understanding of AIDS organizing as a matter of possessing and contributing pre-existing skills and expertise—a sharp contrast to Paul's grassroot, self-help orientation and autodidactic activism. Feeling that she otherwise lacked expertise, she presented her professional training as an administrator as the sole basis of her engagement. Accordingly, she narrated how maintaining AIDS Relief D-Town was primarily a burdensome and arduous financial problem that required her skill and strength.

For both Sandra and Claudia, civic organizing was about supporting Paul rather than directly related to pressing social realities of HIV/AIDS. And yet, while insignificant as a motive of their engagement, these social realities were not entirely absent in their narratives. While they were exposed to these realities, they carefully managed their emotional impact.

The temperate experience of stigmatization

Where the stigmatizing climate mattered for Sandra and Claudia it was mainly as an unavoidable, complicating background circumstance that they somehow had to cope with. For instance, Sandra and Claudia referred to this climate where they constructed their work as successful *despite* such burdens, rather than with respect to them. Accordingly, they felt irritation, vague bewilderment, dread or annoyance and sometimes pity about it, but not outrage. Unlike Paul, they remained passive with regards to the climate of ostracism and stigma.

Claudia, for instance, mentioned that they were not welcome, that AIDS was not seen as a problem by locals and she even linked this to the denial of institutional support (e.g., use of premises). However, she narrated and placed this in the context of Paul's quitting AIDS Relief D-Town to construct a feeling of hopelessness about continuing the organization. Similarly, at another point, she described that there was generally a disapproval of AIDS Relief D-Town. There are a number of curious prosodic markers, indicating an emotional charge and yet, after two long pauses, she resolves this with an accepting conclusion:

> it was in [paul's] apartment, that is in the neighborhood, it was also, it was also also very dis: : : approved actually then, [I: mhm] the whole thing was never welcome, [...] they would have preferred, say, if he had not been there [I: mhm] (4.0) but (1.0) well you'll always have that sometime

Later she attributed the lack of members to the fear of publicly identifying with AIDS Relief D-Town. But this figured chiefly as an elaboration of financial problems rather than as an issue in itself. At the end, when she described Paul's decision to quit and move away she even mentioned his experience of ostracism, but this only served to make Paul's decision plausible and to construct the necessity to disband.

Sandra's narrative was similar in this respect. Information work in the public directly exposed her to local hostility. She described how she had to listen to "strange" things and argued that it is especially necessary to do something in smaller towns. But this served to construct the dissolution as a mere "pity."

Emotion analysis allows for particular insight into this temperate understanding. Interestingly, there was sometimes a latent, never explicit sense of anger to their narrations. Consider, for instance, the following excerpt:

> SANDRA: (2.5) 'cause, that is, of course, my god, the people (4.0) you must not blame anyone, not at all, but the people: (--) are perhaps empathizing with a certain cause, now in this case (---) uhm (1.0) wi: : th h.i.h.i. infected h.i.v. infected people (–) and want to help somehow (1.0) and (---) 't is of

course easier to simply say o.k. i support you with twenty euros or with fifty euros, [I: mhm] which is great, [I: mhm] which also, without this it just wouldn't work but on the other hand you simply need people who just say, i don't know, i sacrifice an evening each week or a day each month or whatever [...] and that was it, that's what that's what caused it [i.e., the dissolution]

Sandra managed anger about bystanders' passivity (which she nevertheless linked to the problems of AIDS Relief D-Town) by diluting blame through explicit denial and elaborately evoking understanding for people's passivity. This managing of anger is particularly evident at the beginning where long pauses, aborted sentences and an exclamation indicated how she struggled with this emotion management.

Sandra and Claudia tempered their lingering anger by individualizing pertinent instances. In the above quote, Sandra constructed passivity as something all-too human (laziness and poor motivation) rather than a problematic structural condition. Similarly, the experience of open hostility was a matter of flawed character for Claudia, a personal insult, which she struggled to put into perspective here:

even if the <<amused>majority> perhaps says ah how weird [I: mhm] are you all sick with aids, such things came sometimes out in the open, then, well, if that's what you think, i mean, that should, can, that if someone thinks that, that you are only then in a position to campaign for this ok then well that is poor minded i mean <st> YEAH! NO! 't WAS fun nevertheless

Essentially, experiences of hostilities, being ignored for support, being not welcome, accepted and wanted etc. came down to an experience of social devaluation—a constitutive aspect of shame (Katz 1999; Neckel 1991; Scheff 1988; Simmel 1992b). Sandra described hostile remarks in public as a traumatic experience, as something she "won't forget." Equally, there is a sense of shamed hurt and bitterness in Claudia's curiously iterative, faltering[6] description of how recognition, let alone support, by the city was absent—something that Claudia seemed to long for:

well that was nothing where the city presented itself and said hurray we have an aids relief chapter [I: mhm] (1.5) that certainly wasn't the case (2.0) it just existed but we were never (3.0) mentioned in any way or supported or whatever

The expression of reproachful anger that is equally conveyed in these excerpts can then be interpreted in relation to shame. Both can be intimately linked as shame theorists remind us (see also Katz 1999: 163; Retzinger 1991; Scheff 1988; Scheff and Retzinger 1991). From this perspective then, Sandra's and

Claudia's ashamed anger is about the withholding of validation by dominant social actors (the city, the general population).

This has to do with another feature of Sandra's and Claudia's narratives: the peculiar construction of success and self-efficacy, i.e., their ascent to a feeling of pride, particularly while facing self-refuting instances of hostility. Both interviews had episodes hinting at the ostracizing climate intertwined with positive conclusions asserting self-efficacy and, emotionally, pride. For instance, after Sandra attributed the lack of volunteers to people's laziness and poor motivation (see excerpt above) and a bit later even to AIDS Relief D-Town's dissolution, she concluded the segment—after a every long pause!—positively:

> (7.0) but it is always worthwhile even if you if you don't get quite big or even if you can't sustain it forever but i do believe it is always worthwhile

She could only substantiate her claim by referring to an attitude change in her father due to her work as well as the persistence of the high school group where she had started AIDS work—things that were arguably not central to AIDS Relief D-Town. Concluding that her time doing AIDS work was "nice," she constructed success and pride while keeping parts of the local social reality of AIDS—the conditions for lacking support—at bay.

In a similar vein, Claudia talked about the general lack of donations for AIDS issues—in her view due to competing social issues and shifting public attention and due to the locals' view that AIDS was a distant problem that did not affect them in their region. But finding this attitude only "a pity" she quickly moved away form this nascent structural understanding to describe how she herself helped improve the organization's financial situation. Again, managing blame allowed for constructions of success and pride.

In the pursuit of pride instances of hostility came to form a burdening condition that complicated possibilities to be successful as volunteers but that remained external to this volunteer work, something that had to be dealt with only out of sheer necessity. Recall, for example, how Sandra felt she *had* to listen to the hostile remarks. Claudia's talk about hostile remarks at open air festivals was embedded into an argument about how nice her time at AIDS Relief D-Town was, rendering hostility a negative, burdening background condition. In this way, the hostile climate remained external to their work and a deeper understanding of it could be eclipsed. The feeling of pride about being successful volunteers rested on this.

Volunteerism vs. activism

To theorize and explain these findings I want to suggest analyzing Sandra's and Claudia's engagement at AIDS Relief D-Town as instances of what I will call volunteerism, contrasting with Paul's activism. Volunteerism and activism serve as a distinction of two different types of civic action. Both are based in certain emotions and thus involve specific forms of sensemaking.

Volunteerism can be viewed as a discourse which defines identities (Stirling 2007) and carries specific feeling rules. Compassion may be one of the most central feeling rules in this respect (cf. Musick and Wilson 2008: 422).[7] For instance, the popular topos of the Good Samaritan functions (in some cultures) as an important narrative template for volunteering (Wuthnow 1991, 1995). It is about individual help inspired by compassion based on fellow-humanness.[8] Research has noted the connection between the individualizing concept of altruism and volunteerism (Haski-Leventhal 2009; Hustinx *et al*. 2010). This is attributable to the properties of compassion. It is an emotional apprehension of individual rather than of collective suffering. It "can comprehend only the particular, but has no notion of the general and no capacity for generalization" (Arendt 2006: 75). This individualizing focus on suffering itself entails compassion's tendency to shun politics (Arendt 2006: 76–7). What is more, volunteerism is also a relatively institutionalized discourse (cf. Musick and Wilson 2008: 420). It is embedded into public policies that try to foster and tap civic resources (e.g., Berlant 2004b) and it connects to powerful normative discourses about, for example, the good citizen/national or gender (Eliasoph 1998; for the gender aspect, see also Nadai *et al*. 2005). It becomes a socially valued ideal that one should in principle aspire to. In these ways, compassion tends to be compliant with, or at least does not significantly challenge, dominant power structures.[9] Eliaspoh (1998: 25), drawing on Gramsci, therefore calls volunteerism a "hegemonic image of good citizenship."

This allows me to pick up the thread from Chapter 1 and to outline activism, the kind of action associated with social movements, and protest, in contrasting terms. As I argued there, activism could be meaningfully defined as antagonistic towards dominant power structures. Certain emotions seem particularly indicative of such antagonism. For one, the burgeoning body of research on emotions and social movements points to anger as one of the key emotions of activism (for a more nuanced view on this see Flam 2004, 2005) along with other oppositional emotions like solidarity, indignation, shock, resentment, vengefulness, etc. (Barbalet 1998: 126–48; see in addition Flam 2005; Goodwin *et al*. 2001; Jasper 1998). The successful management of fear may often be a precondition to challenging dominant power (Flam 1998, 2004). Paul's keenly felt solidarity with (local) people with HIV and/or AIDS involving, as it did, moral outrage put him squarely into the activist category. It was his feelings of solidarity that allowed him to look beyond individual distress and link it to institutional-structural conditions which he then proceeded to challenge through his organizing efforts. This points to another aspect. While volunteerism is embedded in dominant discourses and based on depoliticizing emotions, activism involves emotional liberation (Flam 1993, 2005), that is detachment from cementing emotional structures (together with cognitive liberation, McAdam 1999). As I have argued above, Paul's solidarity diverted from and challenged the emotional climate of dominant AIDS discourse: the fearful and arguably shaming climate of ostracism it created in D-Town or professionalism with its technical-neutralizing bent and its implicitly othering, subtly shaming premises. His feelings of solidarity, the basis of his engagement, involved a rejection of this emotional climate that stifled AIDS work (fear and shame instilling ostracism) or worked to disempower non-professional civic actors (professionalism).

An alternative, unchallenging stance would not necessarily have implied civic passivity as Sandra and Claudia illustrate. They can be analyzed as volunteers. Their decision to get involved was based on their personal relation to Paul and their engagement was in the first place about helping *him* run the organization. Their stories followed the compassionate narrative paradigm of the Good Samaritan: they offered help to an individual in need whom they met, as it were, along the way (Paul). With a focus on individual help, what was largely missing in both narratives *as a driving motive* is a reference to the social situation of people with HIV/AIDS per se, or rather a sense of solidarity. Consider, for instance, how Claudia met Paul in her taxi—almost literally along the way—and thus learned about his problems at AIDS Relief D-Town, and eventually offered to help him out. Compassion with Paul was also at the basis of Sandra's admiration for him:

> time and again there was something, over and over, some illness, we talked on the phone about it and where i thought that's impossible and then to see again how he deteriorated after a stroke and so on how he manages to walk how he manages to [do certain things] because [paul] is [disabled] is by now uhm and that WAS extreme to see all these (tensions) and nevertheless to see how the guy put himself out for for all the other people

Other emotions in their narratives indicated how dominant power structures were in turn affirmatively a central point of reference for Sandra's and Claudia's work. They derived a sense of pride from trying to live up to the socially approved ideal of the active, caring, good-doing citizen. As we have seen, this depended on very specific measures of success and self-efficacy, which in turn were premised on fading out, or rendering peripheral to their work, the local hostile climate around HIV/AIDS. This notion of success and its pride was considerably derived from more abstract civic ideals and relatively detached from the cause it addressed.

Emotions of compassion and of a specific kind of pride help understand why they constructed and sustained a relatively unpoliticized reality, which is why many of the things outraging Paul had only peripheral significance for them. Their work was centrally about living up to relatively abstract and self-referential ideals and taking pride on the basis of these ideals. Potentially outraging instances mattered only insofar as they provided an arduous context for living up to the volunteerist ideal and for taking pride in it. The individualizing focus of compassion was fundamental to this and precluded a generalizing understanding of the realities of AIDS in D-Town. In short, they left the emotional climate of dominant AIDS discourse, its concrete manifestations in D-Town, relatively unchallenged. To be sure, the very fact that they got involved with AIDS Relief D-Town *in effect* posed something of a challenge to it (e.g., helping Paul sustain his more challenging work). However, this was not a central motive for their engagement and it is for this reason that their work constituted a different paradigm of civic action.

Distinctions

This can be linked to another source contributing to the retention of Sandra's and Claudia's approach. As the most committed Paul could have functioned as a role model and inspiration for the others and indeed, as he described, he struggled hard to push others for stronger commitment and, implicitly, to have them follow different feeling rules. His failure at this had to do with how members of AIDS Relief D-Town interactively constructed organizational identities for each other, which in turn related to dominant social meanings of AIDS.

Essentially, his peers framed Paul as the expert and heroic, almost superhumanly strong figure, while denying for themselves not only expertise and strength and the possibility to grow to acquire the same characteristics. Rather, they assumed a supportive role. Paul was initially daunted by AIDS work, too, but unlike his peers he took this as a challenge. Let me re-consider two excerpts:

> when i started out (1.0) NO that was very very strange (-) [barbara] and [petra] said then (-) well you are the [health care worker] you just do that with the people with aids [...] then i said but i must MYSELF first find information on this; [...] and then i bought those folders over there and covered uhm covered myself with expert literature [I: yes] (1.0) but how psychosocial interactions with people with HIV/AIDS are to be (2.5) well you actually didn't read much about that and didn't get much out of it and then i thought well how would you like to have it YOURSELF! [I: yes] as a person with HIV/AIDS; [...] yes and so i began;

> a: nd (--) there was the big question: (-) what do we do when a person with aids comes in; then I said but what should we do [I: mhm] we just talk to him decently [...] you are a [health care worker] you are h.i.v.-POSITIVE [I: mhm] and and also [petra] pushed it all toWARDS me right

Both quotes from Paul show already the key grounds on which other members constructed a fundamental difference between themselves and him: expertise as evidenced by formal qualification and Paul's serostatus. I have already described how this dynamic kept repeating itself—a pervasiveness that testified to more than merely interpersonal dynamics. Sandra and Claudia were no exception to this. Rather than taking the challenge of daunting AIDS work they also constructed a fundamental difference between themselves and Paul and assumed the role of supporting him in his work.

CLAUDIA: because also none of us had the also didn't have the backgroun the background knowledge [I: mhm] to keep going [after Paul's retreat] neither the background knowledge nor also the [health care] skills he also then partly cared for sick persons [I: mhm] and also through his training as a [health care worker] yeah he simply had it down pat the knowledge and [I: mhm] he also has done that forever [I: yes] so but for us it was important that we at least support him enough so that he can continue with it

This insurmountable difference was also evident from the feelings of admiration latent in this excerpt. For Sandra, this amounted to an almost heroic, superhumanly quality of Paul given his own share of illness and the extent of his commitment (see excerpt in the previous section).

This construction of essential difference can be attributed to a particular aspect of dominant AIDS discourse and its emotional climate. Discussing Paul's stance towards professionalization I have already pointed out how the increasing dominance of a medical understanding of AIDS has led to professionalization. A specific aspect of this is that volunteers were positioned in subordination to professional guidance (see also Chapters 2 and 3). This also reflects the more general condition that the volunteer construct or role is to some extent constituted against the backdrop of and in relation to professionals and vice versa (Musick and Wilson 2008: 423, 436–8; Nadai *et al.* 2005). Hence for a number of reasons AIDS and AIDS work have come to be seen as an issue that demands specialized expertise. But another feature of AIDS discourse is pertinent here, the production of and ascription of AIDS to social others (see Chapter 2). It is crucial in our case, that Paul's difference is also attributed to his serostatus. Implicitly this is based on the idea that seropositivity demarcates fundamentally different skills and indeed a different kind of person.

By rendering AIDS an expert and "others'" issue, dominant AIDS discourse constituted part of the very fear and intimidation of AIDS work. At the same time these discourses allocated competency away from volunteers like Sandra and Claudia. Understanding AIDS in terms of expertise and othering thus legitimized their avoiding the intimidating challenge posed by AIDS work. An important condition for this is that their compassionate stance allowed them to sustain this shying away, where Paul's sense of solidarity led him to face the challenges and made it nearly impossible for him to quit. The difference construct prevented Sandra and Claudia from engaging with the social situation of clients directly, retaining their compassionate focus on supporting Paul.

Dissolution

When Paul decided to leave, the other members were very quick to decide to discontinue the organization. In fact the dissolution appeared quite self-evident to the remaining members.

CLAUDIA: so it was a fact that [paul] moved to [the next bigger city] [I: mhm] and thus AIDS relief [d-town] ceased to exist

SANDRA: [paul] decided then that he goes to [the next bigger city] because of the hospital and so on [I: yes] and then it was just clear also because of that lack of active members that we can actually forget the whole thing sooner or later

Sandra and Claudia related emotionally to the demise of AIDS Relief D-Town—with resignation mingled with pitiful regret. Asked how she felt about the dissolution Sandra recalled:

of course you are disappointed that you somehow think like man was it all in vain but my, one had been able to achieve something up till then of course you are disappointed but on the other hand i thought it will somehow continue [I: mhm] [...] (3.0) yes but there was no chance at all not to think of it at all actually

This sense of self-evidence about disbanding can be understood in terms of volunteerism. A central element of Sandra's and Claudia's volunteerism was the orientation towards helping Paul do his work. From this perspective the organization lost its purpose when Paul left.

As the preceding discussion has shown, however, this was a rather contingent orientation in terms of its discursive premises, feeling rules and the ongoing matching of new experience into the volunteerist construction of organizational reality. This rested on a careful management of the significance of the local, ostracizing climate. Subscribing to the volunteerist ideal allowed them to attach rather peripheral significance to this and curb or manage emotions like anger related to it. Central to this was compassion as instilled by a key feeling rule of the volunteer construct, which effectively limited the scope of their political outlook and entailed an individualizing take. This volunteer approach to AIDS work was in turn premised on dominant AIDS discourse rather than challenging it (or its concrete manifestations). It should not be overlooked that this nevertheless mobilized Sandra and Claudia as they both did AIDS work for several years. But their politically limited construction of organizational reality based in individualizing compassion meant that they were quick to disband the organization when Paul had left even though the AIDS situation in the D-Town region had evidently not changed. Emotional apprehensions of the local social realities of AIDS were lacking as a propelling and binding force to their civic action. This formed a sharp contrast to Paul, whose politicized construction of organizational reality based in solidarity made AIDS work a rather compelling affair for him. Like Eliasoph (1998: 6) has argued, political apathy involves an active and productive process:

We often assume that political activism requires an explanation, while inactivity is the normal state of affairs. But it can be as difficult to ignore a problem as to try to solve it; to curtail feelings of empathy as to extend them; to feel powerless and out of control as to exert an influence; to stop thinking as to think. There is no exit from the political world, no possibility of disengagement; human, political decisions permeate human life, whether we like it or not.

Conclusion

In sum then, the extent of politicization varied with different modes of civic action. In this chapter I suggested distinguishing activism from volunteerism as two such modes. A key difference in how modes of civic action differ is in how they configure emotions and emotion management and in how this in turn implies different ways of relating to dominant power structures. This means that either mode encourages certain ways of constructing social reality, of perceiving certain things while rendering other occurrences and conditions irrelevant or peripheral to the self's experience. The basis for this are different emotional registers. At stake is the very emotional apprehension of alternate versions of reality and how this does or does not translate into action.[10] The key dimension distinguishing different modes is how they relate to dominant power structures— in antagonism or in compliance. Emotions serve as the analytical indicators of this. In the present case this was the difference mainly between solidarity and resentment on the one hand and compassion and the pursuit of pride on the other hand. These emotional bases of civic engagement entailed rather different stories, that is they rendered certain things relevant and charged with emotions while other things remained peripheral. Crucially, however, the potential of those relegated aspects of organizational experience to constitute a different story and different emotions were latently present in the narratives. Modes of civic action evolve narratively and reflexively. Civic actors start out on a certain emotional basis which subsequently guides them in finding out what happens to them, how it matters and how they relate to it emotionally. In principle, this either confirms their point of departure or introduces changes to it, such as Paul's realization that the AIDS work he had found so compelling was in fact in vain given his recurring feelings of absurdity. In Sandra's and Claudia's case, the potential for change was continually present as they implicitly indicated awareness of in principle angering local conditions, which, however, they managed to fit into their volunteerist outlook by managing feelings of anger. It is for this reason that volunteerism functioned as a hegemonic organizational device (Clair 1998: 75) that inspired certain blind-spots constitutive of an unchallenging stance towards dominant power structures. This goes in particular given that volunteerism is a social construct that is to significant extents co-produced by dominant social and political actors and institutions (e.g., public policies). This hegemonic function of volunteerism contrasts with how activism involves a degree of cognitive and emotional liberation (Flam 1993, 2005; McAdam 1999) that breaks with patterns of thinking and feeling that otherwise bind civic actors to hegemonic power.

Background differences and the relativity of antagonism

The metaphor of liberation, however, should not gloss over the fact that it is to be understood in relative terms. In fact, liberation may perhaps even necessitate a modicum of reliance on some power structures while challenging others. This has to do with the fact that domination and submission are never dualistic. Hegemony is rather a multifaceted field with numerous power lines running through it in diverse angles constituting actors with multiple, simultaneous subject positions (Clair 1998: 50–4).

Gender is a particularly pertinent dimension in the present case. After all, it may not be entirely coincidental that both volunteers were women, while the activist was a man.[11] Volunteerism has historically emerged with a strong link to women (Eliasoph 1998; Musick and Wilson 2008; Nadai et al. 2005). This was in fact precisely because it was considered unpolitical. "In this respect, volunteer work, because of its close association with women, acquired the non-political connotation it still has today" (Musick and Wilson 2008: 173). While gender differences in civic work—broadly conceived—may have faded a lot in purely quantitative respect, there are still qualitative differences along gender lines: there is a tendency of men to become more involved with political action, while women tend towards caring work for people in need (Musick and Wilson 2008: 175). It can be argued that this has particularly to do with the fact that gendered feeling rules stipulate compassion for women (cf., for example, DeHart-Davis et al. 2006: 876; Wuthnow 1995: 168). Emotions like anger and resentment, in turn, tend to be privileges of men (e.g., Flam 2005; Hercus 1999; Holmes 2004).

Another difference operating in the background here was the difference between urban centers and the countryside. Paul came to D-Town as an outsider with a background of self-help organizing in an urban center. He was in Schütz's (2002) sense an alien and this may in part have eased his sensitivity to local conditions in D-Town. Sandra and Claudia, in contrast, were both from the D-Town region, and in fact they were still living there at the time of the interview. This became explicit when Paul began exploring the situation in D-Town, made first contact with the ostracizing climate and had Barbara, the local physician, explain to him that people in the region are different. Sandra, by contrast, initially got in touch with Paul when she wanted to donate money she had collected with her student group to a local organization.

Finally, Paul identified as HIV positive and gay. Sandra and Claudia were both straight. They did not mention their serostatus.

All these conditions arguably contributed to Paul's feelings of solidarity and resentment. He did not have to detach himself from deeply ingrained loyalties and forms of normality of a largely taken-for-granted life in the D-Town region.

It was easier for him to see the plight of locals with HIV/AIDS given his own serostatus. As a man it was a bit less daring for him to assume a resentful stance. To some extent he was acting from something of a privileged social position.

However, this is not to essentialize the differences between his activism and the volunteerism of Sandra and Claudia. In particular, the background differences listed here do not entirely explain why neither Sandra nor Claudia followed Paul's example given that he pushed hard for his peers at AIDS Relief D-Town to become more involved. As we have seen, a host of other factors contributed to the retention of their volunteerism. However, a different kind of emotional-cognitive liberation would have been necessary for Sandra and Claudia to become activists. Their solidarity would have had to bridge other differences. But this solidarity could have built on other grounds too. Where Paul felt solidarity with locals as an outsider to the region based on compatible experience of living with HIV, Sandra and Claudia could have also built solidarity precisely on the grounds of a regional identity.

Notes

1 Appendix 2 gives details of the notation used in the transcriptions.
2 Arendt (2006: 79) considers solidarity a reasoned principle rather than an emotion, which she generally finds detrimental to public life. This is arguably based on the problematic opposition of emotion and rationality. However, she fails to sustain this throughout the entirety of her work (Heins 2007). In fact, she talks, albeit not conceptually, about a "feeling of solidarity" (Arendt 2006: 61). In contrast, the sociology of emotions has variously conceived solidarity as an emotion (see, for example, Flam 2002).
3 The feeling of the absurd (cf. Camus 1959) is about a "general sense that things simply aren't adding up" (Proulx 2009: 230). It indicates the failure of sensemaking, a feeling of loss and meaninglessness. Outrage, or rather: rebellion, is one way to regain meaning in situations of absurdity (Goodwin 1971). Garfinkel's (1964) breaching experiments are arguably about how emotional responses, such as anger, resolve a feeling of absurdity (Barbalet 1998: 142–3; cf. Flam 2009: 85).
4 See Chapters 8 and 9.
5 Conflicts in the process of splitting away from the Working Group led to the outbreak of an infection and to hospitalization, where he felt he was treated like a "leper," the hospital also disclosed his serostatus to his employer (a hospital) which would only let him work under unacceptable conditions, such as having to wear double face masks, rubber gloves, two coats. He would also have been barred from dealing with patients, instead cleaning toilets only. Paul also described how it was impossible for him as a gay man to argue that he might have contracted HIV through his job.
6 Note the repeated, long pauses.
7 At the same time, it is not the only pertinent feeling rule. Defining volunteerism chiefly through compassion or pity would limit the concept to instances of help in the context of suffering.
8 The story of the Good Samaritan has taken on numerous readings (historically, theologically) that may differ from the popular understanding focused on compassion (cf., for example, Wuthnow 1991: 157–87).
9 It is no coincidence that compassion is invoked by, and instrumentalized for, conservative politics (see, for example, the contributions to Berlant 2004a). Relatedly,

Barbalet (1998: 130–3) has argued that Whites' sympathy with African Americans actually helped maintain the system of lynching in the US. In principle this does not preclude the possibility of compassionate actors gaining forms of political insight over the course of time, perhaps even take action, and their emotional stances shading towards solidarity (e.g., Hoggett 2006). As analysis in this chapter demonstrates, the compassionate-depoliticized stance is by no means static but must be continuously sustained.

10 While Eliasoph (1998) has focused on different rules restricting or enabling political talk in public, pushing it frontstage or restricting it to the backstage (in a Goffmanian sense), my analysis offers an alternative, complementing perspective: reasons for political disengagement are not just found in contextual rules of appropriateness for talk.

11 However, there were also other male members of AIDS Relief D-Town. The interviews with Paul, Sandra and Claudia suggested that they too focused on supporting Paul in his work. They were either unwilling to participate in this study or have passed away.

References

Arendt, Hannah. 2006. *On Revolution*. New York: Penguin Books.

Barbalet, Jack M. 1998. *Emotion, Social Theory, and Social Structure: A Macrosociological Approach*. Cambridge, New York, Melbourne, Madrid, Cape Town, Singapore, São Paulo: Cambridge University Press.

Berlant, Lauren, ed. 2004a. *Compassion: The Culture and Politics of an Emotion*. New York, London: Routledge.

Berlant, Lauren. 2004b. "Introduction. Compassion (and Withholding)." Pp. 1–13 in *Compassion: The Culture and Politics of an Emotion*, edited by L. Berlant. New York, London: Routledge.

Camus, Albert. 1959. *Der Mythos des Sisyphos. Ein Versuch über das Absurde*. Hamburg: Rowohlt Taschenbuch Verlag.

Clair, Robin Patric. 1998. *Organizing Silence: A World of Possibilities*. Albany: State University of New York Press.

DeHart-Davis, Leisha, Justin Marlowe and Sanjay K. Pandey. 2006. "Gender Dimensions of Public Service Motivation." *Public Administration Review* 66(6): 873–87.

Eliasoph, Nina. 1998. *Avoiding Politics: How Americans Produce Apathy in Everyday Life*. Cambridge, New York, Melbourne, Madrid: Cambridge University Press.

Flam, Helena. 1993. "Die Erschaffung und der Verfall oppositioneller Identität." *Forschungsjournal Neue Soziale Bewegungen* 2: 83–97.

Flam, Helena. 1998. *Mosaic of Fear*. Boulder: East European Monographs.

Flam, Helena. 2002. *Soziologie der Emotionen. Eine Einführung*. Konstanz: UVK Verlagsgesellschaft (UTB für Wissenschaft).

Flam, Helena. 2004. "Anger in Repressive Regimes: A Footnote to Domination and the Arts of Resistance by James Scott." *European Journal of Social Theory* 7(2): 171–88.

Flam, Helena. 2005. "Emotions' Map: A Research Agenda." Pp. 19–40 in *Emotions and Social Movements*, edited by H. Flam and D. King. London, New York: Routledge.

Flam, Helena. 2009. "Extreme Feelings and Feelings at Extremes." Pp. 73–93 in *Theorizing Emotions: Sociological Explorations and Applications*, edited by D. R. Hopkins, J. Kleres, H. Flam and H. Kuzmics. Frankfurt am Main, New York: Campus.

Gamson, Josh. 1989. "Silence, Death and the Invisible Enemy: AIDS Activism and Social Movement 'Newness'." *Social Problems* 36(4): 351–67.

Garfinkel, Harold. 1964. "Studies of the Routine Grounds of Everyday Activities." *Social Problems* 11(3): 225–50.
Goodwin, Glenn A. 1971. "On Transcending the Absurd: An Inquiry in the Sociology of Meaning." *American Journal of Sociology* 76(5): 831–46.
Goodwin, Jeff, James M. Jasper and Francesca Polletta, eds. 2001. *Passionate Politics: Emotions and Social Movements*. Chicago, London: University of Chicago Press.
Haski-Leventhal, Debbie. 2009. "Altruism and Volunteerism: The Perceptions of Altruism in Four Disciplines and Their Impact on the Study of Volunteerism." *Journal for the Theory of Social Behaviour* 39(3): 271–99.
Heins, Volker. 2007. "Reasons of the Heart: Weber and Arendt on Emotion in Politics." *The European Legacy* 12(6): 715–28.
Hercus, Cheryl. 1999. "Identity, Emotion, and Feminist Collective Action." *Gender and Society* 13(1): 34–55.
Hoggett, Paul. 2006. "Pity, Compassion, Solidarity." Pp. 145–61 in *Emotion, Politics and Society*, edited by S. Clarke, P. Hoggett and S. Thompson. Basingstoke, New York: Palgrave Macmillan.
Holmes, Mary. 2004. "Feeling beyond Rules: Politicizing the Sociology of Emotion and Anger in Feminist Politics." *European Journal of Social Theory* 7(2): 209–27.
Hustinx, Lesley, Ram A. Cnaan and Femida Handy. 2010. "Navigating Theories of Volunteering: A Hybrid Map for a Complex Phenomenon." *Journal for the Theory of Social Behaviour* 40(4): 410–34.
Jasper, James M. 1998. "The Emotions of Protest: Affective and Reactive Emotions in and around Social Movements." *Sociological Forum* 13(3): 397–424.
Katz, Jack. 1999. *How Emotions Work*. Chicago: Chicago University Press.
Kleres, Jochen. 2015. "Narrative des Mitgefühls. Methodischer Ansatz und Anwendung." Pp. 267–87 in *Die Ambivalenz der Gefühle: Über die verbindende und widersprüchliche Sozialität von Emotionen*, edited by J. Kleres and Y. Albrecht. Wiesbaden: Springer VS.
McAdam, Doug. 1999. *Political Process and the Development of Black Insurgency, 1930–1970*. Chicago, London: University Of Chicago Press.
Musick, Marc A. and John Wilson. 2008. *Volunteers: A Social Profile*. Bloomington, Indianapolis: Indiana University Press.
Nadai, Eva, Peter Sommerfeld, Felix Bühlmann and Barbara Krattiger. 2005. *Fürsorgliche Verstrickung: Soziale Arbeit zwischen Profession und Freiwilligenarbeit*. Wiesbaden: VS Verlag für Sozialwissenschaften.
Neckel, Sieghard. 1991. *Status und Scham. Zur symbolischen Reproduktion sozialer Ungleichheit*. Frankfurt am Main, New York: Campus Verlag.
Proulx, Travis. 2009. "The Feeling of the Absurd: Towards an Integrative Theory of Sense-Making." *Psychological Inquiry* 20(4): 230–4.
Retzinger, Suzanne M. 1991. *Violent Emotions: Shame and Rage in Marital Quarrels*. Newbury Park, London, New Delhi: SAGE.
Scheff, Thomas J. 1988. "Shame and Conformity: The Deference-Emotion System." *American Sociological Review* 53(3): 395–406.
Scheff, Thomas J. and Suzanne M. Retzinger. 1991. *Emotions and Violence: Shame and Rage in Destructive Conflicts*. Lexington, MA: Lexington Books.
Scholz, Sally J. 2010. *Political Solidarity*. University Park: Pennsylvania State University Press.

Schütz, Alfred. 2002. "Der Fremde. Ein sozialpsychologischer Versuch." Pp. 73–92 in *Der Fremde als sozialer Typus*, edited by P.-U. Merz-Benz and G. Wagner. Konstanz: UVK (UTB).

Simmel, Georg. 1992a. *Soziologie. Untersuchungen über die Formen der Vergesellschaftung*. Frankfurt am Main: Suhrkamp.

Simmel, Georg. 1992b. "Zur Psychologie der Scham." Pp. 140–50 in *Schriften zur Soziologie: Eine Auswahl*, edited by H.-J. Dahme and O. Rammstedt. Frankfurt am Main: Suhrkamp.

Stirling, Christine. 2007. *The Volunteer Citizen, Health Services and Agency: The Identity Work of Australian and New Zealand Ambulance Volunteers*. PhD thesis, University of Tasmania.

Weick, Karl E. and Karlene H. Roberts. 1993. "Collective Mind in Organizations: Heedful Interrelating on Flight Decks." *Administrative Science Quarterly* 38(3): 357–81.

Wuthnow, Robert. 1991. *Acts of Compassion: Caring for Others and Helping Ourselves*. Princeton: Princeton University Press.

Wuthnow, Robert. 1995. *Learning to Care: Elementary Kindness in an Age of Indifference*. New York, Oxford: Oxford University Press.

Chapter 7

AIDS politics between compassion and pity

One particular source of frustration for Paul was Bavarian AIDS Relief—the umbrella federation of AIDS Relief organizations in Bavaria—which he found bureaucratized and of little help for what he wrestled with in D-Town. Set up in 1995, ironically, it, too, disbanded (in 2002), after a phase of stagnation running parallel to the decline of its small-town and non-professionalized chapters (such as in D-Town). This is particularly interesting as one of its key activities revolved around providing support to those smaller chapters. In this way, it related indirectly to the local conditions for AIDS organizing in rural Bavaria in which, for instance, AIDS Relief D-Town was embedded. It is interesting, therefore, to analyze how these conditions mattered to actors at Bavarian AIDS Relief and which actions they took to address them. Also of particular interest is that they made connections with Bavarian AIDS policies, a topic that was absent from the narratives about AIDS Relief D-Town. The Bavarian state government was the only regional state government in Germany to oppose new public health policies and it tried to implement more coercive measures, albeit with limited success (see Chapter 3). As one interviewee described, this approach later gave way to the tacit implementation of new public health approaches, especially the inclusion of civic organizations, yet with a crucial difference: with one exception (AIDS Relief Munich) civic partners were not recruited from the ranks of AIDS Relief organizations, historically rooted as they are in the gay movement. Instead the state commissioned other, pre-existing general welfare organizations.

Only two people from Bavarian AIDS Relief agreed to tell their stories. However, these two interviews provide a picture that is rather resonant with the analysis of AIDS Relief D-Town shedding additional light on volunteerism.[1] While one of these interviews allows us to further explore the intricate ramifications of compassion in civic action, the second one introduces a different emotional basis for volunteerism: pity.

Peter: volunteerism, political inclusion and self-confidence

As a board member of a large, urban and professionalized AIDS Relief chapter, Peter helped set up Bavarian AIDS Relief, building on a pre-existing informal inter-organizational network. As for his motives in doing so, however, he remained curiously vague:

> ninety-five (we came to) the conclusion that it would be better, give us more clout, be more effective if we turned this [the informal network] into a formal organization [I: yes] [...] and we decided we should form an umbrella association with those seven [existing local aids relief] organizations [I: mhm] to create a presence at the regional state level [...] so we stood there had an organization and really didn't know what <<laughing> that (would) be good for>

Despite this somewhat combative rhetoric ("clout"), his narrative provided no detail as to what necessitated more clout and made an umbrella organization desirous. His ironic closure was indicative here. This did not change much throughout the interview, even when directly asked about it. On closer inspection, this discrepancy turned out to be no coincidence. His vagueness had to do with the kinds of goals pursued through Bavarian AIDS Relief: rather than politically specific, these were about gaining "presence," the pursuit of recognition, that is, emotionally a quest for self-confidence. Barbalet (1998: 82–102) characterizes self-confidence as the feeling of confidence in self's ability to act effectively in the future. This, he argues, depends on social relations of recognition and acceptance.[2] This ability to act effectively—in the political arena, that is—was also at stake for Peter. He aimed at Bavarian AIDS Relief becoming a significant actor acknowledged by "the media, by the ministries, by German AIDS Relief and so on if we say we are not just the AIDS Relief organizations in Bavaria." The most important goal to him was "recognition, a presence at the regional state level."[3]

The ascent to collective-organizational self-confidence meant that Peter strove for Bavarian AIDS Relief to function as an intermediary association representing its member organizations. On the one hand this involved an orientation towards dominant institutions (mainstream media, state agencies), which in principle included both exerting influence while refraining from downright antagonism. This ambiguous stance can precisely be explained by the emotion of self-confidence, which inherently depends in its presumption of standing and influence on recognition by powerful actors. Only as long as Bavarian AIDS Relief was recognized by them could it act self-confidently as the representative of its member organizations and reliably exert influence for them. The goal was inclusion among the legitimate political actors of the field rather than wrestling with them in an antagonistic struggle. On the other hand, this intermediation equally rested on the ability to represent the base of member organizations.[4] In this dual orientation towards influencing the state and towards the membership base, Peter mirrored a neo-corporatist logic (see Chapter 4). The orientation towards the membership was not instrumental for Peter. To some extent—however limited, as we shall see—he cared about member organizations. When much to his surprise a wave of AIDS Relief chapters emerged in small towns, he tried through Bavarian AIDS Relief to make the expertise of its bigger, experienced member organizations available to the newcomers by offering trainings. When he then came to feel that the small chapters would still not succeed, this led to the appointment of a professional co-ordinator at Bavarian AIDS Relief to support smaller chapters. At this point his narrative followed the Good Samaritan paradigm: the protagonist (Peter) came along some others (small town AIDS Relief chapters), saw their distress and ventured to help out. This compassion was succinctly expressed in Peter's realization "then we (2.0) saw the (---) little ones: ? didn't MANAGE" with its belittling, infantilizing as it were, representation of "the little ones" and an emphasis on their weakness, i.e., their need of protection and caring support.

Decline and absurdity

Over time Peter found these ambitions to be in vain, however. Overall, he told the story of Bavarian AIDS Relief as one of crumbling participation and withering internal support, ultimately leaving no alternative to dissolution. In Peter's understanding this was essentially a matter of members' failure to back the activities of Bavarian AIDS Relief or even to make use of its services. To a large extent this involved attributing blame to volunteers. This operated on the basis of a specific understanding of the tides of volunteer commitment as due to individual idiosyncrasies or the coincidental contingencies of personal situations. As we shall see in the next section, this was conditioned by, and fed back into, a keenly depoliticized construction of organizational reality.

This theme played out right from the beginning in the context of the informal network preceding Bavarian AIDS Relief. Peter hinted at the unreliability of individuals' enthusiasm especially as they move on in their lives.

> yes but even then dissolution was an issue already, there had been three aids relief chapters already in bavaria [...] that had disbanded [I: uhm yes] and it was quite clear in none of those cases, even though finances are always a problem, it was not finances it was the commitment of people [...] in [e-city] there were i believe three uhm enthusiastic students there, when they moved away from ([e-city]) the aids relief chapter was gone

Later it became clear that the support co-ordinator was not succeeding. There was little to no demand for the trainings meant to channel expertise from bigger to smaller chapters. Peter blamed this on local volunteers themselves and their individual characteristics. He saw them as too overburdened with their ongoing local work and too weak to cope with it:

> they simply didn't have the strength, that, [our support offer] was not a facilitation for for the for the local people it was an additional [I: uhum] <<laughing>burden> to talk to us

With participation of member organizations in, and their support for, the activities of Bavarian AIDS Relief declining he found the organization ultimately reduced to a minimum.

> activities at regional state level became increasingly scanty [I: mhm] what we offered was not taken, there were few impulses from the smaller organizations, some said what are we paying membership fees for anyway [I: mhm] if we get nothing out of it and we really saw us mainly to be there for the small ones, the big ones said we can do our work ourselves better actually we don't commission you with anything

When public funding for the paid co-ordinator ended—it was limited from the outset—Peter found Bavarian AIDS Relief "<<chuckles> shrunken> back down to the board members." This was a period, when smaller chapters, too, were now disbanding, leaving only the handful of professionalized organizations in operation in Bavaria—an instance which he equally attributed to the tides of volunteerism: "the founders didn't want to do it anymore." Finally, it proved to be impossible to find new candidates for the board of Bavarian AIDS Relief, which, again, he found to be due to individual circumstances, as one former board member moved away and another possible candidate feared conflicts with her employer.[5] Manifold organizational decline left Peter with feelings of resignation and the conclusion that there was no way to continue. Bavarian AIDS Relief disbanded.[6]

> ok we talked a lot about how much of a pity it would be in the com uh in comparison with other organizations it is not good if we disappear from the map but no one was willing to do something and we saw no alternative

This feeling of resignation was the outcome of persistent and recurring feelings of absurdity. As he pursued his ambitions for Bavarian AIDS Relief he came to "discover" the ever so human qualities and circumstances of the local volunteers'/activists' function, which blunted his efforts—volunteers relocating, simply shifting their interests, running into (understandable) problems with their employers or simply being unable to muster the strength required for AIDS work. In principle, not unlike Paul's case, it was the discrepancy between cherished goals and real-world conditions that left him with a feeling of absurdity. Characteristically, Peter repeatedly interspersed his narrative with chuckling and laughter as some of the preceding excerpts have shown. For instance, the irony of the impossibility to recruit board members from a *state-wide* base made him laugh: "suddenly I was the only, the only person who was willing [to serve] as a board member <<laughing> in this regional state federation>." He concluded his narrative with a segment about browsing through old documents at home some time after the dissolution: "said what rubbish was that and destroyed <<chuckles briefly>> everything." His feelings of absurdity thus took on an emotional shade of bitterness and resignation as he realized the discrepancy between his high, self-confidence aspiring goals and what he saw as the sobering, mundane and idiosyncratic realities among the members of Bavarian AIDS Relief. This combination of absurdity and bitterness was succinctly expressed, for instance in his characterization of the internet representation of Bavarian AIDS Relief as deceptive trickery ("Blendwerk"): "they were beautiful web pages professionally made [...] but <<chuckles>> there was not much substance". However, the absurdities did not agonize him the way they did Paul, although, not unlike Paul, he did try till the very end to keep things going. As we will see, this sense of absurdity and resignation involved a specific understanding of organizational reality.

Compassion, rationalized AIDS discourse and depoliticization

Peter's account may have considerable ad hoc plausibility. Yet, much as we saw in the previous chapter, it rested on contingent premises that rendered some aspects of reality relevant and others peripheral. This is already evident from the rather different story that Paul (of AIDS Relief D-Town) told about Bavarian AIDS Relief. He was a representative precisely of one of those small, rural and non-professionalized chapters that Peter talked about. But this contingency was also evident from Peter's narrative itself which hinted at potential different accounts.

A rationalized understanding of HIV/AIDS functioned as the pivotal premise, that is the discursive reduction of the disease, by and large, to the status of a medical condition. This depoliticizing and individualizing discursive background can be related to the compassionate (rather than solidaristic) stance Peter adopted towards smaller member organizations, and to his specific understanding of volunteers as idiosyncratic while simultaneously averting from all things with potential political significance such as the difficult conditions for AIDS organizing in Bavaria outside the urban centers (cf. AIDS Relief D-Town). From this perspective, his civic organizing can be analyzed as volunteerism. This applies in particular as his engagement evolved in close relation to professionalism which functioned in his narrative as the paradigmatic ideal of AIDS work. Even more than Sandra and Claudia, his narrative evidences this intimate link between volunteerism and professionalism up to the point where volunteerism seems to be a kind of proto-professionalism for Peter (see also Onur in Chapter 9).

What Bavarian AIDS Relief tried to offer to its smaller members was expertise ("knowledge transfer"). This related to, for example, public relations work, legal issues, prevention for gay men or fundraising techniques. Simultaneously, small town organizers signified to Peter deficits of expertise and skill. Rather than local adversities, in Peter's view the problem of small chapters was their lack of competence.

> we wanted to provide a professional for press work for trainings, not really that he would have given trainings himself but organize trainings [I: ja] uhm say knowledge transfer [I: yes] for uhm uhm for the small ones because it was clear to us that they have deficits [I: mhm] and they won't succeed with it on their own they also won't have a paid position and uhm so the idea was this project co-ordinator would [I: mhm] form a switch point a transfer point

Peter put primacy on the ideal of professionalism here—the central importance of expertise and skill to AIDS organizing. Significantly, this ideal held true for him also with respect to the all-volunteer small chapters, which underlines how volunteerism constitutes itself in relation to professionalism. There was a corresponding sense of superiority about professionalized AIDS organizing and the volunteerism embedded into it. Its flip side was a feeling of condescension for all-volunteer-based chapters, as when he described the knowledge transfer:

> in most cases the uhm bigger ones [...] told the small ones a little bit about what they are doing but also partly also vice versa

Professionalism and volunteerism as related to professionalism thus served as the ideal of AIDS organizing for Peter. This was an ideal not of his own making: it has become the legitimate paradigm in the field of AIDS organizing in the wake of shifts in dominant AIDS discourse and has since reinforced this shift—i.e., the shift towards a predominantly medical, socially generalizing understanding of AIDS (see Chapters 2 and 3). On the basis of these discursive premises, AIDS work has evolved into something of a technicality, the application of expertise and skill.

The supremacy of professional AIDS work also contributed to Peter's compassion for "the small ones." Compassion essentially involves a social relation of difference: between superior ability and need. An individualizing emotion without an eye for generalization (see Chapter 6), it inspires helping the needy. Peter succinctly expressed this through the notion that Bavarian AIDS Relief was doing something *for* its smaller members, which came down, as we saw, to a transfer from the professionalized to the non-professionalized and deficient. The legitimized ideal of professionalism in AIDS work therefore was constitutive of Peter's feelings of compassion: it constituted his apprehension of smaller chapters as needy, that is in a specific way deficient, and hence in need of help by the more abled organizations. This specific emotional apprehension and construction of need eclipsed more politicized notions of need, which for instance organizers like Paul in D-Town felt to be at stake in their work.

The primacy of professionalism and the feelings of compassion it engendered shaped Peter's apprehension of the failure of the support efforts. He reported this failure as a cascade of disappointments: he and his co-organizers at Bavarian AIDS Relief installed the co-ordinator to provide advice centrally, "but practically nothing [requests, etc.] came in"; they offered consultation hours, but that "didn't interest anybody"; they offered trainings, but "nobody came or too few came"; and in conclusion: "uhm nobody has the time or didn't fancy it or whatever". In sum, this amounted to feelings of ironic absurdity, frustration and blame.[7] The compassionate shunning of the politics of local AIDS organizing was constitutive of this. Against the backdrop of the taken-for-granted validity and supremacy of the professional and volunteerist ideal he came to understand the poor resonance among smaller chapters in terms of non-professionals' inherent unreliability, or, rather, inferiority. The important point here is that his emotions and sensemaking markedly differed from what small town organizers felt to be at stake as Paul's interview suggests. The problem for Paul was not the lack of expertise and skill but rather the struggle with hostility, stigma and failing support (including Bavarian AIDS Relief). Peter briefly mentioned D-Town (among others) but explained its demise, too, solely in terms of the otherwise uncontextualized waning of mobilization:

> [d-town] was originated by one person [I: mhm] he did manage to get a few other people uhm on board [I: mhm] but when he was gone from [d-town] it was was (crystal) clear there is no organization in [d-town] anymore

Peter's feelings of absurdity given the ironies of his work—the irony of compassionate help extended to the needy, but rejected by them—were thus premised on his subscription to the professionalized ideal of AIDS work and an according understanding of volunteerism as auxiliary to professionalism. It led him to view the problems of smaller chapters in terms that differed categorically from their own perceptions as in the case of AIDS Relief D-Town. These premises—taken-for-granted, institutionalized and based in powerful discourses—also allowed him to resolve this feeling of absurdity by blaming organizations themselves for their failures as volunteers. In this way he could retain his volunteerist outlook.

His narrative betrayed at the same time some degree of awareness of political and social conditions of AIDS organizing in Bavaria, yet he put effort into neutralizing their significance. Most explicitly, politics made itself felt to him through the impact of Bavarian AIDS policies on AIDS Relief chapters.[8] Peter was far from unaware of this but it failed to trigger his solidarity.

In his account the Bavarian penchant for old-public health (see Chapter 3) had given way to involving—i.e., funding and officially recognizing—civil society actors in public AIDS policies. These civic partners were "proportionately" picked from among such organizations as the Red Cross or Caritas (Catholic welfare agency). Munich was the only AIDS Relief chapter included in this even though several other cities had existing chapters as well. These now often found themselves with another, officially recognized AIDS organization in the same city and "had to struggle really hard [I: mhm] with this organization in the same town." For instance, one particular AIDS Relief chapter had its legitimacy constantly questioned by the officially recognized local AIDS organization and eventually "[went] down the drain" and disbanded. This wording—struggling, going down the drain—revealed a great deal of empathy for the plight of those organizations. But this failed to translate into solidarity. Rather, Peter ended up constructing the local conflict in personal terms as due to a mean, ill-intentioned leader of the recognized AIDS organization and a lack of recruitment skills of the leading local AIDS Relief activist/volunteer.[9] This was a rather individualizing take. And again he viewed local organizers through the frame of deficient volunteerism. This functioned to manage the potential for feelings of solidarity and to retain a merely compassionate stance for local chapters lacking expertise and skill. In this way Bavarian AIDS politics both came into view but simultaneously lost its political significance. As we have seen, this understanding of local organizers was centrally tied to the ideal of professionalism in AIDS work, which in turn was embedded into dominant AIDS discourse.

It was on the basis of all of these contingencies that Peter arrived at concluding the immanent and inextricable futility of Bavarian AIDS Relief leading him to a keen feeling of resignation:

> many of those organization were unfit to survive to begin with [I: mhm] i'd say and we have made ourselves a little uhm important we went from seven uhm member organizations to twelve [inaud.] those twelve <<short laughter>>at most half of them were fit to survive

His resignation then was contingent on his efforts at neutralizing the significance of instances that could have inspired a different way of sensemaking—smaller chapters rejecting the help offered to them and the impact of Bavarian AIDS politics on them. It is only on the bases of this management of alternative meanings and emotions that he came to experience a feeling of absurdity about his engagement and eventually a sense of resignation.

Formalization and conflicts

The professional-volunteerist approach pursued through Bavarian AIDS Relief also led to conflicts with grassroots organizers. In theory, this also could have pushed Peter to greater engagement with the politics of AIDS organizing. However, his rationalizing, depoliticized approach allowed him to ward off the conflicts and match them into the frame of lacking support for the umbrella association.

The most significant conflict was about the regular Bavarian People With HIV/AIDS Gatherings.[10] Previously organized by an informal group of activists/volunteers, shifting funding patterns first led Bavarian AIDS Relief to take on financial administration, which in turn led to "dissent between the people who had led this well for years and us [organizers at bavarian aids relief] who were suddenly in charge of the money." In reaction to these tensions Bavarian AIDS Relief decided to take over organizing completely, which only increased tensions. Peter's narrative suggests that this was essentially about a clash of a bureaucratic-rationalized logic with grassroots organizing. However, his understanding of the conflict was rather different. This had a lot to do with his taken-for-granted rationalized, professional-volunteerist approach to AIDS organizing. With AIDS organizing figuring as something of a technicality it became amenable to purportedly disinterested administrative procedures. Essentially, Peter established precedence of what he framed as neutral, apolitical, bureaucratic-formal considerations over substantial issues which he sweepingly rendered peripheral:

> and i believe it was absolutely not about substantial issues ["inhalt"] [...] we felt uhm we dealt with money from others and we were not by any means uhm happy how uhm the representatives dealt with our money and that was also only [inaud.] borrowed money we said that has [inaud.] has to be more formal there was a huge row [I: mhm] one has to say and uhm in the end we found ourselves compelled uhm to revoke the assignment [...] organize it differently [I: mhm] which stirred up pretty uhm bad feelings [I: mhm] and we felt, i believe we had a little bit of support from the at from the aids relief chapters but we as board members had to take the rap for it

> the people who lead that don't understand that it is about money about a good reputation they can damage quite a bit with their way of working [I: mhm] uhm <<clears throat>> and uhm we had tried to set [I: mhm] uhm stricter uhm rules and they held that against us said we know what we do you are only the uhm [I: mhm] office workers anyway [I: mhm] uhm and uhm it became really yes a (2.0) bitter conflict

> they could not comprehend that it had to have a formal frame [I: mhm] and where we had to enforce certain points [I: mhm] even if the substantial work is o.k. that is uhm [I: mhm] that if a bill for professional fees uhm comes in six months six months later we can't account for the whole thing [I: mhm] that means we are simply in debt for six months until you order your affairs [I: mhm] and uhm uhm s they didn't care about such formalities or they di they didn't either didn't believe us or they didn't see that that's a problem [I: mhm] if we are suddenly in debt for ten thousand [I: mhm] and uhm so that uhm yes it was difficult

Though he hints at the power processes at stake here (Bavarian AIDS Relief as setting rules vs. acting as office workers), he constituted the episode as another failure of volunteerism/activism as organizers simply failed to properly grasp or appropriately consider what was at stake. Volunteerism once more appeared as irrational and idiosyncratic, an entanglement of personal, financial and substantial matters as he pointed out. Framing dissent in these terms, based as it was in the specific discursive premises of Peter's outlook, allowed the neglect of its essence and the politics of professionalization and its disempowering effects.

In many respects, Peter can be characterized as a volunteer. His pursuit of self-confidence for Bavarian AIDS Relief, while aiming at a degree of influence, simultaneously involved dependence on powerful public actors. His goal of creating an intermediary organization also related him to the constituency of Bavarian AIDS Relief—its member organizations—but his feelings of compassion based on a proto-professional ideal of AIDS work (expertise, skill) and on rationalized AIDS discourse led him to a relatively depoliticized understanding of the situation of small AIDS Relief chapters and how it related to Bavarian AIDS policies. This was constitutive of his attributing blame on local volunteers and what he understood to be their idiosyncratic shortcomings. In turn, this led him to recurrent feelings of absurdity about his engagement and in the end he gave up in resignation. Overall, that is to say, the challenge to dominant power and its adverse consequences (e.g., for the smaller chapters) were not a central, driving motive to his engagement.

Alfons: pity and avoiding narration

Much like Peter, Alfons became involved with Bavarian AIDS Relief via his engagement with a large, urban chapter, but their stories differed fundamentally. While Peter felt committed to Bavarian AIDS Relief and tried to make it work, Alfons did not see its relevance and necessity. He felt this to such an extent that he struggled to tell a story at all about Bavarian AIDS Relief. Where in Peter's case the pursuit of collective self-confidence and his feelings of compassion made for both a degree of civic action and its limitation, the focus of Alfons' AIDS work was even more limited. A slightly different emotion was central for him: pity. This constituted his engagement equally as volunteerism.

Irrelevance: an urban-professional perspective

> this construct [Bavarian AIDS Relief] simply existed [I: mhm] yes didn't know quite how to deal with it [I: mhm] and it didn't make itself felt also in the day uhm in the normal aids relief work also

From the very beginning, Alfons presented Bavarian AIDS Relief as irrelevant. With just a few sentences he briefly listed that Bavarian AIDS Relief organized the Bavarian People with HIV/AIDS Gatherings; that it gained public funding; its membership assemblies; and an instance of helping a chapter politically to secure public funding. Time and again he interspersed this with arguments that the association was irrelevant and concluded: "that organization didn't make itself felt here [i.e., at his own local chapter]." This forms a stark contrast to

Peter's sincere ambitions for it and raises the question as to the premises that led Alfons to experiencing the umbrella organization as peripheral. After all, as cursory and sparse as these few recollections of Alfons are, they indicate his principle awareness of occurrences that could have mattered.

Recurring references to his own AIDS Relief chapter already hinted at a key background against which irrelevance is constituted:

> there is then probably sometime a period where the whole thing [Bavarian AIDS Relief] became more condensed [I: mhm] (6.5) but it was, didn't appear to me as like an important institution or so [I: mhm] like for the work here in the house [i.e., his own aids relief chapter] yes well I have always, am not passing judgment now [I: ja] that the work itself for for bavarian aids relief [I: mhm] uhm uhm didn't have any value, but for the work here in the house this was more or less well it wasn't important uhm rather that that [his own chapter] well provided practical support uhm services for for other aids relief chapters here in bavaria [...] leave it open whether this would have happened had the bavarian aids uhm state association not been there [I: mhm] i think it would have happened anyway

There was a notable degree of urban centrism, pride and condescension to this. This in turn rested on more fundamental premises. Pride and condescension came down to a feeling of superiority,[11] which in this case was constituted by the advanced profile of Alfons' own chapter, a large organization, with a variety of services, organized into "departments"—in short, a professionalized agency. Tellingly, Alfons employed the language of professionalized AIDS work (my emphases): Bavarian AIDS Relief did not play a role in the "normal *AIDS Relief work*"; "for the *work* here *in the house*[12] [...] it was not important"; and it was his chapter which "provided *services*" to Bavarian AIDS Relief. What is more, to the limited extent that he detailed Bavarian AIDS Relief's activities, he focused on the channeling of expertise from large chapters, like his own, to smaller ones or the securing of funding for chapters threatened by funding cutbacks—concerns of a professionalized paradigm of AIDS work. Even more explicitly than Peter, Alfons shared the professionalized ideal of AIDS work with volunteers relegated into an auxiliary position. As argued before, such professionalist premises are linked to a rationalized understanding of AIDS primarily as a medical problem. While Peter too was indebted to this discursive paradigm, Alfons was arguably even more entrenched in it. As a result, Peter pursued some kind of political ideal notion of Bavarian AIDS Relief as an intermediary organization including what neo-corporatism calls the logic of membership (however limited that was), whereas AIDS work for Alfons entirely exhausted itself in apolitical, technical aspects of service provision. This was evident, for one, from what he felt was at stake when Bavarian AIDS Relief helped to save a local chapter—solely a matter of securing funding and staff positions:[13]

that regional state association made itself felt more intensely when monies were to be secured for one aids relief chapter [...] [I: mhm] or secure its existence altogether <st> it was about I believe half a staff position but it was about staff retrenchments or something [I: yes] where the the uhm the bavarian aids relief association uhm also made itself felt a little politically

The same decontextualized financial focus recurred later with regards to the peculiarities of Bavarian AIDS policies. While Peter was to some extent aware of its adverse impact on AIDS Relief chapters, though did not squarely criticize it, Alfons framed this in purely monetary terms and as a matter of mere regional-administrative differences:

'cause there are just different funding models in bavaria [I: mhm] uhm munich is a recognized advice center [I: mhm] that means that munich has a uhm a different funding [I: mhm] that that that that is institutionally guaranteed [...] takes its place among the other [recognized, non-aids relief] advice centers

[in all other cities] each AIDS relief chapter files its own own application with the district with the city or so on and bargains for itself

and uhm the regulation the funding and so on is different from district to district [...] thus given that it was also the conditions were partly not compati uhm comparable at all and so on [I: yes] one could thus also not create a common stance for all aids relief chapters [...] 'cause there were always regionally different funds

This left political action on a regional state-wide level pointless to Alfons. With AIDS organizing reduced to a technicality, an umbrella organization indeed easily appeared superfluous.

Supporting others and pity

This insignificance was manifested in Alfons' struggle to tell a proper narrative at all. Details were scarce, their significance immediately denied and even the temporal order seemed to be confused sometimes. What is more, he expressed time and again his inability to remember much specific detail often referring me to Peter, even though he later indicated that he was at times personally involved with some activities. There is no story to be told about something that is experienced as irrelevant (Schütze 1976, 1987). Mostly, therefore, he presented descriptions of and arguments about Bavarian AIDS Relief rather than a narrative (on narrativity vs. description and argumentation, see Chapter 5). One development, however, stands out as something of a narrative constituting occurrence. This was the initiative of Bavarian AIDS Relief to support smaller chapters. Alfons' understanding of this initiative, however, owed much to his construction of irrelevance. He essentially presented the initiative as something of a deviating presumption given the pointlessness of Bavarian AIDS Relief: [14]

and yet uhm bavarian aids relief then began uhm yes to institution uhm stitut institutionalize this support for for other aids relief chapters a little [I: mhm] so uhm a part time position just came into being

Premised on his understanding of AIDS organizing as apolitical and of Bavarian AIDS Relief as irrelevant, the initiative to support smaller chapters was stripped of any potential political significances and legitimacy. He arrived at an essentially Michelsian (1989) argument about organizational self-perpetuation, where employment of paid staff led to an increased administrative work load, tying up resources. This ended up in the organization "devouring itself from the inside"— an imbalance of used resources and effective output. And yet, Alfons could not entirely ignore the legitimacy of the plight of the smaller AIDS Relief chapters and of the initiative to redress it. He conceded:

uhm nevertheless it was about support for smaller AIDS relief chapters [I: mhm] so practically so those that were just in need of support [I: mhm] 'cause there just are different funding models here in bavaria

He even began to link the situation of smaller chapters to Bavarian AIDS politics. However, he only hinted at this link and instead elaborated in the following on Bavarian AIDS politics as described above, that is in terms of mere administrative-technical peculiarities and differences and aimed at the conclusion that the support initiative was futile.

Overall, this translated into a specific emotional stance towards smaller chapters and their needs. Where Peter was moved to action by feeling compassion for them, Alfons, in contrast, was not effectively moved to some sort of action. I want to argue that this was due to his feelings of pity for the smaller AIDS Relief chapters. Arendt characterizes pity as feeling "sorry without being touched in the flesh" keeping a sentimental distance from the suffering (2006: 75) and as "enjoy[able] for its own sake" (2006: 79; cf. also Sennett 2004: 158 on sentimental forms of compassion). While similar to compassion as the emotional apprehension of others' suffering, pity, in other words, is less moving the pitier as it operates at greater distance from suffering. The reason for this is in pity's intentional structure. Its intentional object—its "aboutness"—is not the suffering or the sufferer (as with compassion) but most directly something relatively independent from misery. Most immediately pity rather relates to the pitier her/himself. Feeling pity serves the pitier by, for example, promoting the faithful's standing towards God (e.g., forms of Christian charity, see Sennett 2004: 167–72; Ahmed 2004: 20–3), social prestige and acknowledgement, self-justification, etc. It may therefore appear to be an end in itself.[15] Pity thus involves an element of pride as it aspires to meeting hegemonic evaluative standards and to the social recognition that comes with this. While solidarity engages antagonistically with hegemonic structures and while compassion glosses over how these structures cause suffering, pity is emphatically intertwined with them.

In pity, the distance between pitier and pitied is a difference in power which pity, through its intentional orientation, rather stabilizes than blurs (as solidarity and compassion do). Pity establishes a hierarchical relation between both parties (see also Balaji 2011: 54). The aim of pity is "to announce one's virtue by registering one's feeling about such suffering" and it simultaneously develops an authoritative understanding of the plight at stake in which the pitied have little say (Spelman 1997: 64–5). "While compassion's object is the suffering of another, pity uses the suffering of another—any old other will do—to produce or prolong a feeling in oneself" (Spelman 1997: 65). In other words, feelings of pity inspire help that confirms the valuation and superiority of the pitier and thus cements authority over others in suffering (Spelman 1997: 79; Balaji 2011: 51). This is why pity tends to have an extremely condescending ring.

Pity for smaller AIDS Relief chapters was concisely evident from his framing the smaller organizations repeatedly as "needy" and "in need of support" or as

> beneficiaries of bavarian aids relief so who get some support [I: mm] which was more of a substantial kind a a training sometimes to organize a a seminar perhaps uhm to simply aid them in their work

He invoked an imagery of benevolent charity,[16] which functioned more as a purpose in itself than immediately sharing emotionally the distress of others. Alfons was, in Arendt's terms, not touched by the situation in the flesh and he was hardly moved to action, as Peter was.

Pity was linked to Alfons' proto-professional volunteerism, and its discursive bases, on the one hand through the relegation of politics. To the extent that he understood AIDS work as a technicality the problems of other AIDS organizations became, indeed, only a pity. But pity is linked to the professionalized paradigm of AIDS organizing on the other hand also through another emotion. His pity was inflected by a sense of pride about the work and achievements of his AIDS Relief chapter and this pride allowed him to straightforwardly dismiss smaller organizations condescendingly. He thus outlined the dilemma of Bavarian AIDS Relief:

> on the one hand a big aids relief chapter like [city] which that doesn't need to bother with [contributing to Bavarian AIDS Relief[17]] [I: mhm] yes which does its uhm its exchange of experience with others itself through co-operative work [...] [I: mhm] and the small ones which are actually needy [I: mhm] and uhm actually don't have the strength [I: mhm] to keep an entity like that [I: mhm] alive keep an an entity like that an institution like that alive

At another point he dwelled on the sophistication of bigger chapters before he characterized smaller chapters in condescending contrast:

> and with the little ones there there things crumble apart i think into, that is probably not quite right, but crum just crumble then into so a single case

here, some counseling [I: mhm] there uhm perhaps manage some kind of official things [helping clients deal with bureaucracies] or whatever so thus this [I: mhm] yes but they are not so institutionalized specific departments and the like

With professionalized AIDS organizing as the paradigmatic ideal he framed the motives of organizers in smaller chapters as in principle understandable but essentially ineffective and irrational, even wrong, lacking the sophistication of true AIDS organizing. Note how this contrasts and in fact bluntly dismisses several aspects of the organizing experience of activists like Paul:

yes ('t was a) like like a small uhm aids relief chapter where it where it actually it it the (motor) was one person [I: mhm] who was living with hiv/aids him/herself [I: mhm] where where then also uhm probably where there was then also a huge background of drug use [I: mhm] to the story and [where] one needed that [doing AIDS work] then also because one had a good heart

there are really quite small organized aids relief chapters [I: mhm] yes which part partly so just came into being in some town somehow from a self-help vantage point [I: mhm] and then just somehow the strength of the person who built this up then just got [I: mhm] worn out sometime

In sum then, his wholehearted subscription to the professionalized ideal of AIDS organizing meant that he took pride in the fully professionalized, organizations that he himself was involved in as a volunteer, while smaller chapters came to figure as illegitimate, aberrant and deficient as they were peripheral to his pursuit of what he considered true, that is professionalized, AIDS organizing—something to be pitied. Where Peter had some form of understanding and compassion for the cause of AIDS organizing in smaller settings, Alfons had subscribed to the organizing paradigm that AIDS Relief had evolved into—self-help organization, where volunteers are rather auxiliary to the professional core of AIDS organizing. Volunteers are either employed instrumentally by professionals to carry out AIDS work or they merely constitute the membership organization that has professionals do AIDS work. It is for this reason that he bluntly dismisses self-help in the above excerpts.

Dissolution: a minimal tragedy

With Bavarian AIDS Relief construed as irrelevant and the plight of smaller chapters a pity, the initiative to support smaller chapters came down to a presumption of a political posture and something of hubris. In turn this cast the downfall a tragic inevitability. Alfons directly linked the support initiative to the dissolution of Bavarian AIDS Relief. Given that he barely identified with Bavarian AIDS Relief its demise lacked any gloom but took on a matter-of-fact tone in Alfons' narrative—to him it was the right ending.

so actually, the interest in the life of bavarian aids relief [I: mhm] [was] rather low and towards the end tended towards zero [I: mhm] yes this certainly had reasons so but m uhm even the reasons one has to say it just tended towards zero so in in the end 't was not possible for bavarian aids relief any longer to somehow appoint a board [I: mhm] yes and and with this the affair had finished itself off

Having established the futility of the support initiative in the preceding segments, the irrelevance of Bavarian AIDS Relief became even more evident to him. From this perspective dissolution was indeed without alternative. However, as analysis has shown, this rested on a number of contingencies: Alfons' strong subscription to the professionalized ideal of AIDS organizing informed as it was by dominant AIDS discourse; and the management of how the problems of smaller chapters mattered to him, neutralizing their emotional impact and significance.

This contingency on a specific construction of reality, including distinct omissions, was once more evident from how Alfons ends his narrative. In the above quote he explicitly glossed over reasons for declining interest. But these conditions continued to weigh on him and he evidently felt that his presentation needed further support. Thus he took up the failure of the support initiative once more:

[the] dilemma that people uhm said yes i don't want to know how i uhm uhm how i recruit sponsors for my work [I: mhm] but they just say then said i thought you get me some money [I: mhm] right so now to say it [I: mhm] quite in a nutshell but that's about [I: mhm] about how it went that yes i have underst standing that that also from the small aids relief chapters and there were or are in bavaria [...] there are really quite small organized aids relief chapters [I: mhm] yes which part partly so just came into being in some town somehow from a self-help vantage point [I: mhm] and then just somehow the strength of the person who built this up then just got [I: mhm] worn out sometime and then [I: mhm] there is of course nothing like that you go someplace and still listen attentively [at workshops of Bavarian AIDS Relief] [...] and see to it that you find a sponsor or whatever

It was only at this late point in the interview, by way of an epilogue, that something of the dire situation of smaller AIDS Relief chapters like in D-Town, became almost explicit. Remarkably, there was even a degree of compassion and understanding for their plight. However, Alfons swiftly moved to managing compassion, and its impending intrusion of politics: the excerpt is followed by Alfons' characterization, already described above, of the larger chapters' sophistication and the crumbling activities of their smaller counterparts.

In sum, Alfons can equally be analyzed as a volunteer, although slightly different emotions were central to his narrative. Like Sandra, Claudia and Peter he left the power processes affecting AIDS organizations in Bavaria largely unchallenged. In fact, he is even less perceptive of them. Where Peter elaborated at some length on Bavarian AIDS policies and how they created adverse conditions for smaller chapters, this issue was only vaguely hinted at in Alfons' narrative and remained latent for the most part (yet was not entirely absent either). Pity and its greater distance towards suffering explains this politically more limited outlook and his relatively greater political passivity. It was embedded into a heightened subscription to the professionalized paradigm of AIDS organizing. This additionally illustrates the interlinking of volunteering and professionalism.

Conclusion

Bavarian AIDS Relief operated within a political frame that was in some ways not conducive to local AIDS organizing (whereas the regional state government had always been supportive of Bavarian AIDS Relief, as Peter felt). Volunteerism, much like in D-Town, however, prevented organizers such as Peter and Alfons from directly challenging this. For Peter, this was a matter of compassion for local chapters. This meant that he was aware of their plight but it also led him to make sense of it in a way that made no links to larger political power processes but instead attributed blame to local volunteer organizers. In Alfons' case, a different emotion was fundamental—pity—which removed political conditions even farther out of sight. In fact it largely delegitimized the cause of smaller chapters for him. Like in D-Town, volunteerism thus functioned as a hegemonic device on an organizational level as it produced silences that helped conserve a certain status quo (Clair 1998).

Both Peter and Alfons added additional illustration of how volunteerism is constituted in relation to professionalism and is thus ultimately embedded into cultural contexts of dominant AIDS discourse. However, they also gradually differed in this respect as Alfons subscribed much more to the professionalized ideal of AIDS organizing with volunteers having an even more peripheral and merely auxiliary role. This did not only play out in the difference of compassion vs. pity as emotional bases of their engagement with Bavarian AIDS Relief. It also meant that Peter felt sincerely committed to the organization trying till the very end to make it work out. In contrast, Alfons, although an organizer of Bavarian AIDS Relief, denied its necessity and seemed barely engaged with it. His heightened emphasis on professionalism in AIDS work left little space for volunteers like him to assume an active role, not even that, as in Peter's case, of organizing the channeling of expertise. In fact he talked about his present volunteering as a representative of his own AIDS Relief chapter on a federal level and described how he cannot really see the purpose of that given that much of the work of his chapter operates on a professional level.

In both cases, a key background condition was the cleavage between countryside or small towns and the urban centers. Both Peter and Alfons came from large cities and in their narratives there was a more or less explicit sense of superiority about the degree of sophistication that AIDS organizing had achieved there. The center–periphery cleavage and the ideal of professionalized AIDS work, that is to say, were intertwined. This contrasted in interesting ways with Paul in D-Town whose activism, through feelings of solidarity, aimed at bridging this cleavage, moving to D-Town, as he did, from the next bigger city. Living with HIV himself and in fact experiencing discrimination and ostracism in D-Town personally were one basis for this. Crucially, neither Alfons nor Peter mentioned if they were living with HIV. If they were, it was not explicitly relevant for their experience at Bavarian AIDS Relief.

Notes

1 Further details must be omitted here in order to secure a sufficient degree of anonymity.
2 Pride in contrast is the emotional apprehension of valuation.
3 One of the few straightforward successes he recalled was Bavarian AIDS Relief's role in warding off renewed political debate about introducing compulsory registration of people with HIV/AIDS, which he evaluated in relatively marked terms: "that was impeccable press work." Peter's conclusion about the dissolution negatively later buttressed this point, as Bavarian AIDS Relief's demise turned self-confidence into shame: "it was also an ignominy [blöße] for bavaria for uhm in with german aids relief [...] it was but a confirmation that we did not want to have <<short laughter>> [I: mhm] but there was no way around it." As he felt, this reverberated with the general image of Bavaria as politically backwards.
4 For instance, this is evident from Peter's sense of boredom—the emotional apprehension of social meaninglessness (Barbalet 1999)—which he felt when participation of local chapters in the activities of Bavarian AIDS Relief declined.
5 Peter dispelled any potentially disquieting qualities of this instance by providing details that made both the board candidate's as well as her employer's stances plausible: he pointed out that the candidate was employed with a public health department and her boss feared a conflict of interest had she assumed a role on Bavarian AIDS Relief's board.
6 Apart from the focus on volunteers/activists in the smaller chapters, there are also instances of blaming the larger member organizations for not giving sufficient support to Bavarian AIDS Relief. But this plays a much more limited role in the narrative. At one point he talked about how the smaller chapters failed to make use of support offers while at the same time larger organizations refused to rely on Bavarian AIDS Relief in any respect, such as lobbying. Together this refuted the purpose of the umbrella organization. The principle attribution of blame to the bigger chapters, however, is immediately mitigated in the narrative by elaborating certain details—e.g., the superior networks into political institutions of some bigger chapters—to make the attitude of the larger members plausible.
7 Peter speculated that more efficient work flows in the local organizations would have given them the time to make use of support programs. Blame was also about a lack of gratitude for the help offered as expressed through neglecting the offer. Gratitude can be said to be the feeling rule for receivers of compassion. He recounted how Bavarian AIDS Relief helped one chapter counter criticism for how it used its resources. However, as he added, the same organization was particularly outspoken about not seeing an adequate return from Bavarian AIDS Relief for the membership fees.
8 In addition, some of the stigmatizing local climate came into some degree of relief when Peter gave the example of Bavarian AIDS Relief pushing for an accepting approach to drug politics, while smaller organizations feared any public identifications with illicit drug use might compromise their local standing and thus impact their

ability to raise funds. However, this mattered to Peter as indicating the latter's inability to live up to the ideal of sophisticated AIDS politics and resulted, in his experience, in yet another instance of failing to support Bavarian AIDS Relief.
9 The possibility of solidarity immanent in his narrative came into some limited relief as he briefly hinted at the role of lacking official recognition in the difficult development of AIDS Relief organizations. Despite that, however, the segment overall failed to constitute a story of unjust state action. The depiction of state policies rather form the background only for what he constructed as a conflict in individual terms.
10 In Peter's description these involved about four–five gatherings per year with about 20–25 participants.
11 On the emotional nature of superiority, see Neckel (1991, 1996).
12 A social work metonymy referring to an institution that provides personal social services.
13 As the quote indicates, for Alfons such staff reductions were quite readily tantamount to an existential matter for the organization in question. This reduction of AIDS organizing to its core of paid professionals was itself indicative of the taken-for-granted validity for Alfons of the paradigm of AIDS service organizing.
14 Note the opener ("and yet" ["nur hat dann"]) and the negative framing as institutionalization.
15 The difference to compassion may still be one of emphasis. As we have seen, Sandra and Claudia derived a sense of pride from living up to the socially sanctioned ideal of volunteerism—an end only indirectly related to the suffering they felt compassionate about. At the same time, this pursuit of pride was arguably not a constitutive element of their feelings of compassion. They did not feel compassion because they wanted pride, but rather were proud because they felt compassion and acted on it.
16 Alfons frequently used variants of the somewhat antiquated word "bedürftig" ["needy"], which carries distinct connotations of traditional/Christian charity and benevolence. Sennett (2004: 167–72), for instance, discusses the Christian tradition of *caritas* as oriented not so much to redressing suffering but as a purpose in itself and in relation to God. Ahmed (2004: 20–3) provides a non-Christian interpretation of this aspect of charity.
17 His German wording sounds particularly condescending: "so ne große aids hilfe wie [city] die das nicht nötig hat"

References

Ahmed, Sara. 2004. *The Cultural Politics of Emotion*. New York: Routledge.
Arendt, Hannah. 2006. *On Revolution*. New York: Penguin Books.
Balaji, Murali. 2011. "Racializing Pity: The Haiti Earthquake and the Plight of 'Others'." *Critical Studies in Media Communication* 28(1): 50–67.
Barbalet, Jack M. 1998. *Emotion, Social Theory, and Social Structure: A Macrosociological Approach*. Cambridge, New York, Melbourne, Madrid, Cape Town, Singapore, São Paulo: Cambridge University Press.
Barbalet, Jack M. 1999. "Boredom and Social Meaning." *The British Journal of Sociology* 50(4): 631–46.
Clair, Robin Patric. 1998. *Organizing Silence: A World of Possibilities*. Albany: State University of New York Press.
Michels, Robert. 1989. *Zur Soziologie des Parteienwesens in der modernen Demokratie. Untersuchungen über die oligarchischen Tendenzen des Gruppenlebens*. Stuttgart: Kröner.
Neckel, Sieghard. 1991. *Status und Scham. Zur symbolischen Reproduktion sozialer Ungleichheit*. Frankfurt am Main, New York: Campus Verlag.

Neckel, Sieghard. 1996. "Inferiority: From Collective Status to Deficient Individuality." *Sociological Review* 44(1): 17–34.

Schütze, Fritz. 1976. "Zur Hervorlockung und Analyse thematisch relevanter Geschichten im Rahmen soziologischer Feldforschung—dargestellt an einem Projekt zur Erforschung von kommunalen Machtstrukturen." Pp. 159–260 in *Kommunikative Sozialforschung*, vol. 159, edited by Arbeitsgruppe Bielefelder Soziologen. München: Fink.

Schütze, Fritz. 1987. *Das narrative Interview in Interaktionsfeldstudien I*. Hagen: Fernuniversität.

Sennett, Richard. 2004. *Respekt im Zeitalter der Ungleichheit*. Berlin: Berlin Verlag.

Spelman, Elizabeth V. 1997. *Fruits of Sorrow: Framing Our Attention to Suffering*. Boston: Beacon Press.

Chapter 8

Cuddly easterners, professionalism and the west

Based in eastern Germany, Positive Relief[1] was the post-1989 continuation of a more or less informal HIV/AIDS self-help group. It was part of official GDR AIDS prevention structures. The East German state response to HIV/AIDS[2] rested strongly on the public sector and the medical system, specifically testing for HIV antibodies and, institutionally, a web of so-called consultation centers in larger cities. Positive Relief's informal predecessor was annexed to one of those centers. Although led by what would nowadays be called a social worker the group had a rather informal internal structure and relied on self-help as one of its original members described.

This group survived the changes of *Wende*[3] and reunification and turned itself into a formal association. As such it came to operate within a mixed field of eastern and western AIDS organizations and catered to eastern German gay men with HIV or AIDS. Formalization also meant professionalization, which effectively bifurcated the internal structure into a team of employed AIDS workers and a membership association as its carrier and volunteer/activist base. This did not come without internal frictions. Professionalization also meant reliance on public subsidies. In the mid-1990s the Regional Association of AIDS Organizations (hereafter "the Association") was commissioned by the regional state to distribute the gross amount of public funding for the region's AIDS organizations among its member organizations. With this, the state essentially short-circuited political conflict. When HIV was no longer seen as potentially spreading on a large scale outside minorities, the regional state government decided to gradually decrease each year the funding for AIDS organizations over the course of several years. Having the Association administer the gross amount of public funding meant to leave the contentious decisions of allocating cutbacks among its members to the Association itself.

The regional field of AIDS organizations was marked by some disparities. It included some large, western organizations already in operation for many years. Others, like eastern German Positive Relief, were not only smaller and newcomers to the field (and western politics in general). What is more, Positive Relief represented a group that was marginalized not only for living with HIV/AIDS and being gay but also as eastern Germans.

Positive Relief disbanded in the late 1990s when cutbacks reached a degree which, as several interviewees phrased it, would have severely circumscribed the essence of Positive Relief. Technically, the cutbacks in question would have left the organization as such intact, but much reduced in scope. This indicates that cutbacks alone are insufficient to explain the group's dissolution. In fact, Positive Relief actually did not quite disband. One of its professional AIDS workers decided to continue its work with a new host organization as a carrier for the project. This meant that Positive Relief became a purely professional project, losing its membership-based organizational form. The following analysis looks at the stories of three Positive Relief actors to show how budgetary cutbacks reverberated in diverse ways through their respective organizational experience, leading to a range of different individual outcomes—from retreat to continuation. I will show that the distinction of modes of civic action via their emotional bases provides the analytical lens through which these differences can be made explicable. An important emotional dimension of this was the east-west divide which produced a dynamic of shameful inferiority and the counterbalancing pursuit of pride. I will focus here on three central organizers, although the story of Positive Relief is more complex than I can describe in the limited space of this chapter. They highlight the tension between activism and professionalism and allow me to introduce and conceptualize the latter as a kind of civic action.

Professionalization as a tragedy of activism: Adam

Adam was perhaps the most pivotal actor in Positive Relief as its co-founder after 1989, its executive director and lead social worker, and as advocating the organization's dissolution. Overall, he straddled an activist orientation and professionalism. As I will show here, resolving the ambiguities of this hybrid, embedded as it was in an emotional climate of eastern inferiority/western superiority, the political dynamics of an organizational field and shifting AIDS discourses, was central to his experience of Positive Relief's demise.

Community and its preservation in changing times

Two points of departure mark Adam's entry into civic organizing as an activist, providing key motives for his engagement. One was a keen valuation of grassroots community building. The pre-1989 group was a key point of reference for his activism. What mattered most about it to him was the group's communal, informal-personal character: he cast it as a self-help group, based in a community of people with HIV/AIDS,[4] emphasizing an emotional climate of intimacy, "friendship," "sympathy," and interpersonal care. This, however, was endangered as the institutional changes of re-unification meant that the group's hosting institution was

> crushed after the fall of the wall [...] like so much else uhm where people acted according to the slogan, do we have this in the west, ah nope, well, then we can just do away with it

This left group members without a "home" ("Heimat"). This did not only threaten the group's existence, but also entailed the experience of shameful inferiority as easterners: for Adam it was an experience of utter disregard, denied acknowledgement ("just do away with it") and powerlessness ("crushing"). Experiences of devaluation and disrespect are in turn at the heart of shame (Simmel 1992), especially when it combines with powerlessness to constitute feelings of inferiority (Neckel 1991). This—"like so much else"—evolved in the emotional climate (Barbalet 1998) of re-unification, which established the west as the norm to which the east by and large was to adapt ("do we have this in the west"). Crucially, however, shame translated into a sense of anger as he constructs an image of unjustice, brutality and blatant neglect (on the transformation of shame see, for example, Katz 1999: 163; Munt 2008: 2; Scheff 1988). This proved to be pivotal for his engagement with Positive Relief. Assuming an angry stance, countering western domination, Adam became the group's spokesperson and the main organizer of its transformation into Positive Relief as a formal organization. His antagonistic orientation persisted as a baseline of his unfolding activism, but would later undergo crucial transformations.

Life in the face of death

A second motivating point of departure became evident as he connected with the more radical parts of the western gay and AIDS subculture/movement. He felt energized by the issues intersecting there—the political struggle about AIDS policies and the moving issues converging in AIDS ("like sexuality like death like like ostracism like subversion"). He met with crazy ("schräg"), "maladjusted," "wild," "combative," and "solidaristic" activists who took "great strides forward" and pushed to make AIDS Relief a significant force in society, part of "a breathtaking development." In short, he felt the appeal of what he termed the "power of the movement"—the excitement, the thrill, the titillation, the eroticism (cf. Gould 2009: 192–6). He described this with various metaphors of life, invoking an imagery of energy, power, pressure, heat and unchecked dynamism, freedom and movement, indicating a divestment from stifling contexts of stigmatizing AIDS discourse and politics and homophobia. Crucially, this liberated aspect of "life" interlinked with his anti-institutional, communal orientation.

"Life" was central to Adam's activism and to him a foundational principle of Positive Relief. He recounted how the first public presentation of Positive Relief by way of a party at a local gay bar coincided with the news that a pivotal Positive Relief activist had just died. Yet drag performers managed to turn grief into a celebration. Adam framed the entire episode in terms of life: a bar brimming with hundreds of people (a hyperbole); only a shoehorn could have squeezed in more people; the exhilarating weirdness of drag queens; a place bursting with "assailing" "insane power" and with "energy and vitality and fag power and AIDS work." As a result people had the feeling that there is intensity in pleasure and in celebration or like uhm a feeling of closeness to life

an unbelievably intense feeling of life and also a form of happiness that we shared together, it is not always so easy to describe, [...] why did you dance on the graves, why was there so much fun and joy, too, but this was exactly it, it had this intensity, this feeling of being so close to life to the desires to the concerns [that make up] life [...] we lived unbelievably intense

How can we disentangle the complex and opaque emotional dimension of Adam's life metaphors? What Adam evocatively conveys is the emotion of *joie de vivre*. It is opposed to suffering (Elster 1996: 1396) but also depression—the emotion of emotionlessness (Barbalet 1998: 24) which is in turn related to status deficits or the denial of acknowledgment (Kemper 1978: 35–6). Pertinently, his life metaphors were intertwined with narrating the successful establishment of Positive Relief. His sense of *joie de vivre* thus related to overcoming the shame-inducing complex of westernization, marginalization and institutional domination. In another way it contrasted with a sense of hopelessness in facing illness and dying ("dancing on the graves"). In these ways, it indicated an emotional liberation (Flam 1993, 2005) from conditions that denied or limited his agency. It is the joy derived from asserting one's self, that is self's capacity for agency. "Joy [...] can be liberated by slipping out from underneath shame" (Munt 2008: 4). And yet, as the following sections will show, Adam's anarchic, joyous activism could never quite bypass the specter of shame, as the pursuit of pride became a dominant motive for him.

In the west: ambivalences of building an eastern German AIDS relief chapter

A key objective for Adam was to reconstitute the pre-1989 group as a formal, eastern German AIDS Relief organization—the dominant institutionalized form of AIDS organizing in western Germany at the time (see Chapter 3). Paradoxically, this involved both gradually abandoning his joyful sense of anarchy and holding onto it as he began embracing the legitimized organizational paradigm and its evaluative matrix of the field of AIDS work. Establishing Positive Relief was very much a matter of proving themselves to, and gaining acceptance and recognition by, the west. Essentially, this aimed at achieving pride as a substitute for shameful inferiority:

only at rare times were we [organizers at positive relief] an autodidactic bunch of easterners ["*Osthäufchen*"] we were very quickly relatively fit in all those affairs [such as of dealing with state funding agencies]

He boasted about Positive Relief as something of a star in the field of AIDS work at the time. "Life" and communal orientation now turned into a competitive advantage and distinguishing trait rather than an end in itself as he expressed numerous times in the interview:

> our joint was buzzing [I: mhm] and we had uhm really just a lot of ideas for uhm (-) cultural events for panel discussions so that was really such a brimming LIFE and for some TIME we felt, (--) as i then realized later even the estABLISHED WEST uh uhm institutions, so like the stirrer[5] who [I: mhm] just somehow [brings in] a little fresh LIFE and they [the western organizations] were the established and old ones.

Notions of Positive Relief's uniqueness allowed for feelings of pride and even superiority. Where the west initially signified a source of shame about eastern inferiority, Adam endeavored to counter this with a sense of Positive Relief's uniqueness, turning shame into pride. Subtly, however, this meant that his emotional orientation shifted away from the community as an end in itself towards the western-dominated organizational field as an arbiter of recognition.

Ironies of community organizing: professionalization

This turn towards pride through recognition in the western-dominated field led to the professionalization of Positive Relief as a way of reconstructing it as a legitimate organization. Yet this ascent to pride was not straightforwardly possible for the communal character of Positive Relief effectively changed in the process:

> this process was rather painful for some who then just had to miss very much this this this this cuddle positive relief this this uhm couch circle f uhm feeling as we just wanted to open ourselves to a larger number of people [I: mhm] and be there for them and this was linked to uhm processes of professionalization uhm in the course of which it was NOT successful to always include EVERYBODY who wanted to also keep this this card game circle feeling and that that that uhm uhm everybody knows everybody [I: mhm] we are something like a group of four five friends and we do something for us; [I: mhm] there were unbelievable attacks [...] by people with hiv/aids who uhm (1.0) then had somehow like like like lost that CUDDLE island

Professionalization meant that his work was increasingly about doing something for rather than with people. Indicatively Adam's use of the first person plural increasingly referred to the active organizers—i.e., the professional team—rather than the organization as a community. Also note the feelings of contempt for his critics in the above excerpt—derogatory terms such as couch circle—indicating a sense of primacy and superiority of professionalism over grassroots organizing. And yet, there remained a sense of lingering guilt as he was at pains to detail how they tried to retain a sense of community, though now professionally organized. As community figured instrumentally as part of Positive Relief's legitimation, there was a decoupling in neo-institutionalist terms. The communal orientation became a competitive advantage in Adam's quest to reverse feelings of eastern inferiority and take pride in Positive Relief vis-à-vis western counterparts—a kind of pride that usurped and instrumentalized the initial climate of life. Throughout the interview he kept casting Positive Relief in terms of a community-based organization. At the same time this also implicitly hinted at practice falling short of this ideal:

> so this CORE idea [I: mhm] soliDARity and and and and EMpathy and and mutual HELP and so that these things indeed that is (--) uhm (--) for a LONG time now made up (4.0) the the corporate identity [sic!];

> at at only very RARE times (-) uhm (-) somehow had it that smack of of of aids relief wel WELfare work [I: mhm] like it had to be so inEVItably in those BIG INstitutions;

Adam is at pains to show how the retention of community succeeded. Yet he struggles to make his point and gloss over its ambiguities: solidarity, empathy and helping were only central for some time, however long; the smack of institutionalized care was only absent most of the time; community became "a corporate identity." Adam tried to straddle his intimate and joyous grassroots beginnings and his proud professionalism.

The woes of normalization[6]

Paralleling professionalization, Positive Relief's activities declined and its clientele changed. "All those cultured creative middle-class gays" increasingly left and with them Adam's sense of life as he found Positive Relief turn into a "social service center." Theoretically, this decline can be easily linked, among other things, to professionalization and its disempowering effects (see Chapter 2 and Michels 1989; Zald and Ash 1966) and indeed the process caused significant frictions as we have seen. How did Adam make sense of this decline? How did it resonate with his dual communal and western-professional orientation?

Indicatively, it was precisely when he narrated his fragile straddling of community and professionalism that Adam abruptly changed the topic and in fact stopped narrating to continue in a argumentative-theoretical mode (see Chapter 5). This is where he introduced and elaborated on the normalization of AIDS following the advances of highly active anti-retroviral therapies in 1996. Perceptively, he argued how this shifted the power of dealing with HIV and AIDS from AIDS workers towards the hitherto more or less impotent medical professions. In fact he resented this as an injustice and power assertion:

> that is since THAT moment when those (-) uh combiNATION therapies were preSENted and (-) uhm (---) the white coats came back onto onto onto the podium and now now we will tell you again what to do;

He reflected here the initial lack of treatment options and the subsequently increased medicalization of HIV/AIDS when effective therapies later became available in terms of professional power shifts between social workers and physicians. Where the former had been central actors of AIDS work, they became increasingly irrelevant and replaced by doctors as the centrally pertinent profession. Adam described this essentially as an injustice: he depicted the medical system as being at first impotent about AIDS, and ignorant and negligent of the messy human issues of HIV/AIDS, leaving these issues to others, whom they now pushed aside again. This sense of injustice was in fact conveyed expressively, for instance, when he talked contemptuously of "white coats" telling people in an authoritarian way what to do.

Perceptive and interesting though Adam's theory is, its insertion into the narrative by way of a thematic leap and a switch from narrative to argumentation indicates a different significance for Adam. He used it to explain the loss of a sense of life in Positive Relief, which is rather attributable to professionalization, too. Where he had felt lingering guilt about this, and was indeed attacked for it by others at Positive Relief, the focus on medicalization rendered him a tragic victim of higher and, as he put it, unjust powers.[7] Resentment about medicalization served to manage his feelings of guilt. This shielded his efforts at combining community organizing and professionalization, when both were in conflict at Positive Relief.

Medicalization, community dynamics and dissolution

Adam's understanding of the medicalization of AIDS work and its effect on Positive Relief are pivotal as this sets the stage for his experience of the dissolution. The receding vibrancy of Positive Relief came down to a loss of meaning for Adam, that is to a loss of emotional intensity, or rather of *joie de vivre*—as we have seen, a central motive of his engagement:

> so then also (-) uhm for US the engine was kind of BROken at some point [...] that is actually [a] danse MACAbre[[8]] [...] it it it was uhm not this this this uh: : brimming life anymore

> of course that had ALSO quite a lot to do with us at positive relief saying at some point well first off nobody quite wants us here [...] and we did have also the clear feeling (2.5) uhm (1.0) that an agency of THIS size (1.0) would probably probably NOT be necessary in the long run

As long as Positive Relief flourished and grew this afforded him a sense of self-confident *joie de vivre* that was soon usurped by feelings of pride. With the decline of community participation these emotional foundations of his engagement dissolved. The professional orientation of doing something for others meant that he came to find the organization, as much as it had grown, and himself as its personification, obsolete: nobody quite wanted them anymore as it were. Where the internal climate of *joie de vivre* was initially an end in itself, it subsequently formed the means to and object of Adam's professionalized engagement, which in turn lost its central point of reference when community members went away. This constituted a reversion of his sense of *joie de vivre* into a feeling of depression, the emotion of emotionlessness (Barbalet 1998: 24). The loss of relevancy of the self—of purpose and meaning—expressed in the above excerpt underlines this (cf. Barbalet 1999: 635). Crucially, however, this was contingent on how the pursuit of pride usurped a communal orientation and how feelings of resentment about the medicalization of AIDS work helped to manage feelings of guilt.

Funding conflicts

Positive Relief disbanded in the late 1990s after a series of funding cutbacks administered by the Regional Association of AIDS Organizations (hereafter "the Association"). As the key external representative, Adam was the most involved actor at Positive Relief to participate in the negotiations about cutbacks within the Association. Adam talked only hesitantly about this and his emotional take on it was highly ambivalent. Identifying the cutbacks as the primary cause of dissolution he is at great pains to dispel any concrete blame for them. He constructs cutbacks in terms of fate as unavoidable given the necessity to allocate shrinking public funding. Actors in western AIDS organizations had no bad intentions but were merely a small part of large immutable processes:

> you could have put there the meekest lambs that were around in the west in social work at the time (-) would have come out the same [I: mhm] […] those are power structures that are outside of (-) uhm (-) uh human character wise uh project uh uh uhm political uh uhm: : : considerations; these are these are matters which (-) uh are to be understood in a much (-) bigger (-) social CONtext; THAT's HOW IT WAS [I: mhm] the uh uh persil-starched[9] west-shirt was shoved onto the east [I: mhm] and [the east] had to arrange itself with the things which uh uh came as new conditions onto (the people) for better or worse [I: mhm] there were hardly any ch: ances (--) uh to contribute uh GROWN uh uh structures, considerations: : uh ways of thinking: : uh uh uh principles (---) uh to: : this work

Blaming the state for outsourcing cutbacks ("a clever move to keep the rabble at distance") the consequences among AIDS organizations were merely "logical":

> the gates [were] of course uh uh pushed open to (-) so that now (-) uh also (-) the uh (--) more professional fundraising and and and and uh uh use of POWER (-) uh by the by the [western] aids projects uh could become more effective; […] LOgically this had to be to the disadvantage of the somewhat weaker ones (-) in the [association] these were [I: mhm] without doubt the

eastern projects; and the o and the OTHer smaller ones; [...] relative to the somewhat bigger [i.e., western] tankers

And yet, at the same time, there is a latent sense of anger in his narrative as well, for instance, when he introduced the aspect of power and coercion—the "persil-starched west-shirt" forced onto easterners—with the insistent exclamation "that's how it was." The construction of larger organizations turning against the smaller, weaker ones conveyed a sense of injustice. But this anger remained latent in the narrative, expressed only via distanced, ironic and black humor-style insertions. More overtly, he instead expressed a sense of sadness and fatalist resignation: he felt increasingly worn down ["abgegessen"— "gnawed off"] and unable to muster the strength to "somehow counter the very very uhm multiple attacks on the project's existence." In fact, as he described, in a way he eventually threw his hands up in the air and accepted, without any outward indication of resistance, what funding changes were suggested to Positive Relief.

Much like at the beginning, he felt that the west had destroyed eastern organizing, but now he ended up in resignation rather than trying to angrily reassert Positive Relief. How can we understand this sharp contrast? What accounts for this laborious management of anger?

Shame

I want to argue that shame about eastern inferiority was the pivotal emotion underlying how Adam constructed cutbacks and their relation to the dissolution of Positive Relief. Emotionally, Adam's organizing was an effort at countering such shame by striving for pride, its dialectical counterpart (e.g., Scheff 1988; Flam 2010; Gould 2001, 2009). Resorting to a mix of professionalization and a claim to community organizing, he strove for Positive Relief to be included into the west-dominated field of AIDS organizations. The validation and recognition that such inclusion entailed was the evaluative basis of his pride. Subtly, however, the very organizational community by whose evaluative standards he had tried to prove the validity of Positive Relief now gradually withdrew funding, which had symbolized membership in and validation by the organizational field.

Tellingly, Adam's narration of cutbacks and dissolution was interspersed with references to the shame of eastern inferiority. For instance, it is in this context that he recalled how quickly and successfully he adopted western mannerisms and how proud he felt when people told him he did not appear to be an easterner; how quickly he learned to speak "west German"; that he "wanted to be like them"; and so on. This indicates how the funding conflict was significant precisely in terms of his ambition to overcome eastern inferiority. This is also evident from how he proposed the decision to disband to his colleagues, highlighting a neglect of Positive Relief's significance:

162 Positive Relief

> [and the other colleagues] ah are you crazy, i say yes, i say well i (-) i i if they [western organizations represented by the association] don't see by themselves how important [we are] and what we do here

In fact, the theme of shameful inferiority recurred several times. Continuing the project under a different host organization "wouldn't have been bea: : rable" given the claim to being a community organization. He recounts how western organizers directly expressed their superiority over "that bit" of eastern AIDS work:

> and of course there were uhm enough people also from western projects and such, said well that bit that they do in the east there, we can easily cover that too

The Association's declared intention was to retain Positive Relief, but on a much smaller scale—to Adam an "undignified ending" and a "betrayal of their authenticity" and communal roots. But the overt goodwill of the Association made the shame expressed in this particularly insidious as a kind of double bind:

> so so there was there was [...] nobody who seriously questioned the quality of our work [I: mhm] or the fact that we uh during our entire existence uh uh uhm uhm always also also provided ideas and impulses for the entire aids work [in the regional field] [...] i don't believe it was calculation [I: mhm] calculation was uhm all must give up something [...] and uhm let's just create a small small aids project and [adam] can keep meddling somehow a little with his three folks and uhm play around and he will agree to continue [...] and we are [I: mhm] not the evil ones [...] it WAS clear [...] that the association smashed [positive relief] [I: mhm] so they were surprised also by it [I: mhm] so they had assumed somehow that we rather <<naive-benign tone>well it may be bad but then we just continue with a half-time position and so and [I: mhm] and shall we rent a small broom cupboard somewhere where we continue for a year then we just do that>

Adam combines here an exculpating take on the cutbacks that seemed to involve a neutral calculation, with a sense of shame about their practical consequences and implicitly resurfacing anger about this. At stake for Adam was the validation of Positive Relief's work, which was both acknowledged in principle while subverted in practice. In this constellation, the dissolution became a means to a proud reassertion. Feelings of anger were held in check by the alleged neutrality of cutbacks and a sense of shame.

Adam's sense of ashamed resignation and subdued anger was additionally compounded by the fact that the community of Positive Relief had already declined. This was something he constructed in fateful terms in connection with the normalization of AIDS. Community decline deprived him not only of a sense of *joie de vivre* as a source of energy to help him fight cutbacks. It also meant that he lost a source of legitimation to counter any lingering sense of eastern inferiority. It is no coincidence that Adam switched in a second interview from the funding conflict at the beginning to detailing Positive Relief's successes in sustaining its community character. This extended for more than half of this second, three-hour interview.

The feeling of alienation and activism

In sum, the funding conflict angered Adam, but this anger remained latent as it was stifled by the reversion to feelings of shameful inferiority. As he tried to refute the inferiority of eastern Positive Relief and prove its validity as a legitimate AIDS organization to the regional field of AIDS work he remained unconditionally subscribed to the evaluative matrix valid there. In his pursuit of pride, he was ultimately dependent on the other organizations granting recognition and validation of Positive Relief. The initial experience of shame when the pre-1989 group was "crushed" therefore left him in a "wounded attachment" (Brown 1993) to the west: in his effort to overcome the wound of shameful inferiority he remained attached to the wounding west in his quest to disprove inferiority to and receive recognition from the west. Even though he seemed to succeed in this for a while, he could be quickly recommitted to shame. When validation was withdrawn in the course of funding conflicts his engagement turned out to be a failure to him by the very evaluative standards that he himself harbored. Rather than resulting in straightforward anger, therefore, his organizational experience resulted in the feeling of frustrated resignation and alienation.

> i had increasingly the feeling there is some circus happening and but i am but uh only i was only like like off off stage so i am somehow i sit there but I was somehow not anymore couldn't present myself there anymore [I: mhm] didn't want that anymore uh it somehow was impossible [I: mhm] difficult to describe it was like a perspex pane that came down and they talked about something [I: mhm] and i found the words familiar but i couldn't participate anymore

Adam set out as an activist, emotionally liberating himself from stifling contexts of "crushing" westernization and dominant AIDS discourse and politics. However, his efforts to counter eastern inferiority with a claim to pride led him to professionalize Positive Relief, effectively turning community organizing into a means rather than an end. The discourse of the normalization of AIDS allowed him to neutralize the significance of the resulting communal decline. But when funding conflicts turned his attachment to the west against him, he was left defenseless to the shaming it involved.

164 Positive Relief

Professionalism: Erwin

As Adam struggled to retain an activist stance while professionalizing the organization, one of his colleagues was firmly professionalist. This is Erwin, the only[10] employed AIDS worker at Positive Relief who dissented from the decision to disband and continued its services, joining another host organization. As closer analysis reveals, professionalism is central to understanding his deviating decision. Dissecting the contingent premises of this decision and how it emerged from his sensemaking will allow me to carve out some characteristics of professionalism precisely as a kind of civic action and of the kind of sensemaking this may engender.[11]

"My first job as a social worker": professionalism

Erwin's professionalism was evident in a variety of ways. The overall point of his story was about him becoming a social worker. Large parts of the narrative were structured like a resume/CV, as a succession of occupational positions; detailing job descriptions at some length; arguing he was suitable for the position at Positive Relief because he had matching qualifications acquired at university, etc. His concluding exclamation about starting out at Positive Relief was equally indicative:

> that was <<ral> my FIRST position as a SOCIALworker> as social pedagogue? and uhm it was all quite new and exciting for me?

By contrast, Positive Relief's pre-1989 and eastern German roots figured only in practical terms—a specific context of and object for his professional practice— as the mere presence of "clients with a special, eastern socialization[!] with very special needs and uhm (-) wishes." From this perspective his work at Positive Relief signified to him as a period of acquiring new professional skills (legal knowledge, counseling techniques, etc.). But perhaps more importantly, professionalism was manifest in Erwin's positioning himself in his narrative as endowed with professional competences and expertise. This has several aspects.

The professional approach

One aspect of this was the unfolding of his professional identity in contrast to what he dubbed the "cuddle approach" dominant at Positive Relief:

> i'm exaggerating now, the pros in the WEST they do a WONDERUL JOB uhm but WE [at positive relief] we CUDle here a little with the CLIents and help them a bit THIS way.

He rejected this approach as unprofessional because it would colonize clients rather than giving them the advice they need—the normative ideal of respecting clients' autonomy, a central trait of professionalism in social work (Steinbacher 2004: 102–3).

> well (-) i believe it was (-) uh uh it was over a little bit with CUDdling (-) when I uh joined in? (--) because it is not my STYLE (--) uhm (1.5) well i am more someone who: (-) tries to LOOK precisely what is needed by WHOM (-) in which situation and i had (-) especially in the FIRST years at [positive relief] ninety-five the imPRESSion (-) that that inteRESted people [i.e., incoming clients] (--) where IMMEDIATELY TURNED! into CLIENTS and iDEALly then also right away into volunTEERS! too uh (--) and the they should also even become MEMbers [of positive relief] that is ALL! at ONCE!;

Erwin implied here an essentially professional model, where professional services are carried out by virtue of superior, exclusive expertise on the basis of professional autonomy (Freidson 1994: 157–63, 174; Macdonald 1995: 30; e.g., Nadai et al. 2005: 19). Much in line with this he positioned himself as a vicarious expert interpreter of clients' needs—what Parsons (1975, 1991) dubbed the fiduciary responsibility of professionals. The "cuddle" metaphor highlighted what he felt was a contrast between his expert rationality[12] (his quest for precision; his penchant for orderly and carefully crafted role structures) and the "cuddly" emotionality dominant at Positive Relief.

Professionalism vs. volunteerism/activism

Erwin's irritation about the messy role structure had another cause. Professionalism in nonprofit organizations and social work constitutes itself in an (often hierarchical) social role-relation to "lay" actors, i.e., volunteers and activists (see Musick and Wilson 2008: 422–3; Nadai et al. 2005; Nelsen and Barley 1997; Steinbacher 2004). I have discussed this already in the preceding two chapters from the perspective of volunteerism. In line with this, Erwin recurrently aimed at carving out his superiority to volunteers/activists. At the outset, for instance, he found himself ordering the chaos they had caused:

> my predecessor [on his position at positive relief] <<ral>had already> left for uhm a couple of months? [...] and in the MEANtime a [volunteer] board member had done that work temporarily [I: mhm] was actually overSTRAINED with it so that when i arrived [...] at [positive relief] i first had to uhm order the CHAos; it was pretty chaotic

The chaos metaphor underlines here the rationality of his own (ordering) work by virtue of his superior expertise in contrast to (overstrained) volunteers.[13] At the same time, this constructs superiority over lay members and thus implicitly established for him a feeling of pride in being professional—an emotion that was a driving motive of his civic work. But this pride had another, perhaps more important source.

Pride and the professional community

Professionalism has often been characterized, among other things, as the autonomous self-regulation of an occupation (e.g., DiMaggio and Powell 1991; Freidson 1994, 2001; Macdonald 1995). This implies a community of professional peers who set rules and standards, regulate entrance for newcomers and thus assign status, prestige and legitimacy (Goode 1957).

This element of a professional community allocating prestige figured prominently in Erwin's narrative, which was centrally about his gaining professional standing and acknowledgment and, fundamentally, the pride attached to that. Consider, for instance, his proud exclamation "my first position as a social worker" when he started out at the organization. Much later, he expressed deep gratitude when he set out to reconstruct the project after its demise and was met with what he felt was generous acceptance, support and openness by his *professional* colleagues from the new host organization. His gratitude when approval was granted showed how much Erwin accepted the standards of these professional peers and aspired to meet their requirements. The fact that his narrative was essentially about his becoming a full social worker indicates that pride, achieved through professional standing, prestige and superior skill, formed the central emotional motive of Erwin's involvement with Positive Relief.

The professional lens

The salient point here is that Erwin's proud and rationalistic professionalism entailed specific perceptions and omissions in his experience of the organizational process. Overall, this amounted to a relatively depoliticized outlook and a focus on technical-administrative matters.[14] To sustain this outlook the significance of other, potentially politicizing issues had to be carefully managed. As the subsequent two sections will show, this pertained to internal conflicts about bureaucratization and the funding conflict.

The burdens of grassroots participation

Internal conflicts, which others, like Adam, related more or less explicitly to professionalization, overall hardly mattered to Erwin with one notable exception. This was his description of how he was confronted with postings of open, anonymous letters which in no uncertain terms berated Adam, the executive director, and demanded that he leave. It irritated and shocked Erwin that the founder of a project like Positive Relief had opponents who would not publicly identify themselves.

Feelings of irritation and shock indicate that at first the incident did not make sense to Erwin. Curiously, these tensions lacked any context for him and the reason for these hostilities remained unclear in his interview. This had much to do with his professional lens. As we have seen, social service delivery was for Erwin a disinterested professional practice based on rationalized expertise and objectivity. These premises made it indeed unthinkable that, and why, the beneficiaries of such professional practice criticize and attack it. Professionalism stripped internal conflicts of possible significance, such as disempowerment or changing internal emotional climate, and turned them into mere irritations. Later on he managed to resolve shock and irritation through extending his critique of the cuddle approach. Internal tensions would thus have been an outcome of colonizing clients and creating a messy role structure, that is a lack of professionalism. Using such a psychologizing theory helped him fit internal conflicts into his professional sensemaking, thus neutralizing the critical potential of these conflicts.

Precisely because he conceived of his work as professional practice, the dynamics of a membership association mattered to him essentially as a burden to his work, a complicating and annoying nuisance rather than an integral part of his civic organizing. Comparing the old, membership-based Positive Relief to its continuation as a purely professional project without a membership base, he stated:

> but I am very glad that positive relief is NOT! a registered association any more [I: mhm] because the (3.0) the energy and the time that was uhm consumed for this associATION management uhm membership relations ARguments with with BOARD members uhm that that was not pleasant;

Engaging with the organization as a community was not part of his work as he saw it in purely professionalist terms as the application of his superior expertise. This buttressed his disengagement from conflicts when they emerged. In turn, although shocking and irritating, the internal conflicts which had thereby been neutralized could not push him out of his professionalism to make him engage with the issues others found at stake in the professionalization of Positive Relief. While he aspired to the pride attached to being a professional endowed with superior rationalized expertise, the internal communal dynamics failed to engage him significantly.

Personal or political? Funding conflicts

The professional lens had a very similar effect on Erwin's experience of the funding conflict. On the one hand he described cuts as the direct trigger for the dissolution of Positive Relief. Yet he was at pains to neutralize any wider significance of the conflict. While he implicitly indicated an embryonic awareness of some of the political contexts, he tried to cast this conflict in psychologizing and individualizing terms, effectively decontextualizing it.

Essentially, Erwin understood the funding conflict as a personal, private struggle, a clash of personalities between the executive director of Positive Relief—Adam—and the executive director of the Association. For instance, he spoke of a "private war" between the two; a matter of antipathy independent of facts and real givens; a clash of personalities doomed to become fatal; and an interpersonal dynamic of fear and of targeting the other's weaknesses, etc. Note how this psychological perspective builds on professional social work paradigms of social psychology as a vocabulary of sensemaking (see Chapter 5). In Erwin's perspective, letting the personal interfere with practice and giving emotions precedence over facts formed a breach of professional rationality.

This entailed a specific emotional stance. His psychologizing professional lens meant that he kept the conflict and its potential, mobilizing significances at bay. Rather, he related to it emotionally with annoyance as a nuisance, a burden and an external impingement on his work:

> BUT uhm (1.5) COUNTless supersivion sessions were uhm used IN ORDER to work on this conflict [...] i focused more on my WORK and that simply was not part of my tasks [...] but of course i did hear a lot about it [...] and that was a burden that was a burden
>
> i really (-) tried to stay clear from it i have (--) uhm it was enough how much uhm (-) how much i heard about it (--) that i uhm: couldn't uhm (--) escape from so to speak <<laughing> that is what>, the uhm atmospheric things, information that overTOOK me uhm [...] what i couldn't avert; because i worked in the project; (-) uhm that was already enough for me

Political work was not part of his job description and, implicitly, not part of his idea of being a professional. In fact, his reference to a misuse of supervision sessions indicated he experienced this as a breach of professional norms, that is a deviation from the (professional) essence of Positive Relief's work as a service provider. His annoyance, the fact that he saw these conflicts as a burden rather than as part of his work, something he would have preferred to escape from, particularly underlined this.

Managing alternatives

Significantly, elements of potential alternative understandings of the funding conflict were latently present throughout the interview text as Erwin put active effort into managing their significance. For instance, when he talked about being accepted into the new host organization, he also framed the new host organization in terms of its larger size which would protect small and vulnerable Positive Relief against cutbacks. Implicit in this is an embryonic moral understanding of the funding conflict in terms of larger organizations overpowering smaller ones, that is as an injustice.

He also talked about other AIDS organizations' reacting negatively to his continuation of Positive Relief, which he attributed to their disappointment that its share of public funding would not be reallocated to them. Tellingly, this became significant in the narrative only in the context of him continuing with Positive Relief's work, that is as a condition of continuation rather than of the dissolution of Positive Relief.

At another point he briefly critiqued the funneling of public subsidies through an umbrella organization as conducive to conflicts among member organizations. But he quickly evaded the issue again by pointing out that he was far removed from what was going on and instead he essentially naturalized the process as logical:

> but it was of course also CLEAR tha: : t uh little projects (--) uhm were much MORE threatened (-) by this scythe of funding cuts than uh than LARGE ones that's logical

In sum then, some of the political contexts and implications of the funding conflict did not fail to register with Erwin. These could have plausibly inspired a different, political take on the political process leading to the dissolution of Positive Relief and a different emotional stance: for instance, moral outrage and resentment about smaller organizations being overpowered by bigger ones. The professional lens—its rationalizing bent, buttressed by pride—effectively neutralized any such emotional potentials and the political action they might motivate.

Dissolution

Erwin's understanding of the dissolution continued this pattern. Though cuts were the immediate context of the dissolution in his narrative, he hastened to point out deeper reasons, with the cuts functioning only as a trigger. Central for him was rather what he theorized in individualizing/psychologizing terms as his colleagues' burn-out syndrome.

> that uhm parTICularly projectleader [adam] [...] was burnt OUT; that they (2.5) especially he was INcredibly engaged [...] and for him [positive relief] was like like a second HOME; [...] and uhm that was suddenly enDANgered [...] i believe he was really he was also exHAUSTED exHAUSTED from from struggling time and again with the project FUNders

While exhaustion from persistent struggles with the funders hints at a more politicized, solidaristic understanding, this is neutralized through a psychological theory of burn out and (unprofessional) over-identifying with the project ("second home"). Accordingly he could attribute guilt and responsibility for the dissolution to his former colleagues:

> THAT executive director of [the association] [...] (7.0) never had the inTENtion that [positive relief] would be closed. that is, the thing with the

cutback directive that that was indeed his responsibility uhm (1.5) NEVER had the inTENtion that the project uhm would be closed. i believe that believed him at the time and today too. uhm and yet uhm leaders at [positive relief] decided for it [i.e., for the dissolution]

Specifically, Erwin argued that Adam simply (!) did not want a pragmatic solution for allocating cutbacks among team members. Significantly, he could not achieve this attribution without conceding the responsibilty of the Association's executive director. But highlighting his good intentions devoid of the conflict's contexts allowed him to continue constructing the decision to disband as an idiosyncratic lack of will, buttressing his attribution of blame.

Phoenix from the ashes: continuation

This sheds considerable light on Erwin's decision to continue. He recalled his considerations at the time:

and i also didn't want it [the dissolution]. didn't want it beCAUSE i uhm didn't want to lose my job again so soon after four years? i didn't want to become unemployed and secondly uhm i didn't deem the the timing good i found that was not a good point of time to close the project.

In one way, Erwin quite simply and pragmatically did not want to lose his job. This had a professional aspect: access to an enlarged professional community of colleagues and the increased professional pride that joining the new host organization made possible. But this would not entirely do Erwin justice. His reference to timing concisely indicates he felt a continued necessity for Positive Relief's work. This is also why he declined the offer of one organization to host the project:

which i found rather UNpleasant and where it became clear in the end? that [aids relief] was NOT so much interested in in [positive relief] [...] or let ALONE in this EASTern location BUT in the end in in this in my POSITION <<pp> and uhm and the money that came with it>

The eastern German focus of the project now became significant: in line with his professionalism, he identified a persisting need and set out to organize so that this need be met. Just as at the outset, he relied on his professional, superior competence to clear the chaos caused by a lack of professionalism:

thus uhm i w: as AT LEAST TWICE [...] busy with REconstruction. that was at the very beginning ninety-five when i [I: mhm] had to resuscitate those working areas and basically ninety-nine again when i had to start over again hm it's striking me right now phoenix from the ashes

Professionalism

Professionalism emerges from this analysis as a kind of civic action in nonprofit organizations. It centrally involves an element of rationalized expertise and affords professionals feelings of pride about their status. As Erwin's case illustrates, this has a keen depoliticizing potential, neutralizing the mobilizing emotional potentials of some aspects of organizational realities through the recursive process of professional organizational sensemaking. Alternative renditions of organizational reality and their emotional implications need to be continuously managed. Yet, we have also seen that this needs to be qualified. Professionalism also meant that Erwin continued to cater for what he found to be a continuing need, where, for instance, Adam lost much of his *joie de vivre* as Positive Relief's clientele changed to what he found to be a much less exciting demographic. Still, it meant that Erwin did not engage with internal conflicts of professionalization nor with the political conflict over public funding.

The following chapter will continue to explore and develop the notion of professionalism as a kind of civic action in more detail. For now, I would like to recall, as I have argued throughout the preceding analyses, that professionalism and its core element of rationalized expertise are particularly embedded into dominant, medicalizing AIDS discourse as a cultural context and source of power. It is on this discursive basis that professionals can claim primary competence for dealing with HIV/AIDS and, that is, superiority over other forms of AIDS work (activism, volunteerism), as Erwin did. If AIDS is understood in scientific (and also social-scientific) terms, its political significations become delegitimized and AIDS work emerges as a technicality, the application of expertise. The focus on administrative aspects throughout Erwin's narrative was particularly expressive of this. Professionalism in nonprofit organizations is thus not neutral in its relatedness to power structures. In this way professionalism involves specific, fundamentally contingent notions of which causes matter and need to be addressed, how they matter, in what way they are to be dealt with and who should deal with them. It is also for this reason that professionalism is to be considered a mode of civic action, even though its claim to expert objectivity denies this.

Solidarity and communal organizing: Benjamin

I will only briefly and selectively outline the case of a third organizer of Positive Relief—Benjamin. This is to highlight how a different emotional basis led in his case to rather different ways of making sense of some of the aspects that were crucial in both Adam's and Erwin's narrative, especially the professionalization of Positive Relief and the funding conflict. Crucially, this had very different consequences for his activism: He was a board member of Positive Relief for a couple of years, but quit this position before the dissolution, remaining a rank-and-file member. But while Adam retreated by and large from civic organizing after the dissolution and Erwin simply continued, Benjamin retreated from Positive Relief and went on to pursue his activism with other organizations.

Positive identifications

Central to Benjamin's civic organizing were emotions of solidarity, in his case with people living with HIV/AIDS. This was based on his own experience of being HIV-positive and overcoming feelings of hopelessness and despair after testing positive. Having received support from Positive Relief at the time, he wanted to help others achieve the same. This rendered his AIDS-work a matter of self-help organizing based on his feelings of solidarity with others living with HIV/AIDS. In his opposition to the suffering caused by HIV/AIDS as such, this was initially a subjectively relatively apolitical stance, only implicitly related to the emotional regime of dominant AIDS discourse. But the abstracting, generalizing quality of solidarity was reflected in a particularly communal thrust, a strong emphasis on creating a social space for people with HIV/AIDS to counter the incapacitating and isolating despair of living with HIV/AIDS, which he described with some urgency (note the iterations), referring to a community of people with HIV/AIDS ("we"):

> emphasis was always these social offers' where we said we must get people out of their (-) like we must get people out of their (-) we must get people out of their iso isolation [I: mhm] that just is the decisive thing (--) and there was uh (1.5) the cafe [of positive relief]

The primacy of his identity as living with HIV also meant that his eastern German background was relatively insignificant to him and so were the dynamics of shameful eastern inferiority that took their toll on Adam.[15]

But whose identity? Inertia and dissolution

Though initially oriented towards combating despair and isolation, Benjamin's solidarity and his penchant for creating an inclusive community for all living with HIV/AIDS later provided the basis for a critical potential as he apprehended a number of developments in Positive Relief with feelings of resentment. For one, he found himself pitted against a practice of catering to gay men only, which persisted despite his interventions. It was at this point that his feelings of solidarity led him to critique AIDS organizing at Positive Relief and beyond. He cast Positive Relief's focus on gay men as a neglect of the changing demographics of AIDS, and in turn he linked this to dynamics in the regional field of AIDS organizing where the claims were staked for good. He felt that Positive Relief was pressured by dynamics of the regional field of AIDS work into the specialized role of catering to eastern gays and this contrasted sharply with his solidarity-based objective of "constructing an atmosphere that actually uhm builds the bridge for EVERYONE to [be able to] go there [i.e., to positive relief]". In contrast to Adam, the changing social face of HIV/AIDS was not a threat to his activism nor a resort for managing feelings about communal decline at Positive Relief.[16] Instead it led him to engage critically and in anger with the ongoing politics among the regional AIDS organizations, its inertia and, implicitly, with the dominant AIDS discourse, as retained by AIDS organizations, that continued to provide gay connotations to AIDS. A rhetoric of inclusiveness at Positive Relief, paying lip service to his demands and purportedly valuing his input, only added to his feelings of anger:

> i said then that, why are we now actually clarifying things? if then in the end nothing comes out of it; [...] i feel bullSHITTED! when somehow uhm they act like tell us your opinion that would be really important here and so [I: mhm] and then nothing happens in the end; [I: mhm] that's shenanigans; i can do better things with my time.

Target group issues were a protracted and lasting conflict for Benjamin. Given the persistence of gay-focused organizational practice at Positive Relief, Benjamin found that it was not a suitable place for him to realize his objective of a solidaristic community by and for all people with HIV/AIDS. Eventually he quit his post as a board member. And when the organization finally disbanded, this only demonstrated to him the obsolescence of Positive Relief—its inability to progress in tune with the changing social reality of HIV/AIDS. He continued his AIDS work with other organizations instead.

Critique of professionalization

His solidaristic critique of the lack of progress at Positive Relief and beyond was also a critique of professionalization and bureaucratization. He attributed the inability to change to the self-interestedness of professional staff members.

> simply well that organizational development OUT! of itself uhm that doesn't happen. and like i said that didn't happen at positive relief. uhm that is because that also just would have meant for the acting staff to let uhm go und that wasn't there.

This became even more explicit as he drew a sharp contrast to his present AIDS work with a different, "self-help" (!) organization.

> hm well like i said i see this from a self-help organization where i NOW am still involved (--) and we try OUT OF! ourselves well people do this there really as volunTEERS; [...] cause we have increasingly also the feeling the BIG organizations don't CARE! about this; [i.e., the changing situation of people with hiv/aids] they also don't even SEE! this (--) and apart from (--)

well a political adVO!cacy also doesn't happen which was originally connected with [aids organizing]

Based on his solidarity and concomitant communal orientation in his organizing efforts he came to cast Positive Relief and the field of AIDS work more broadly as a neglect of people with HIV/AIDS and specifically attributed this to professionalization—the bifurcation of AIDS work into professionals and clients. Solidarity afforded him a critical potential to disengage with the taken-for-granted operations of existing AIDS organizations. Implicitly, this also involved a disengagement from dominant constructions of HIV and AIDS. Rather than a medical issue requiring professional handling it was to him a deeply human issue as his foundational concern with helping others overcome despair and hopelessness indicates.

The funding conflict: east vs. west?

Benjamin was not oblivious to east–west issues, but they took on significance to him on the basis of his feelings of solidarity with people with HIV/AIDS rather than through dynamics of eastern shame and pride. Through his feelings of solidarity (and as an easterner himself) he came to understand what he described as the specific needs of easterners living with HIV/AIDS as they had to cope with the economic, social and cultural disruptions of a system change.

> for THEM positive relief was an ANCHOR; [...] to give them at least the feeling (-) well (-) YOU too MATTER! somehow? (--) right (--) you too are OK [...] to give people ALWAYS' the opportunity to find their PLACE in this new society;

This notion of specific eastern needs that Positive Relief catered to was the basis for him to relate to the funding conflict. To him, it came down to other, larger organizations denying the necessity of a separate organization catering to this special need. Rather than being about the west overpowering the east, Benjamin understood this as a lack of understanding for people in a different situation—a lack of solidarity. This was part of his critique of AIDS organizing as detached from constituent communities and their need rather than about an eastern shame/pride-politics. The above excerpt continued accordingly:

> well, god, i don't want to become abusive BUT well this IS pretty DIFFICULT uh (--) there IS no understanding let's put it THAT way; so the people [in western organizations] simply cannot emp empathize with such a situation that is (--) how that IS: (-) when you suddenly somehow: (1.5) like when suddenly everything is totally different; <quiet chuckle> than how it still was the day before;

The funding conflict failed to outrage him as such since he was already disenchanted about detached, professionalized AIDS organizing. He rather found the debates within the association "too SILLY!", having "nothing in common anymore with SEN!sible debates; (-) they were in fact (clear power) things." It is for this reason that he did not choose a side in this power struggle but agreed to dissolving Positive Relief.

> but MUST say that this uh well that i have consciously supported (-) uh (-) this deCISION at the time to dissolve [positive relief] [I: mhm] uhm (--) because i found that right then at some point to just simply say uh (--) NOW not to maintain no masquerade here

He framed the dissolution as a means to break through the encrusted structures of AIDS organizing at Positive Relief and beyond. Specifically, the continuation of Positive Relief's services under a different host organization ensured him not only that the needs of people with HIV/AIDS would continue to be met, but that organizational inertia would be overcome.

In sum, this brief outline of Benjamin's narrative demonstrates the contingency of both Adam's and Erwin's approach to AIDS organizing. Benjamin shows how yet another emotional basis for civic action entails a different way of making sense of some of the same issues. Adam endorsed professionalization as he strove to counter eastern shame with pride. Erwin struggled to make sense of internal conflicts related to professionalization given his focus on rationality and expertise. Benjamin's feelings of solidarity in contrast meant that he grew critical of the disempowerment of people living with HIV/AIDS through professionalized and increasingly ossified AIDS organizations. This extended to how he related to the funding conflict as well. It also meant that the dissolution of Positive Relief was not the end of his AIDS organizing. Rather, he pursued his cause of solidarity with people with HIV/AIDS in other organizational settings.

Conclusion

The analysis of Positive Relief has highlighted a number of additional emotions as the bases of activism and brought professionalism into relief as a mode of civic action. Adam's *joie de vivre* meant an emotional liberation from being shamefully crushed by westernization as well as from the discursive regimes that converged in AIDS. He also engaged with the emotional climate of reunification—its implication of shameful eastern inferiority—through the pursuit of pride. These were the emotional bases of his engagement and of his sensemaking. They prefigured what mattered to him, how it mattered and how he reacted to it. The paradoxes of the emotional basis of his engagement, however, also meant that he promoted the professionalization of the organization which involved its transformation in a way that disempowered its constituent community, changing the internal climate. Equally, these paradoxes meant that he related antagonistically to the funding conflict but eventually accepted it and ended up preferring to dissolve the organization. In these ways, his liberation from dominant power structures turned out to be limited. What is more, his sensemaking was based in his not being HIV positive but giving primacy to being an easterner. In this sense, on a fundamental level his organizing was more about eastern emancipation than about AIDS work. This was a crucial foundation to his dismissing internal dissent about professionalization and to his disbanding the organization (leaving certain needs possibly unmet).

This last point came into particular relief with Benjamin for whom the experience of living with HIV took primacy over his background as an easterner. His engagement was based in solidarity with people with HIV/AIDS quite generally. This equally entailed specific ways of sensemaking for him. He grew critical of professionalized AIDS organizing—at Positive Relief and beyond—and how it operated in relative detachment from its constituent communities. In this way it provided an emotional liberation from the power structures that dominant AIDS organizing had evolved into.

In different ways, both Adam and Benjamin were activists. But the fundamental differences and thrusts of their stories also highlight the relativity of activism and its antagonistic-liberating element. As we have seen in previous chapters, power structures are always multidimensional and critical engagement with one dimension may very well involve the covert acceptance and even building onto others.

Finally, Erwin presented professionalism as a unique mode of civic action. It was based in the pursuit of pride that professional prestige involves. A second basis was rationalized expertise as the essence of professional practice. This set-up entailed again a different story about Positive Relief, which by and large remained ignorant of any potential political implications of Positive Relief and the political process it was embedded in. Professionalism thus emerged as firmly compliant with dominant power structures. The following chapter will add additional nuances to our picture of professionalism as a mode of civic action.

Notes

1 The following summary of Positive Relief's history is deliberately kept vague in several respects so as to ensure a certain degree of anonymity while still providing the salient context information.
2 The incidence of HIV and AIDS was relatively low (Herrn 1999: 20–1): 16 registered cases of AIDS by October 1989, i.e., one month before the *Wende*; in 1987–1989 respectively 29, 27 and 21 new HIV infections (West Germany: 9027, 8423 and 6817); but a sharp increase in positive tests after reunification (55 in 1990 to 307 in 1997) in eastern Germany (decline in western Germany: 6308 to 4287 over the same period).
3 *Die Wende* was the political and economic process which took place during 1989–1990 in the German Democratic Republic and culminated in the fall of the wall and the reunification of Germany.
4 This is something of a hyperbole, see note 2.

5 He used an idiomatic expression here that literally translates as "the pike in a carp pond." It evokes imagery of greater power and superiority (of the predatory pike over its prey) resulting in moving the other fish about at will.
6 On the normalization of AIDS, see Chapter 3.
7 In ways I cannot elaborate here, it matters in this context, too, that Adam identified as untested and presumably HIV-negative. This co-shaped his resentful understanding of the normalization of AIDS.
8 The German word literally translates as "death dance."
9 Persil is an iconic, laundry detergent associated with West Germany.
10 This, and the fact that another interviewee, a former board member, represented a dynamic of eastern shame/pride similar to Adam, suggest that Adam's sentiments were in fact shared by others at Positive Relief.
11 The character of social work as a profession has been debated (see, for example, Etzioni 1969; Nadai et al. 2005; Steinbacher 2004). For present purposes, we can eschew this debate, rather drawing on pertinent theories of professionalism to carve out some characteristics of this kind of action in nonprofit organizations.
12 This indicates an important feeling rule of professionalism that I will elaborate on in the next chapter.
13 This is resonant with Peter's view of volunteers as unreliable.
14 He elaborated with considerable detail, for example, on the team structure, number of colleagues, respective responsibilities, or the administrative-technical aspects of re-organizing after the dissolution. In turn, he barely talked about political contexts.
15 This may also be for biographical reasons, as he was of a younger generation, joining Positive Relief in the early 1990s when he was in his early twenties.
16 In fact, at another point in his narrative he constructs the introduction of effective treatments as an opportunity for AIDS organizing and criticizes how AIDS organizers rather felt fear about their now threatened status quo.

References

Barbalet, Jack M. 1998. *Emotion, Social Theory, and Social Structure: A Macrosociological Approach*. Cambridge, New York, Melbourne, Madrid, Cape Town, Singapore, São Paulo: Cambridge University Press.
Barbalet, Jack M. 1999. "Boredom and Social Meaning." *The British Journal of Sociology* 50(4): 631–46.
Brown, Wendy. 1993. "Wounded Attachments." *Political Theory* 21(3): 390–410.
DiMaggio, Paul J. and Walter W. Powell. 1991. "The Iron Cage Revisited: Institutional Isomorphism and Collective Rationality in Organizational Fields." Pp. 63–82 in *The New Institutionalism in Organizational Analysis*, edited by P. J. DiMaggio and W. W. Powell. Chicago, London: Chicago University Press.
Elster, Jon. 1996. "Rationality and the Emotions." *The Economic Journal* 106(438): 1386–97.
Etzioni, Amitai. 1969. *The Semi-Professions and Their Organization. Teachers, Nurses, Social Workers*. New York: Free Press.
Flam, Helena. 1993. "Die Erschaffung und der Verfall oppositioneller Identität." *Forschungsjournal Neue Soziale Bewegungen* 2: 83–97.
Flam, Helena. 2005. "Emotions' Map: A Research Agenda." Pp. 19–40 in *Emotions and Social Movements*, edited by H. Flam and D. King. London, New York: Routledge.
Flam, Helena. 2010. "Emotion, and the Silenced and Short-Circuited Self." Pp. 187–205 in *Conversations about Reflexivity*, edited by M. S. Archer. London, New York: Routledge.

Freidson, Eliot. 1994. *Professionalism Reborn: Theory, Prophecy, and Policy*. Cambridge: Polity Press.
Freidson, Eliot. 2001. *Professionalism: The Third Logic*. Cambridge, Oxford: Polity Press.
Goode, William J. 1957. "Community within a Community: The Professions." *American Sociological Review* 22(2): 194–200.
Gould, Deborah. 2001. "Rock the Boat, Don't Rock the Boat, Baby: Ambivalence and the Emergence of Militant AIDS Activism." Pp. 135–57 in *Passionate Politics: Emotions and Social Movements*, edited by J. Goodwin, J. M. Jasper and F. Polletta. Chicago, London: The University of Chicago Press.
Gould, Deborah. 2009. *Moving Politics: Emotion and ACT UP's Fight against AIDS*. Chicago: University of Chicago Press.
Herrn, Rainer. 1999. *Schwule Lebenswelten im Osten: Andere Orte, andere Biographien. Kommunikationsstrukturen, Gesellungsstile und Lebensweisen schwuler Männer in den neuen Ländern*. Berlin: Deutsche AIDS-Hilfe.
Katz, Jack. 1999. *How Emotions Work*. Chicago: Chicago University Press.
Kemper, Theodore D. 1978. "Toward a Sociology of Emotions: Some Problems and Some Solutions." *American Sociologist* 13(1): 30–41.
Macdonald, Keith M. 1995. *The Sociology of the Professions*. London, Thousand Oaks, New Delhi: SAGE.
Michels, Robert. 1989. *Zur Soziologie des Parteienwesens in der modernen Demokratie. Untersuchungen über die oligarchischen Tendenzen des Gruppenlebens*. Stuttgart: Kröner.
Munt, Sally R. 2008. *Queer Attachments: The Cultural Politics of Shame*. Aldershot, Burlington: Ashgate.
Musick, Marc A. and John Wilson. 2008. *Volunteers: A Social Profile*. Bloomington, Indianapolis: Indiana University Press.
Nadai, Eva, Peter Sommerfeld, Felix Bühlmann and Barbara Krattiger. 2005. *Fürsorgliche Verstrickung: Soziale Arbeit zwischen Profession und Freiwilligenarbeit*. Wiesbaden: VS Verlag für Sozialwissenschaften.
Neckel, Sieghard. 1991. *Status und Scham. Zur symbolischen Reproduktion sozialer Ungleichheit*. Frankfurt am Main, New York: Campus Verlag.
Nelsen, Bonalyn J. and Stephen R. Barley. 1997. "For Love or Money? Commodification and the Construction of an Occupational Mandate." *Administrative Science Quarterly* 42(4): 619–53.
Parsons, Talcott. 1975. "The Sick Role and the Role of the Physician Reconsidered." *The Milbank Memorial Fund Quarterly. Health and Society* 53(3): 257–78.
Parsons, Talcott. 1991. *The Social System*. London: Routledge.
Scheff, Thomas J. 1988. "Shame and Conformity: The Deference-Emotion System." *American Sociological Review* 53(3): 395–406.
Simmel, Georg. 1992. "Zur Psychologie der Scham." Pp. 140–50 in *Schriften zur Soziologie: Eine Auswahl*, edited by H.-J. Dahme and O. Rammstedt. Frankfurt am Main: Suhrkamp.
Steinbacher, Elke. 2004. *Bürgerschaftliches Engagement in Wohlfahrtsverbänden. Professionelle und organisationale Herausforderungen in der sozialen Arbeit*. Wiesbaden: Deutscher Universitäts Verlag.
Zald, Mayer N. and Roberta Ash. 1966. "Social Movement Organizations: Growth, Decay and Change." *Social Forces* 44(3): 327–41.

Chapter 9

Professionalism and the limits of migrantic activism

Migrant AIDS Group (hereafter "the Group") catered to immigrants from Turkey and their descendants—the largest migrantic[1] community in Germany—and later to Muslims in general. International governmental contacts stimulated state agencies in the late 1980s to foster AIDS services for ethnic minorities. They recruited an association of Turkish health professionals to set up and host Migrant AIDS Group. Facing persistent clients' demands, the Group soon widened its initial focus on information and education only, to include also counseling services.

Much like in the case of Positive Relief, the normalization of AIDS led the respective regional state government to commission the regional state-wide umbrella organization Federation of AIDS Organizations (hereafter "the Federation") to distribute the gross amount of state funding among its member organizations. This gross amount was set to decrease annually by fixed rates over the course of several years, leaving it to the Federation how to allocate annual cutbacks among its members. A number of smaller organizations disbanded in the process, including Migrant AIDS Group after a protracted conflict. Its budgets and staff were consecutively reduced until even the last remaining social worker had to be dismissed and the Group thus ceased to exist.

Migrant AIDS Group itself was a professional social work project rather than a membership organization, although it did try—with limited success—to mobilize volunteers for its work. The following analysis will thus provide further insight into professionalism as a kind of civic action. However, there were also instances of activism and volunteerism, which highlights the fluidity of the distinction between types of civic action (see also discussion of Adam).

Medical professionalism: Sarah

Sarah was the co-founder and served as executive director of Migrant AIDS Group through most of its history. A trained physician, doing general health education work professionally in migrantic contexts got her involved with issues of sexuality and HIV/AIDS and eventually led to the opportunity to set up and lead a Turkish-migrantic AIDS project. The funding conflict, resulting in her dismissal, figured centrally in her narrative. Professionalism and its emotional implications were fundamental to her experience of this, though with some specific twists.

Getting involved: discoveries of medical professionalism

Similar to Erwin's story, Sarah's was about becoming a professional physician though failing at it in the end. This had an equally rationalist element. Her narrative starts out as a career description, how her first professional steps led her into health eduction in migrantic settings and how this had her "discover" a necessity of migrantic AIDS work. For her, too, professionalism was a means to construct a need and she presented it in line with her rationalist premises much like a diagnosis: "deficits existed in this area" and required professional interventions. She found this confirmed by a professional audit. Sacrificing initial family concerns, she accepted the offer to start and lead the Group, significantly after colleagues pointed out her skills to her (professional experience, cultural competence). In short, not unlike Erwin, her nonprofit organizing emerged from professional aspirations, on the basis of professional, rationalized expertise, and with reference to professional social contexts (auditors, colleagues). Rationalism defined how she related emotionally to the social issues at stake: an immediate experience of, and moral engagement with, some kind of a pressing social problem was mostly absent. With Turkish-migrantic AIDS work as an objective necessity, Sarah's work took on the quality of a duty and in turn, to some extent, a burden (e.g., affecting her family life), which she shouldered based on her sense of duty. She described setting up the Group as a series of objectives and tasks that emerged impersonally from the material logic of the abstract subject matter at hand, with herself acting as dutiful, passive executioner. Turkish-migrantic AIDS work figured as a merely objective rather than political necessity.

Medical professionalism and civic action

As an instance of medical professionalism, Sarah's case highlights some specific aspects of professionalism that elucidate her inclination to care about the cause at hand and her objectifying perspective. Medical professionalism has different strands that lend themselves in various degrees to political activism (for a more comprehensive discussion, see Dagi 1988). Pertinent to the present purpose, it may inspire a kind of heroism in pursuit of exemplary virtues, such as rational judgment, moral principles, risk-taking, independent thinking, assuming responsibility, pursuit of knowledge or improving society (Dagi 1988: 56–7). Sarah's dutiful sacrificing of her (significant) family concerns can be read as an example of this and there were other instances where she made considerable private sacrifices for the Group. This relates to notions of duty in medical professionalism, where the sense of an exclusive possession of specialized, even life-saving skills translates into a duty and devotion to make their benefits widely available (Merton 1976: 68–9; e.g., Sidel 1998: 363–4). Altruism thus forms a central element here (Evetts 2006: 519; McCally 2002: 147; Mieg 2005; Parsons 1939: 458, 1968: 536; Ritzer and Walczak 1988: 6). This altruistic element bestows a potential on professionalism to serve as a basis for civic action and political empowerment. But this potential may at the same time be curbed (McCally 2002; cf. also Wynia *et al.* 1999): medical professionalism also emphasizes the individual patient and limits the identification with her/his plight, which discourages a broader focus on political responsibility beyond the individual. As Merton argues, the physician is supposed to remain emotionally detached while avoiding callousness by maintaining "compassionate concern for the patient" (Merton 1976: 68). The norm of medical neutrality or impartiality in providing services is another depoliticizing element (e.g., Caldicott *et al.* 2003; List 2008; Merton 1976: 68–9). Fundamental to this is an understanding of professional practice as the application of objective, rationalized expertise. "To the professional [wo]man the other party is a 'case' or a 'client,' [...] the relevant questions do not relate to *who* the patient is but *what* is the matter with him" or her (Parsons 1939: 462 original emphasis).[2] In effect, political contexts are thus construed as external to the essence of medical practice. From these considerations, rationality (Barbalet 1998: 45–54) and, based on the concomitant banishment of politics, individual compassion—rather than more political emotions like solidarity—emerge as central feeling rules of professionalism. This helps explain Sarah's sense of a call to duty overriding private concerns; her self-sacrificing caring while phasing out political contexts; and her rationalist, scientific expertise-based take on AIDS organizing.

Community dynamics, the burdens of professional work and professional pride

In line with this paradigm, Sarah told in many respects a story of perseverance and enduring adverse, burdensome conditions rather than of engaging with these politically or otherwise. She emerged from this as the physician providing professional services and care under great difficulty—the heroic paradigm of medical professionalism. This is in fact similar to Erwin's understanding of membership dynamics as a burden, though Sarah constructs her burdens as part of her professional work. One particular example of adversities were conflicts with her colleagues soon after starting out. These were about representation of migrantic community members in the staff. Sarah dismissed this as cultural machismo and thus framed it as a burdensome condition of her professional work:

> such a difficult undertaking that is leadership of an intercultural project with turkish co-workers where i also always had to listen in the project, who are you anyway yes you are a german woman and you want to tell us, so it is

always also about who can reach his compat that is who can reach turks better [I: mhm] so you have to stand an enormous potential for tensions in the team

Sarah resolved the conflict by turning to the host organization (as the formal employer) and had a particularly hostile co-worker replaced. Political issues, such as minority community empowerment (Turks, gay men) or professionalization, were embryonic in this excerpt ("you are a german woman and you want to tell us") but failed to become significant to her under her dominantly professional outlook. With her civic organizing uninformed by such emotions as political solidarity, she understood tensions as a struggle about competence and hence an attack on her professionalism ("who can reach turks better")—yet, something "you have to stand" precisely as a professional.

Instead, Sarah related to the needs of the Group's target community through the professional feeling rules of rationality and compassion. This was also at the basis of the Group's decision to include counseling services (rather than only educational work). Sarah recounted the story of one gay client with HIV suffering severe stigmatization.

nevertheless, right from the start [...] there were inquiries by affected people and that is with with a high mental strain [...] and this man called so that he was massively well he was simply injured and traumatized and he sought so some uhm shelter and or also counseling from us and then we said well we must make up our minds now [...] but we see that these inquiries come in, can't evade that and also want well we wanted to accommodate that

Feelings of compassion[3] for individual clients affected by HIV/AIDS initiated this rethinking. And again, tangled up with compassion, rational professional practice led her to the discovery of social realities and a diagnosis, as indicated by such expertly rational descriptors as mental strain, injury, traumatization, etc. Again, this appealed to her sense of professional duty to provide care. She *couldn't evade* the caller's request. At the same time, she did not relate to and engage with the political conditions of what she discovered: stigmatizing social climates or the lack of support by non-migrantic institutions.

A story about perseverance, her narrative was simultaneously about succeeding at becoming a practicing professional. She concluded the first project phase with how Migrant AIDS Group gained prominence in the Turkish immigrant community and became institutionalized (rather than a limited pilot-project). She could take relieved pride in living up to the sanctioned professional ideal.

and then you can say the first project phase, as difficult as it was, was successful [...] that is we had taken the first hurdle for now uhm to install ourselves make ourselves kn: : own to the population and uhm succeeded so much that that we continued to be funded that was all o.k.

Inclusions and transformations

In the early 1990s Migrant AIDS Group began seeking membership in the regional state-wide Federation of AIDS Organizations. For Sarah, this mattered in terms of overcoming her professional isolation and gaining acknowledgement through the inclusion into the professional community of AIDS work—not unlike Erwin. This was equally a pursuit of pride. She thus talked about the intake procedure in terms of a professional examination where she had to appear before a meeting of other project representatives to have her eligibility for membership assessed.

The Group's membership request was met with resistance in the Federation. But Sarah's professional vantage point also informed how she related to this. She understood reservations as a matter of not being sensitized for migration issues; as general fears of contact; and as an understandable reaction of the predominantly gay representatives given their experience of homophobia and violence from people with a Turkish migrantic background. Feelings of political solidarity with a group marked by multiple forms of exclusion might have informed a critique of these resistances as racist. But based instead on her compassionate concern for her clientele and a rationalizing understanding of their issues, Sarah rather engaged in rationalizing discourse to simply prove any concerns counter-factual. As she concluded the segment, tellingly, Federation membership, once granted, heralded a positive phase for her in terms of—chiefly personal-professional—inclusion into, acknowledgment, and mutual support by the professional community of AIDS workers. Refuting reservations, she could feel proud to have passed the professional test.

Things changed with the transformation of the Federation into a semi-public funding agency as described at the beginning of this chapter. In her narrative this formed a stark contrast to the previous inclusion into the federation, again, against the backdrop of Sarah's ambitions for professional inclusion. She described a climate change in the Federation: mutual support vis-à-vis the regional state gave way to gay organizations closing ranks while marginalizing others. Indicatively, she related this to her being a physician and a woman:

> we were no pure gay project […] and as a physician i completely stepped out of line that is i believe within the whole [federation] there was one other physician […] and then there was also one person working on women

Again, this illustrates her wish for professional inclusion rather than a migrantic identification.

What is more, it is in this professional context that Sarah now attributed blame through her framing of the Federation's transformation as "project egotism" and, a bit later, a reversal of the social exclusion of gays to them being agents of exclusion—a scathing irony. It is now that she reacted with resentment. As she understood encroaching exclusion primarily in terms of her professionalism, rather than politically, for example, as an instance of racism, this resentment related to her own professional ambitions more than to how exclusion mattered in terms of the Group's constituency.

Emerging conflicts

Emerging conflicts with the Federation made Sarah's professional disengagement with political processes particularly acute. As she told it, Federation representatives tried to transfer the Group to a different host organization. When she declined to support this and stood by the host organization, she recounted an attempt to drown the Group in a surge of bureaucratic stipulations typically to be met within short notice. While she herself was on maternity leave at the time, the host organization asked her to return prematurely in order to "fight together." She returned and managed to work off all the stipulations for the time being.

Throughout narrating this she almost completely omitted political or any other backgrounds that would have elucidated what was going on. Accordingly, she rendered the conflict a mere "power struggle"—an interpersonal fight, that is, between the Federation's executive director and the host association, and mostly focused on how she came to be in the line of fire. Interspersed references to the internal climate change among Federation members (see above) indicated how emerging conflicts mattered for Sarah—as an exclusion from the professional community and the pride it affords.

Broader political contexts were also absent from her decision to side with the host-organization. Her loyalty signified heroic professionalism. When she prematurely returned from maternity leave she once more gave professional demands precedence over her private ones—a physician whose professional skills were called for by someone in need and who dutifully responds to this call[4] for help in a neutrally caring, that is depoliticized way.

There were latent expressions of anger and resentment in this: the Federation's bad intentions,[5] a big and strong organization overpowering a small and weak one and a decline of solidarity. Professionalism contributed to managing anger and resentment as she constructed the emerging conflict as yet another burden, and hence condition for, her living up to the impartial professional ideal. Indicatively, she chose to counter the Federation's assaults by trying to meet its stipulations, which in turn represented the standards of the professional community it embodied.

Conflicts continued after this. For instance, the inception of an intercultural, multi-lingual telephone helpline led to further attacks from the Federation. This figured in her narrative merely as "power struggles like anywhere else," devoid of any political contexts. Instead, these attacks took on meaning for Sarah in relation to her professional aspirations as a denial of acknowledgement:

> so i only want to tell you with this, actually any creative work that comes out of such a project was m: : aybe well that too was part, imagine if you

find ten volunteering people who are [I: mhm] native speakers who are willing to uhm voluntarily or for a small fee to man a helpline then you just, you just say first man how great [I: mhm] and if then however the responsible state uhm [federation] director says what you are doing is shit that was actu uhm that was so to speak not agreed on and you have to come to an agreement with us then uhm the i had the feeling that was not anymore about well simply anything what we did was unappreciated

The recurrence and persistence of these conflicts were tantamount for Sarah to a denial of her professional standing. It was therefore a reversal of the pride that professional success would have allowed into humiliation and shame as expressed through her desperate bemoaning the denial of appreciation and the stifling of her creativity—a devaluation of her exposed (professional) self (Simmel 1992).

Cutbacks and gradual dissolution

The emotional configuration of Sarah's professionalism continued to inform her sensemaking throughout the actual funding conflict. Increasing cutbacks entailed successive reductions of the Group's staff until it ceased to exist when the last social worker had to be laid off. Like before she portrayed this in terms of personalized, irrational aggression and, even more explicitly, a denial of her professional standing and of inclusion into the professional community. She described how step-by-step cutbacks led up to her own discharge:

then it came to the physician's position physician's position, was said the no physician is needed in the project [I: mhm] he [the director of the federation] also always told me that and you know it's like this if you have built up a project like this and with a background like i told you that is first so to speak actually growing into it a little and doing pioneer work and practically developing everything and developing each [I: mhm] brochure yourself, o.k. that often had not so much to do with physician's work but the content nevertheless had to well s uhm and it was then also always like i then had to say somehow why i was nevertheless needed and tell him yes listen you, the turkish clients have confidence in me

Retaining the physician's position was the central aspect of the conflict in her narrative indicating that her professional identity and its pride ("pioneer work") were at stake for her. Understanding AIDS work in essentially apolitical, rationalized terms as the impartial application of professional expertise, casting much contextual conditions as mere adversities to be dealt with professionally, she indicated no conception of political power processes. What is more, her striving for professional recognition left her vulnerable: in the above excerpt she has to concede that her work is not strictly medical in nature and she was left to try to refute the attack on equally rational grounds referring to clients' confidence. She thus remained attached to the professional universe as it not only promised pride but simultaneously contained the seed of shame when the professional community withdrew recognition. And it is this shame that had Sarah eventually give up as her efforts at proving herself as a professional failed.

> and it was then at some point not to be prevented anymore [the federation] said in the project no physicians are no physician is needed but only social workers

In a way, professionalism was empowering Sarah. It provided a basis for relating emotionally to what she constructed as a social need. This was a compassionate rather than, for example, a solidaristic emotional basis. As such it was part and parcel of the emotionality of professionalism where compassion is intertwined with a feeling rule of rationality to prevent the emotional apprehension and engagement with the political contexts of AIDS organizing. In turn, this is further buttressed by professionalism's promise of pride and an orientation of the professional to the professional community as the arbiter of this pride. In Sarah's case this meant she remained attached to this community, desperately trying to prove herself to it rather than countering the successive curtailment of her project and the politics behind that to the point of the Group's dissolution.

Professional volunteerism: Onur

Other actors at Migrant AIDS Group were professionals, that is physicians, too. Yet, their organizational experience differed significantly. In the case of Onur—at the time a board member of the host organization of Migrant AIDS Group—this was because unlike Sarah he also had emotional ties with the Turkish migrantic community. This gave his engagement a different, that is, volunteerist basis constituting it as a hybrid between both modes of civic action.

Intermediating difference: professional volunteering

> we are [...] physicians [...] and we thought uhm that is we are a group of turkish fellow citizens [...] and then also german institutions [I: mhm] that is the most important [I: mhm] we also played this bridging role in this way

> in a country where uhm uhm the turkish or the foreign scientists [I: yes] that they bring help to their compatriots in this foreign country

These two excerpts contain the essence of Onur's engagement in a nutshell: helping compatriots in a foreign country by intermediating between them and German institutions. They also succinctly indicate the bases for such engagement: on the one hand, his being a physician, that is possessing professional expertise and skills; on the other hand, Turkish migrantic feelings of solidarity with his "compatriots," facing the difficulties of living in a foreign country. Finally, the resulting objective of institutional bridging reveals, on closer examination, a fundamental premise: the notion of a fixed ethno-national difference, which, accordingly, can only be intermediated on the level of a professionally enlightened elite.

Self-confidence through "guest worker" solidarity

This premise is attributable to the politics of "guest work" immigration, perhaps the single most dominant paradigm of post-war, "non-German"[6] immigration into West Germany. Mainly in the 1960s–1970s this meant the large-scale recruitment of workers, mostly from southern Europe, with the idea that they would return after a few years. But people stayed, had family members follow and thus constituted de facto mass immigration, not only but especially of Turkish citizens—today the largest migrantic group in the country. Nevertheless the illusion of "*guest* work" has for the most part remained an important element in German discourse and policies on migrants (see, for example, Flam 2007). This has resulted in a persistent othering of migrantic denizens framed until recently as aliens ("Ausländer") (e.g., Flam 2007; Sökefeld 2004; Terkessidis 2000). This was arguably a formative context for Onur's essentializing construction of difference. Configuring and essentializing identifications and differences, migration discourse constituted an emotional climate, shaping Onur's emotional stance of ethno-national solidarity.

This essentializing bent meant that his feelings of solidarity merely opposed the negative consequences of living in a foreign country. Problems of the Turkish-migrantic community, in Onur's view, were not problematic from a normative point of view but an inherent, inevitable and natural outcome of migration. At its basis, it was thus an apolitical form of solidarity and it led Onur to construct a relatively depoliticized organizational reality as we will see. The professional element of Onur's civic action contributed to that, entailing an elitist orientation with him as the elite vicarious representative of his constituent community, as I will elaborate later on.

This also related to a second key emotional aspect of Onur's engagement. The emotional climate of migration discourse and its element of othering bears a shaming potential—the deviating non-normal. Strikingly, Onur told the story of his bridging activities as a story of self-confidence and pride, the dialectical counterpart to shame (e.g., Gould 2009; Munt 1998: 4). Throughout his narrative he evoked the picture of interacting with considerable agency on an equal footing with the highest levels of German institutions such as governments, ministers, regional state administrations, etc. The Group's host figured as the elite representative of its constituency. This brought him into dependence on those very institutions and their acknowledgment—something that ultimately contributed to his failure.

Professionalism as volunteerism

Turkish migrantic solidarity took primacy in Onur's civic organizing over his professionalism. The latter was instrumental (yet nevertheless significant as analysis will show), putting him into a position to "help compatriots." At the basis, his civic action operated as volunteerism, compliant as it was with dominant power structures: through his specific version of solidarity and his pursuit of self-confidence, ascending to acknowledgment by dominant German institutions. In fact, he repeatedly emphasized the volunteerist quality of his work and sharply contrasted it with the professionalized (i.e., involving formal employment) nature of the other member organizations in the Federation: "we are uhm volunteer workers uhm [at the host organization]." He thus represents a hybrid civic actor: his professionalism enabled him to transform his feelings of solidarity into volunteer action in the form of institutional-elite bridging, pursuing a sense of self-confidence from the acknowledgment by dominant institutions.

Constructions of success: bridging in action

This fundamental set-up was the basis of Onur's narrative. He talked extensively about successes in doing bridge work. One success story started with the "observation" of fears among the Group's clients with HIV/AIDS to visit Turkey for what Onur constructed as inhumane[7] tendencies. He then used his professional contacts in Turkey—professors of medicine—to initiate an AIDS organization there and what he described as the first international congress on HIV/AIDS in Turkey. With much detail he described how a delegation of himself, Migrant AIDS Group representatives, and the state minister of health participated in the conference, including a meeting with the Turkish prime minister. This was essentially bridging in action, including feelings of solidarity (compatriots barred from home visits by mere "inhumane tendencies"), elite intermediation and pride (impressive results, his framing of it as a "turning point," interactions on highest political levels).

But his professionalism also made for a rationalist element: he "observed" clients' fears, relating them to "inhumane tendencies" necessitating enlightenment of the Turkish migrantic "population":[8]

> but in this manner that it uhm we also explained our population [I: mhm] turkish population that homosexuality is a a human right

Essentially, the problem to him was a lack of knowledge and information—a technical problem as it were, requiring scientific objectivity and explanation.

Professionalism entailed that his feelings of solidarity operated on an elite level, somewhat removed from the life-worlds of the Group's constituency. For instance, when clients successfully insisted that Migrant AIDS Group offer counseling, tellingly he framed this as a burdensome difficulty he found himself unable to reject, and a problematic complication to his overall bridging project:

which was of course incredibly demanding [I: mhm] and we couldn't send them away [I: mhm] and they said you are an aids group [I: mhm] but we couldn't explain to them what is prevention what is care [I: mhm] and that was difficult [a] difficult (time) for us

Dismissing clients as failing to understand and even as "not so intellectual," he quickly moved past the issue in his narrative. Onur did not relate emotionally to the immediacy of personal suffering given the essentializing premises of his solidarity, his professional rationalism and his pride-pursuing orientation towards elite bridging. These emotional bases were retained by constructing clients' insistence as a burdening condition. The significance and emotional, mobilizing potential of the conditions for clients' distress remained peripheral, although they were latently present: at other points in his story he did indicate that clients felt sheltered at the Group (implying a threat). Also, they frequently returned after having been referred to German institutions because of what Onur called language and mentality problems. There was an embryonic sense here that migrantic clients were excluded from mainstream social service organizations and specifically AIDS organizations (e.g., Tovar Reyes 2006). But the emotional bases of his sensemaking meant that this remained only latently significant.

Conflicts and dissolution

Onur's professional bridging paradigm was also fundamental to his experience of the conflict with the Federation. This conflict eventually led him to the conclusion that a fruitful co-operation or dialog—bridge work—were no longer possible and he resigned himself to Migrant AIDS Group's dissolution.

First off, Onur's professional emphasis on rationality meant that he understood politics as alien to his civic organizing. He explicitly highlighted the impartiality of his work. He conceived of his engagement as professional (volunteer) practice based in rational, objective and value-neutral expertise, replacing politics. The Federation thus figured as an intrusion of politics, which, however, he did not have any understanding of nor engage with emotionally as such.

His narration of the funding conflict is similar to Sarah's where cutbacks increasingly reduced the Group's staff to the point where it dissolved. He also constructed the Federation as having exploited the Group's weakness by overburdening it with bureaucratic stipulations—a "barrage of faxes." This hinted at a story of injustice. But in line with his depoliticized understanding of the position of Turkish migrantic people in Germany he framed this in individualistic-moral terms of ill will of the Federation ("exploiting weak spots"). What is more, it is a story of shame for Onur as he experienced membership in the Federation as hierarchical subordination and hence a break with the ideals of his bridging paradigm:

we didn't find any contacts [in the Federation] that way from the beginning [I: mhm] first that is we always said we are a bridge between german

> institutions and turkish [I: mhm] fellow citizens but on equal grounds [I: mhm] that is otherwise you can't do it

Hierarchical subordination involved a loss of status for Onur. Working off the bureaucratic overload "we all started working like secretaries." This contrasted with earlier phases when Migrant AIDS Group was still receiving subsidies directly from the regional state rather than via the Federation (as it initially did): "then we had a balance right they didn't uhm see us let's say as employees."[9] The funding conflict was thus an experience of shame for Onur. Significantly, his narrative was interspersed here with numerous episodes reasserting pride about Migrant AIDS Group's achievements. He concluded that it may well have been among the best organizations of its kind in Europe.

With the inclusion into the Federation Onur saw his bridge work paradigm eventually collapse. Rather than co-operative intermediation among equals on an elite level and acknowledgment allowing for pride and self-confidence, Federation membership entailed not only subordination and status loss but in fact the gradual breakdown of a social relationship as he experienced difficulties establishing full contacts at the Federation—all in all essentially a configuration of shame (Katz 1999; Kemper 1990; Neckel 1991; Scheff 1988, 2000; Simmel 1992). When a last appeal to the regional state government failed, this resulted in resignation, something he framed precisely in terms of the breakdown of bridge work.

> it is was cut back over and over and at some point we saw NO possibility to collaborate was no dialogue there and nothing anymore

There was another layer to this. Although overall a story of shame and resignation, it was at the same time nevertheless interspersed with attributions of blame. In the context of Migrant AIDS Group's problems of establishing viable contacts within the Federation, he identified what he called a monoculture which he found predominant in the Federation, that is essentially the dominance of gays:

> because at the time they also thought that it (is) a uhm homosexual disease [I: mhm] and uhm with a homosexual disease or it is disease of homosexuals [I: mhm] and they must also lead this [i.e. the Federation]

> and we were sequestered [I: mhm] that is uhm for example you couldn't just go there and (get along) with the people and talk because they were sequestered that means this monoculture homosexual monoculture

Onur developed here a blame-attributing, anger-inspiring theory of structural conditions that he found to be at the basis of the conflict with the Federation. However, this did not change his overall resignation or inspire acts of resistance. One reason for this was that this theory was embedded into his reasoning about the necessity of a *migrantic* organization doing AIDS work for a *migrantic* community. This was not based in normative considerations like entitlement, empowerment or the fight against exclusion and discrimination. Rather it was based in his professionalism. For Onur, the necessity of a migrantic organization was first and foremost a technical requirement given the greater expertise of elite migrantic representatives about their community, which in turn was based in his notion of essentialized alterity.

> and then then we said we are actually uhm we know this population [I: mhm] and uhm [...] what habits and customs they have [I: mhm] and we can forge this project together with [the foundation] [I: mhm] but we lead that we must lead that

At its core, Onur's theorizing of monoculture thus related to what was centrally at stake for him in the conflict with the Federation: the claim to expertise and its acknowledgment. It was part of a reassertion of this claim where Federation cutbacks and social exclusion effectively subverted it. Not unlike Sarah, as he strove for self-confidence and pride, the very actors he looked to for acknowledgment effectively subverted it and thus turned it into shame. His shame, that is to say, was predicated on his seeking acknowledgment by those very institutions and sticking to this orientation as he tried to re-establish his claim to acknowledgment.

Hybrid activism: Anıl

Each in their own ways, both Sarah and Onur ended up with a sense of exclusion from what they found to be the gay-dominated field of AIDS work. This also reflected the simple fact that neither of them identified as gay (although this does not sufficiently explain their sense of exclusion). Anıl, by contrast, started out from the hybrid positioning as a gay Turk. His concern for migrantic AIDS work began in a migrantic gay organization, which led him to volunteer and later to work as an employee for Migrant AIDS Group until he too was dismissed and the organization thus disbanded. He told a rather sparse narrative that made it often difficult to extract his emotional orientations, but this was a datum in itself.

Hybrid identifications

> so <<clears throat>>i came uhm via an uhm different group uhm named [group of international gays] so as a gay turk i am uhm also engaged uhm with: : in uhm (a) gay organization that calls itself [group of international gays] and uhm we uhm also just kept thinking uhm about aids prevention in the context of migrants here gay migrants that live here

> and we were two three uhm gay turks who said gosh we must uhm do something realize also because friends affected it is uhm more and more are affected

With these statements Anıl concisely described key motives of his AIDS work. Fundamentally, he hinted at solidarity with migrantic gays with, or threatened by, HIV/AIDS. In turn, a dual identification as both gay and Turkish was at the basis of these concerns. As these excerpts indicate his engagement constituted in one way an extension of gay AIDS work—the dominant paradigm of AIDS organizing in Germany (see Chapter 3). Notably, it was within a gay, migrantic context and as a gay, migrantic man that he came to construct in these excerpts the necessity of including a migrantic aspect into AIDS work. This was all the more significant as it formed the beginning of Anıl's narrative, its point of departure. The beginning of Anıl's concern for migrantic AIDS work thus involved a widening of the framing of AIDS as a gay disease, that is a migrantic inflection. Dominant AIDS discourses about the gay nature of AIDS—however diluted they had become by this time—and the inscription of AIDS into gay identities were thus fundamental to Anıl's "discovery" of AIDS as a gay, migrantic problem. It is therefore not coincidental that he subsequently first turned to German AIDS Relief, the institutionalized embodiment of AIDS work intertwined as it has been with the gay construction of AIDS (see Chapter 3). Through this he came into contact with Migrant AIDS Group.[10]

The fundamental role of notions about the nature of AIDS was also evident from a critical stance Anıl adopted towards Migrant AIDS Group and its host organization. He found that they tended to neglect gay issues in favor of a more generalized understanding of AIDS, which he attributed to the conservatism of the physicians involved. By way of a tacit take-over he strove to change this:

> so we want so to speak to get into uhm like the trojan horse uhm conservative uhm physicians and uhm how can we uhm with uhm raise this taboo subject there yes [...] [the] majority also within [the host organization] for them the subject was initially also was very uhm uhm uhm strange so that they didn't want to [I: mhm] have to do a lot with it so it affects prostitutes [inaud.] just uhm prostitutes uhm gay men and and uhm with this that was it they were then uhm partly stigmatized uhm we just uhm tried there bit by bit uhm move closer to the [I: mhm] to the physicians

At the same time, Anıl's Turkish migrantic identification meant that his engagement was more than just an extension of gay AIDS organizing. Where his gay identification allowed for a critique of the approach pursued at Migrant AIDS Group, his migrantic identification meant that he equally took critical distance towards dominant, non-migrantic AIDS organizing. This became particularly salient in the course of the conflict with the Federation. Anıl talked about it right at the beginning, where he contextualized his joining the Group with a phase where the organization and its host had once again been "torpedoed" when it was audited:

> and uhm we had the impression that is we folks from uhm the migration sector that it that this uhm instrument of auditing could also function to just

also uhm uhm destroy the project [I: mhm] so already in ninety-five the first uhm so to speak efforts uhm of of [the Federation] uhm to wind up the project [I: yes] [...] to some extent we had the impression as if the questions [during the audit] had been chosen to well let's feel quite directly uhm if the project uhm can stand up to the questioning uhm it just was a trial of strength we passed it

It was on the basis of his migrantic identification ("we folks from the migration sector") that he developed a sense of attack and threat and came to understand the processes at hand as indeed a kind of power struggle. And yet, even in this context of attacks, there were significant ambiguities. The question of whether a medical host-organization is appropriate for migrantic AIDS work—one of the issues in the conflict—weighed on him:

there just was soon also the problem uhm is that that is a conceptual uhm pro problem is the project uhm uhm well located in the realm of medical uhm authorities [I: mhm] right or in a context of prevention work shouldn't it uhm be located uhm rather with a lower-threshold uhm at a different host that is which does social work [I: mhm] in that sense, so this this consideration continues to be present [inaud.] also until the end it was we just discussed it right if if prevention so to speak uhm is to be done from a medi: : : cal perspective uhm or if it should rather just uhm be hosted with a lower threshold like uhm an educational project

There was a degree of understanding for the critique of Migrant AIDS Group's set up. However, the question remained unresolved for him. Significantly, in the interview text his pondering over this was followed and resolved by his experience of the audit and the feeling that this came as an attack.

These ambiguities may be the reason why his emotional stances were difficult to extract from his narrative. On the one hand, there was a sense of resentment in his critique of stigmatizing negligence of gays and prostitutes, but this remained limited and indeed in practice he addressed it by avoiding an open confrontation (Trojan Horse). Arguably, it was feelings of solidarity based on a shared Turkish migrantic identification that had him manage his resentment, a solidarity based in a sense of the marginalized social position of migrantic denizens and their organizations in Germany. Resentful solidarity was at the basis of his experiencing the auditing as an attack from outside the migrantic community which the torpedo metaphor succinctly expressed. While Anıl's hybrid identification may overall have made for a certain amount of timidity, the more salient point is that it allowed him to assume a politicized stance that was equally multi-dimensional and whose emphases shifted according to the tides of political processes. It afforded him a certain degree of independence from both Migrant AIDS Group and the dominant AIDS organizing embodied in the Federation. However, the specific dynamics accompanying his organizing efforts also posed considerable

194 Migrant AIDS Group

limits to this activism which ultimately made for a degree of resignation as Migrant AIDS Group disbanded.

Navigating conflicts

Facing hegemony

Anil recalled how the conflict with the Federation revolved in part around the Group's failure to refer clients to other institutions for counseling services, rather offering such services itself. For the Federation this was a lack of professionalism. But rather than antagonism as in the audit episode, a sense of suffocating dilemma prevailed for Anil.

> people stuck [with us] [...] the rule was [...] referral uhm seeing to it that you just come to grips with the problems uhm more or less and then referral onwards to [...] the respective institutions [inaud.] which however were in german uhm uhm struc uhm uhm structures of regular welfare services there are hardly any migrants (there) who also [...] have knowledge about aids in the end people stayed with us

His feelings of solidarity with migrantic people with HIV/AIDS afforded him a sense of their problematic position within dominant structures of welfare delivery. Yet, he persistently failed to find understanding for this in the Federation.

> until today they have (why) do they stay with you, like that, uhm why don't you refer them onwards, right it was uhm there was no-one we could have uhm referred them to [I: mhm] well it just was such such culture <<laughs>specific> i think so or like that's sort of intercultural uhm communication difficulties right uhm that didn't work out and the insight to say [inaud.] we can't refer them onwards uhm but the [large other local aids organization] says well but uhm that really is unprofessional or [the federation]

There were a number of emotional layers to this. There is a latent sense of anger about the unwillingness of the Federation to acknowledge the impossibility of referrals and its conditions, stubbornly holding the Group responsible. Simultaneously, however, the persistence of Federation criticism blunted his arguments and made for a sense of suffocating powerlessness, disbelief and resignation. There is also a sense of shame given the lack of acknowledgement for his position: indicatively, he interjected his narrative right at this point with an episode of success in a completely unrelated respect.

This pattern of anger being managed by resignation recurred when he described the successive funding cuts:

with its cutbacks uhm the federation started <<laughing>> I believe from ninety-seven on, that is so to speak also through pressure from the [regional state government] [I: mhm] uhm (it was) urged to, [I: mhm] uhm where the small projects were uhm uhm so to speak bit by bit uhm uhm closed down away cut away right this centralization towards bigger projects a phenomenon of large associations well

An embryonic sense of an angering injustice (overpowered small projects closed down, cut away) is kept in check here by diluting blame: splitting agency between Federation and state and constructing a disagreeable but inevitable phenomenon.

How can we understand this blunting of anger? A key condition is the rationalized form that the Federation's charges took, namely that the Group was not professional. Professionalism had become the taken-for-granted ideal in the field of AIDS work (see Chapter 3), bestowing a disinterested, objective quality on any recourse to it (see Chapter 4). Given this, Anıl's alternative understandings and latent anger simply bounced off.

The power of the organizational field made itself felt to Anıl in another way. The Federation pushed the Group to compensate for cutbacks by increasing the use of volunteers.

> but it just simply was the case that uhm people participated only to a certain extent right [...] volunteer work is a phenomenon of the the middle class right so so to speak you work somewhere uhm at a bank and so and say hey i want to be involved uhm in social stuff on top, but this middle class just isn't there in the turkish community [I: mhm] uhm well so that we could work with little volunteers uhm from the outset uhm

Self-help has indeed been another institutionalized principle of AIDS organizing in Germany (see Chapter 3).[11] Though Anıl developed an interesting theory here, there is a defensive, ashamed quality to this segment. He presents this theory by way of excusing the Group's mobilization failure. Next, he immediately switched over to describing a number of instances of successful volunteer mobilization. Then he argued that other migrantic communities had similar problems. This climaxed in an attack on what he described as the decision of the state that culture-specific AIDS organizing was to be closed down and included in other welfare agencies, even though those lacked sensitivity to the needs of migrantic clients—the final trigger of the Group's dissolution. Yet he came to a relatively modest conclusion:

> which in my view is a political issue uhm uhm one says uhm that is just on the one hand one just says uhm there is ghettoization integration deficits uhm have resulted [I: mhm] uhm uhm but on the other hand uhm one just also says uhm despite these deficits uhm yes there should not [be] aids preven uhm uhm there are those ghettos [I: mhm] there should not be any

aids prevention for those ghettos [I: mhm] which i find rather social darwinist [I: mhm] so uhm and uhm there just was simultaneously that uhm yes i do think that (is) discrimination that is on an institutional level, was carried out by [the federation] in the end then also by [the regional state] because it said there should not by any culture specific uhm uhm work

uhm the challenge just was uhm will be in the future too to (enforce) uhm a health political uhm uhm uhm lobby work here in the [regional state] to say hey we have here this we pay taxes here and we want corresponding uhm counseling services

There is considerable politicized anger in these excerpts together with a sense of collective entitlement (unlike Onur). And yet, in his narrative this did not result in angered action but a timid call for lobbying. Expressions of anger rather served more the purpose of deflecting shame about the failure to mobilize (cf. Scheff 1988 on shame–anger dynamics). In shame, there is an acknowledgment of the validity of evaluative standards levied against the ashamed and in this case, the Federation's criticism was rationalized by the legitimized ideals institutionalized in the field of AIDS organizing.

In sum, Anıl felt moral anger and resentment at the Federation and the regional state government behind it for how they dealt with Migrant AIDS Group. However, these emotions were effectively held in check given that these dealings were based in institutionalized ideals of AIDS organizing whose legitimacy he in principle shared.

Inside/outside: the Trojan horse

Anıl was not only critical about the Federation, but equally about the Group's host-organization. In the context of the dissolution he pointed at the inertia and weakness of the host organization regarding pressures from the Federation, leaving administrative work for the Group to take care of. Yet, at the same time he softened any blame by framing extra burdens as "only strenuous"; by normalizing internal problems ("like in any other project"); and by referring to the good intentions of host organizers. Hence, while there was a degree of anger he equally tried to limit and manage it.

Similarly, there was a sense of anger as he constructed the host organization's failure to form effective alliances and how this contributed to the demise of Migrant AIDS Group. But then he developed a detailed theory, diluting blame: a strong Turkish migrantic organization and possible ally would have had an incompatible focus; the insight into the need for alliances came too late; or generation conflicts leading to rivalries among Turkish migrantic associations. And yet, this did not quite neutralize his anger, leaving a residue of blame:

but uhm, this would have been solvable but that didn't happen especially because just also i think on the one hand the [other turkish organization] did relatively much in the social sector and uhm [the group's host organization] in my view played out too much the elderly prince card [...] so uhm they were el: : : derly gentlemen but still wanted to come across as youthful [I: mhm] saying they deal with it nevertheless

As his hopes were disappointed he resorted to sarcasm ("elderly prince")—combining feelings of powerlessness, resignation, and yet anger.

Anger was more subtly managed as Anıl interjected this section with a longer description of what he presented as successes of the Trojan Horse against the backdrop of continuous tensions around his propagation of gay issues within the Group—a struggle about the meaning of HIV/AIDS:

(i) always got to hear well you as a gay man you just always do uhm exclusive uhm prevention for gay men [I: mhm] so you should so to speak use uhm ten percent[12] of your work for gay men and ninety percent uhm proportionately for the heterosexual population uhm so which however was uhm so to speak not backed by statistics [I: yes] affectedness uhm uhm among also the gay turks is many times higher

Anıl took pride in circumventing this by integrating gay issues into his general-focus activities (e.g., information work in schools): "so the issue of sexuality i have also introduced it there as a topic." To a certain extent he complied with the dominant marginalizing of gay issues at Migrant AIDS Group or at least did not squarely and openly counter it—much in line with the Trojan Horse strategy. Although he was in principle driven by solidarity for migrantic gays affected by HIV/AIDS he curbed these motives in favor of compliant compromise. Constructing this as a success not only afforded him personal pride, but also, through its narrative embedding into Anıl's critique of the host-organization, functioned to mediate anger and disappointment about the shortcomings of the host-organization.

Anıl's management of anger about the Group's host organization was embedded into a situation where Migrant AIDS Group was under siege through constant attacks from the Federation that resulted in the gradual shrinking and eventual dissolution of the Group. The audit episode illustrated how this threat led Anıl away from a critique of his organization towards feeling solidarity for it. This linked to his more fundamental solidarity for migrantic gays affected by HIV/AIDS. Indeed Migrant AIDS Group was the only institution that promised some attendance to this concern of his as he found mainstream welfare and AIDS agencies ill-attuned to a culturally diverse clientele.

Dissolution

Anıl's civic action was based in his feelings of solidarity with migrantic gays affected by HIV/AIDS, based on his dual ties with both gays and Turks. It allowed him to be critical towards Migrant AIDS Group and the Federation. At the same time, juggling his multiple allegiances and critiques effectively curbed his political feelings. Anger and resentment about the Group, its host and the Federation were either blunted by institutionalized rationales or counterbalanced by loyalty to his own organization under siege. This had him eventually end up with a sense of resignation. The following excerpt sums up some of this:

> uhm why the project was wound up i think just was uhm a consequence of of yes uhm within the project uhm up to personality issues too [I: mhm] right there were personalities being acted out there rather than substantial issues i think [I: mhm] uhm and uhm one should have focused more strongly on the health political uhm aspect right from the beginning we should have worked political uhm more politically right [I: mhm] and see to it that uhm we uhm achieve good uhm networking also in health policy respects but uhm the day has only twenty-four hours and we just have also seen our task uhm to be there for counseling and also to be there for prevention which just uhm uhm takes a lot

But here too, his resignation did not entirely stifle his anger. He continued the segment by pointing out how the Federation had promised to distribute cutbacks so that the substantial quality of none of its member organizations would have been compromised—a reduction of services only in quantity not in quality. This promise, he pointed out, was betrayed with the dissolution of Migrant AIDS Group—the only project in the Turkish migrantic community that addressed issues of HIV/AIDS as he emphasized.

Anıl set out to act on his solidarity with migrantic gays affected by HIV/AIDS but he felt himself increasingly tangled up in the mundane political realities of conservative physicians unwilling to fully take up the fight and on the other hand the threat of the Federation presenting itself in rationalized terms. This ultimately led to his sense of resignation but it did not entirely do away his solidarity and moral anger. In fact, as he indicated at one point, he has since tried to pursue issues of HIV/AIDS in a new organization with an albeit general/not AIDS focused queer Turkish migrantic focus.

Anıl thus shared some characteristics of activism—his solidarity with migrantic gays affected by HIV/AIDS or his moral anger at disempowering conditions. But he remained enmeshed with these conditions, too, ultimately limiting his resentment.

Conclusion

Migrant AIDS Group adds a number of nuances to our picture of different modes of civic action. Sarah's story resonates in many respects with that of Erwin at Positive Relief. This goes both for her pursuit of pride through gaining inclusion into a professional community—a central, driving motive; and for the rationalizing element of expertise. This provided her with a lens to construct and relate emotionally to clients' need. Professionalism also empowered her to defend and retain the Group for some time. This professionalism kept her from relating emotionally to, and making sense of, the power processes at stake, such as community disempowerment through professionalism or, more importantly, the intricacies of the funding conflict. Others in the Group spoke of monoculture, racism or institutional discrimination. Instead, the funding conflict signified for her chiefly as a struggle for professional pride against the withdrawal of recognition through the professional community of AIDS work. Accordingly, when her efforts to prove herself on rationalized, expertise-based (rather than political) grounds failed her engagement ended as it did in collapse. Without more politicized understandings she had no means to otherwise counter the denial of her work.

Onur was a more hybrid case as a professional doing volunteer work. Professional skill and expertise were fundamental to, yet only instrumental for his volunteerism. He was rather driven by feelings of solidarity based on essentializing diasporic ties with the Turkish migrantic community. In many ways, this prevented him from relating emotionally to ongoing power processes and making sense of them. Professional elitism had him eschew concerns for community empowerment. His premises of naturalized ethno-national difference meant that some conditions for clients' distress did not register with him in a way that would have spurred his civic action (e.g., exclusion from German welfare institutions). Nor did his professional rationality and expertise focus enable an apprehension of the politics behind the funding conflict. His objective of self-confident elite intermediation had him depend on dominant institutions and actors for acknowledgment. When acknowledgment was withdrawn by way of encroaching cutbacks his feelings of self-confidence thus reverted to shame and resignation.

Finally, Anıl emerged as something of a proto-activist. Though formally employed, his solidarity was unmediated by professionalist premises. His feelings of solidarity were based in his dual ties as gay and Turkish. This allowed for an expanded political outlook and a critique of Migrant AIDS Group, its host and the Federation. However, the tides of the funding conflict, polarized along lines of both sexuality and ethnicity (straight/Turkish Group vs. gay-/German-dominated Federation), led his solidaristic allegiances to shift, effectively curbing his critical potential and barring him from addressing head-on the power processes on either side. This ultimately resulted in his resignation. But his feelings of solidarity have also led him to continue pursuing his concerns at a different organization.

The modes of civic action enacted at Migrant AIDS Group in turn related to cultural-discoursive conditions. I have already variously argued how professionalism in AIDS organizing is ground in the medicalized paradigm of AIDS discourse. This was a pivotal basis for Sarah and Onur to make expertise central to their civic action. It also was a basis for some of the Federation's charges against the Group. Second, Sarah's and Onur's professionalism was premised on the notion that AIDS is not a gay disease and they found that to be implicitly at stake in the funding conflict—to them a matter of gays asserting their dominance. For Anıl, in turn, the Group neglected the gay dimension of AIDS. To him AIDS matterd both in terms of ethnicity and sexuality. This analysis thus confirms earlier findings (see Chapter 2) that AIDS organizations are sites where the meaning of HIV and AIDS is negotiated and implemented into communities.

Notes

1 The neologism "migrantic" refers here to both actual immigrants as well as those who are dominantly perceived as, and may or may not identify themselves as, (descendants from) immigrants.
2 As Merton (1976: 68) indicated, this is in fact more ambivalent: there is a balance between emotional detachment and compassion.
3 She constructs a situation of suffering (high mental strain, massive, traumatized, seeking shelter, injured). The excerpt is contextualized by an opposition construct with a Turkish community cast as denying compassion.
4 An indicatively impersonal call: "there was then the request for me to come back."
5 Although those intentions remained unspecified.
6 Other key forms of post-World War II immigration have been people from eastern Europe classified as ethnic Germans as well as people applying for political asylum.
7 He only briefly hinted at debates about coercive public health measures, a climate of homophobia, etc.
8 The German word "Population" has a distinctly scientific ring.
9 Significantly, this was followed by a brief description of dealings with ministerial representatives, that is interactions on a high hierarchical level.
10 Compare this to Sandra and Onur who started out independent from, and only later sought contact with, pre-existing structures of AIDS organizing.
11 As Sarah recounted, Federation membership was predicated on proving the self-help nature of Migrant AIDS Group.
12 This referred to notions about the statistical prevalence of gays in the general population.

References

Barbalet, Jack M. 1998. *Emotion, Social Theory, and Social Structure: A Macrosociological Approach.* Cambridge, New York, Melbourne, Madrid, Cape Town, Singapore, São Paulo: Cambridge University Press.
Caldicott, David G. E., Jamie Isbister, Ruth Das and Geoffrey K. Isbister. 2003. "Medical Activism, Refugees, and Australia (the Land of the 'Fair Go')." *Emergency Medicine* 15(2): 176–82.
Dagi, T. Forcht. 1988. "Physicians and Obligatory Social Activism." *Journal of Medical Humanities and Bioethics* 9(1): 50–9.
Evetts, Julia. 2006. "Introduction: Trust and Professionalism. Challenges and Occupational Changes." *Current Sociology* 54(4): 515–31.
Flam, Helena, ed. 2007. *Migranten in Deutschland. Statistiken—Fakten—Diskurse.* Konstanz: UVK Verlagsgesellschaft.

Gould, Deborah. 2009. *Moving Politics: Emotion and ACT UP's Fight against AIDS.* Chicago: University of Chicago Press.

Katz, Jack. 1999. *How Emotions Work.* Chicago: Chicago University Press.

Kemper, Theodore D. 1990. "Social Relations and Emotions: A Structural Approach." Pp. 207–37 in *Research Agendas in the Sociology of Emotions*, edited by T. D. Kemper. Albany: State University of New York Press.

List, Justin M. 2008. "Medical Neutrality and Political Activism: Physicians' Roles in Conflict Situations." Pp. 237–53 in *Physicians at War: The Dual-Loyalties Challenge*, edited by F. Allhoff. New York: Springer Publishing.

McCally, Michael. 2002. "Medical Activism and Environmental Health." *The Annals of the American Academy of Political and Social Science* 584(1): 145–58.

Merton, Robert K. 1976. *Sociological Ambivalence and Other Essays.* New York: Free Press.

Mieg, Harald A. 2005. "Problematik und Probleme der Professionssoziologie. Eine Einleitung." Pp. 11–46 in *Professionelle Leistung—Professional Performance: Positionen der Professionssoziologie*, edited by H. A. Mieg and M. Pfadenhauer. Konstanz: UVK.

Munt, Sally R. 1998. "Introduction." Pp. 1–11 in *Butch-Femme: Theorizing Lesbian Genders*, edited by S. R. Munt. London: Cassell.

Neckel, Sieghard. 1991. *Status und Scham. Zur symbolischen Reproduktion sozialer Ungleichheit.* Frankfurt am Main, New York: Campus Verlag.

Parsons, Talcott. 1939. "The Professions and Social Structure." *Social Forces* 17(4): 457–67.

Parsons, Talcott. 1968. "Professions." Pp. 536–47 in *International Encyclopedia of the Social Sciences*, edited by D. L. Sills. New York: Macmillan.

Ritzer, George and David Walczak. 1988. "Rationalization and the Deprofessionalization of Physicians." *Social Forces* 67(1): 1–22.

Scheff, Thomas J. 1988. "Shame and Conformity: The Deference-Emotion System." *American Sociological Review* 53(3): 395–406.

Scheff, Thomas J. 2000. "Shame and the Social Bond: A Sociological Theory." *Sociological Theory* 18(1): 84–99.

Sidel, Victor W. 1998. "The Social Responsibilities of the Physician." *Journal of the Royal Society for the Promotion of Health* 118(6): 363–6.

Simmel, Georg. 1992. "Zur Psychologie der Scham." Pp. 140–50 in *Schriften zur Soziologie: Eine Auswahl*, edited by H.-J. Dahme and O. Rammstedt. Frankfurt am Main: Suhrkamp.

Sökefeld, Martin. 2004. "Das Paradigma kultureller Differenz: Zur Forschung und Diskussion über Migranten aus der Türkei in Deutschland." Pp. 9–33 in *Jenseits des Paradigmas kultureller Differenz: Neue Perspektiven auf Einwanderer aus der Türkei*, edited by M. Sökefeld. Bielefeld: Transcript Verlag.

Terkessidis, Mark. 2000. *Migranten.* Hamburg: Rotbuch Verlag.

Tovar Reyes, Jaime Danilo. 2006. *Erfolge und Defizite bei der Aids-Selbsthilfe-Arbeit mit MigrantInnen in Berlin.* Master's Thesis, TU Berlin, Berlin.

Wynia, Matthew K., Stephen R. Latham, Audiey C. Kao, Jessica W. Berg and Linda L. Emanuel. 1999. "Medical Professionalism in Society." *New England Journal of Medicine* 341(21): 1612–16.

Chapter 10

Conclusion

The meaningful, emotional and powered nature of nonprofits

By way of conclusion I want to briefly reconsider the key issues raised in my argument. I will start out by discussing the problems of third sector theories in light of my findings, outlining an alternative take on nonprofits. Next, I will summarize my argument about modes of civic action—the key dimensions of distinguishing them, their function in the production of organizational realities, their contexts and conditions, their significance for understanding dissolution processes and their usefulness for distinguishing types of organizations.

A different take on nonprofits

Prevailing scholarly views on nonprofits understand them either as virtually automatic responses to needs unmet by states or markets or as a means of state action. Individual organizers tend to fall out of the theoretical picture. Theories of volunteerism do not function as theories of nonprofit organizations and predominantly suffer from a too limited, rationalistic analytical focus. Analysis of the field of AIDS organizing illustrates these limits and proposes different understandings of nonprofits.

Nonprofits are intricately embedded into dominant meaning systems, i.e., discourses, and the emotional climates they constitute. Discourses constitute the very reality that nonprofits address and they prefigure how to emotionally relate to this reality. Nonprofits emerge and evolve (or fail to emerge) as their (potential) organizers navigate these meanings and emotional climates. This is to say that civic organizations depend fundamentally on how organizers understand, apprehend emotionally and respond to—in short: constitute—both a cause to be addressed through a civic organization and the specific forms and ways in which this should be done. In the face of existing social problems—i.e., unmet needs in terms of third sector research—nonprofits are fundamentally contingent, as Chapters 2 and 3 demonstrate and as the empirical case studies explore in greater depth. The evolution of the four organizations studied in Chapters 6–9 fundamentally depended on the meaning-emotion making of their individual members and on how they related to discursive-emotional regimes and the politics they animated.

Evolving discourses and shifting emotional climates may engender opportunities for nonprofit organizing and specifically modulate relations with the state and its different agencies. To the extent that this leads to shared constructions of interdependence and a climate of mutual fear this may result in the political inclusion of nonprofit organizing into public policies. Essentially, such settings can be understood and analyzed using elements of neo-corporatist theorizing. This helps us not only to understand how civic organizations may enter into compliant, rather than opposing, relations with dominant power structures, but also how civic organizations function as a power structure themselves. AIDS service organizations carry the dominant, depoliticizing AIDS discourse and its concrete implications into the life-worlds of their constituent communities. Nonprofits need to be analyzed in terms of how they form what neo-corporatism calls private interest government—a means of regulating constituent communities. The empirical case studies (Chapters 6–9) explored this finding from Chapter 2 in detail, highlighting the wider discursive-emotional bases of private interest government in organizations.

In this way, discursive-emotional regimes impact on the internal organizational dynamics of nonprofits. This is evident from how the professional transformation of AIDS organizations was found to be premised on dominant, medicalizing AIDS discourse and was precipitated by emerging state–nonprofit relations. This is a particular way in which nonprofits may be implicated with dominant power structures. Professionalized AIDS organizing constitutes a shift away from other paradigms of civic organizing, namely grassroots and self-empowerment principles. Within the paradigm of AIDS service organizing it involves the differentiation of organziational roles into professionals, volunteers and clients. In comparison to egalitarian grassroots organizing this constitutes in principle a relative disempowerment of the rank-and-file members (however mitigated by, for example, shared communal identifications). What is more, Chapters 6–9 demonstrated how professionalism and volunteerism function as depoliticizing, hegemonic organizational devices.

Comparative analysis shows that findings hold true not only for the US, but in principle also for German AIDS organizing. But it also shows that what can be analyzed in terms of neo-corporporatist inclusion of nonprofits into public policies may have degrees of variation in different countries. National patterns of state–nonprofit relations are thus to be seen as another formative condition for the evolution of nonprofit organizations.

In sum, nonprofits are constituted and shaped through discourses and emotional climates. Nonprofit organizers navigate dominant meanings and emotions as these constitute causes for organizing, prefigure how to relate to these causes emotionally and how to address them practically/organizationally. Discourses and emotions shape political processes and the specific opportunities for nonprofit organizing that these processes offer. This already gives some indications for how nonprofits can be conceptualized as different from social movement organization insofar as they are compliant with, rather than challenging, hegemonic power structures such as dominant, depoliticizing AIDS discourse and public health policies. Through their inclusion in public policies nonprofits may function as a means to regulate constituent communities while in turn exerting more or less influence on public policies.

But how exactly do organizers navigate discourses and emotions? How do they come to understand and emotionally apprehend a cause to be addressed through civic organizing? And how do they relate to dominant power processes through this? These are the central questions in the empirical part of this study. Answering these questions is essential for addressing the lacking microfoundation of nonprofit theorizing.

Three modes of civic action

The meaning-emotion making of civic organizers can be grouped into three categories: activism, volunteerism and professionalism. Key to this distinction is how these modes of civic action relate to dominant power structures. Emotions function as central indicators for this.

1 *Activism*. The key dimension of activism is an antagonistic relation to dominant power structures, involving cognitive and emotional liberation (Flam 1993, 2005; McAdam 1999). Emotions such as moral anger, resentment or political solidarity can be particularly indicative of this. What is more, through its emotional bases activism does not simply relate on an individual, interpersonal level to people affected by some kind of social problem. Rather, it connects a concern for affected individuals with a generalized, abstracted sense of what is at stake. The contrast between solidarity and compassion or pity especially highlights this.

2 *Volunteerism*. Volunteerism can be seen as activism's non-antagonistic, unpaid counterpart. To put it this way, however, would be yet another instance of using a negative logic to define civic action outside of social movements (e.g., as non-antagonistic). A focus on emotions allows a conceptualization in logically positive terms. Compassion and pity are typical bases of volunteerism. These emotions have a strong potential to engender a relatively depoliticized, decontextualizing, unresentful and individualizing understanding of the cause pursued through civic organizing. For instance, in D-Town or Bavarian AIDS Relief, compassion and pity hindered dominant power processes like ostracism or the implications of Bavarian AIDS policies to register with volunteers *in ways that spurred civic action*. Rather, volunteers are affirmatively oriented towards dominant power structures or remain oblivious of them. Pride in living up to a socially sanctioned ideal of the engaged citizen or the pursuit of recognition by powerful institutions and political actors, and a sense of self-confidence derived from it, can be particularly indicative of this. In contrast to activism, these central motives implicate volunteers with hegemonic power rather then leading

them to counter it. Finally, as a civic ideal, volunteerism is discursively constructed, not least also by powerful political actors. It may be fostered through public policies (e.g., welfare devolution) and it is shaped by dominant discourses on, for example, the nation, citizenship and gender. The inscription of feeling rules about such depoliticizing emotions as compassion and/or pity into the volunteer construct is an important aspect of this.[1] It is a key means to keep the volunteer experience relatively depoliticized.

3 *Professionalism.* Introducing professionalism as a kind of civic action may be counter-intuitive given professionals' claims to objective and disinterested practice. This seems to remove them from anything civic or political. But the significant role that professionals (broadly conceived) play in non-profit organizations in quantitative terms amply justifies considering professionalism as a kind of civic action and calls for an investigation into professionalism's unique nature precisely as civic action. After all, a key finding in this study is that professionalized AIDS organizing is far from neutral in civic/political respects and this is often due to its taken-for-granted claim to expert objectivity. Formal criteria such as paid, formal employment are insufficient to characterize professionalism as civic action. One key element is an understanding of organizing as the application of formal expertise. This functions as a powerful source of rationalizing organizational experience, casting it in seemingly neutral, objective and often technical ways. A central feeling rule inscribed into professionalism concerns rationality (Barbalet 1998). From this rationalized outlook, the civic organization's actual cause may be only an indirect or relatively insignificant motivation for the professional. There may be a compassionate sense of the necessity of professional services and of the duty to provide them based in an expert understanding of clients' needs. But more important as driving motives of professional organizing is the aspiration to professional status and prestige granted by the professional community—a pivotal reference point for professionals. That is to say, pride forms a central motive for professionals. Through this pride professionalism is intimately implicated with dominant power structures—the professional community and ultimately the state that grants professional autonomy. This is a fundamental reason why professionalization tends towards disempowerment. More subtly, its objectifying lens depoliticizes and serves to leave dominant power structures unchallenged. They fail to matter for professional practice.

Modes of civic action, narrativity and sensemaking

Modes of civic action emerge and evolve narratively in the ongoing process of organizing. Their fundamental emotional bases configure what matters to civic organizers and how it matters to them. Subjectively significant occurrences in turn feed back into organizers' understandings of what is at stake and how they feel about it, thus retaining or transforming pre-existing organizational realities. Modes of civic action are thus about different ways of constructing organizational realities. It is within this dynamic, recursive process that de/politicization, the dis/engagement with ongoing power processes, is continuously (re-) produced.

Crucially, rather than being absent, alternative organizational realities and emotional stances may be latently present in civic organizers' experience. Sustaining one mode of civic action depends on keeping such alternative understandings at bay by managing their emotional implications. As we have seen in the case studies, volunteers and professionals are often not entirely oblivious of what causes, for example, anger in activists. But these aspects matter only peripherally to them. They make a constant, active effort to subjectively cast such potential sources of alternative emotions in ways compatible with their depoliticized stances. That is why volunteerism and professionalism function as hegemonic organizational devices (Clair 1998) that produce relative political silence and acquiescence. Volunteers and professionals thus emerge as short-circuited selves (Flam 2010; see Chapter 5).

This perspective also shows how emotions are an inextricable part of the sense-making process. It is the emotional basis of civic action that renders some occurrences significant to civic organizers while other register only peripherally with them. As civic actors continuously construct organizational realities in a specific way, this in turn feeds back into the emotional basis of their engagement.

Hybridity and interrelatedness

Modes of civic action are to be seen as ideal types. In empirical reality it may be more difficult to make equally clear-cut distinctions. In fact, organizers may be characterized by more than one mode of civic action. Professionalism can be embedded into, i.e., can be a means to, volunteerism (such as in the case of Onur, the board member of Migrant AIDS Group's host organization, Chapter 9). Or the aspiration to professional acknowledgment can still involve an antagonistic element (such as with Adam, the executive director of Positive Relief, Chapter 8). Elements of different modes of civic action may also predominate at different points in time (such as in Adam's case as he shifted from activism to professionalism).

More fundamentally, we should be cautious about relating modes of civic action unequivocally to specific emotions. Emotions are key indicators of how organizers relate to dominant power structures. But empirical analysis in this study also points at paradoxes, such as countering and depending on powerful actors simultaneously (such as in Adam's case with Positive Relief, Chapter 8). Importantly, emotions need to be analyzed in full context and in their complexity. While solidarity constituted Paul, the key organizer of AIDS Relief D-Town (Chapter 6), as an activist, it constituted Onur, the board member of Migrant AIDS Group's host organization (Chapter 9), as a volunteer. While there was arguably still a qualitative difference between their feelings of solidarity, Benjamin's solidarity at Positive Relief (Chapter 8) had much in common with Onur's. Yet, Benjamin was more of an activist as he aimed at community building and resentfully countered bureaucratization.

The three modes of civic action relate to each other. Volunteerism and professionalism are complementary to each other. As civic action in nonprofits they are constituted in mutual relation to each other. They involve implicit assumptions about a division of labor between them. This aspect is more complex than I have been able to show with my empirical material. In practice at least the formal-hierarchical relation between volunteers and professionals in any one nonprofit organization may vary (e.g., Nadai *et al.* 2005: 84–98): a volunteer board may be in a formally superior position to and have a controlling and decision-making function over employed professionals; volunteers may work under the guidance of professionals; volunteers may also be part of the target group of professional services. Informal practice within an organization may considerably inflect or distort such formal configurations.

Activism claims self-empowerment, which is particularly incompatible with professionalism and its claim to superior competence. It is no coincidence that interviewed activists were critical of professionalism (e.g., Paul at AIDS Relief D-Town, Chapter 6; Benjamin and, to some degree, Adam at Positive Relief, Chapter 8). Volunteerism forms less of an antagonism to activism but differs in its political purview. The difference between volunteerism and activism was implicit at AIDS Relief D-Town in Paul's critique of his co-organizers' passivity.

Contexts and conditions

Modes of civic action are ultimately grounded in discourses about the causes they pursue. They may build on, and feed back into, dominant understandings of what the nature of any given cause is or constitute deviations from it. In the case of AIDS organizing volunteerism and professionalism both relate to dominant, medicalizing AIDS discourse, configuring the division of labor between them as well as their respective depoliticizing potentials. Activism differs precisely in these discursive premises, as it understands AIDS also as a human or political issue.

But discursive contexts are never one-dimensional. Not only are discourses always co-constituted by and embedded into other discourses, but in nonprofit organizing relatively unconnected discourses may additionally inflect civic action. Examples from this study include the east-west divide after German reunification or immigration discourse and racism. These discourses co-constitute the emotional climates that organizers navigate. These discursive contexts form ultimate power structures to which civic action relates more or less directly or indirectly.

Finally, public policies can directly foster specific modes of civic action. Public funding is an effective tool to promote volunteerism and professionalism in nonprofit organizations even when this is not the explicit goal of funding programs (see Chapter 2). This may be part of policies that aim at devolving the welfare state through greater reliance on volunteers. However, some of my interviews (e.g., Anıl, the gay Turkish activist at Migrant AIDS Group, Chapter 9, Adam at Positive Relief, Chapter 8) also suggest that organizers might differ in their mode of civic action from their formal position as professionals, indicating degrees of agency and autonomy from political programs. After all, formal employment is not to be confused with professionalism as a mode of civic action.

Modes of civic action and civic organizations

Distinguishing modes of civic action and considering their emotional bases makes it possible to characterize forms of non-activist civic action in logically positive terms rather than casting them as a residual category. The question remains however, how this distinction of forms of civic *action* could inform categorizations of civic *organizations*. After all, there was a diverse mix of civic modes in all four organizations.

To be sure, the distinction between NGOs and SMOs (social movement organization) may often be less clear empirically than in theory—more or less hybrid forms are certainly a possibility (Flam 2002). Much like modes of civic action, NGOs and SMOs are thus to be understood as ideal types. Concrete, empirical organizations verge between the two depending on which kinds of civic action predominate in them: activism (SMO) or volunteerism/professionalism (NGO).

Crucially, the predominance in any organization of one or the other mode of civic action may be more than just an aggregate artifact. This points to another condition for the formation of civic action and its emotional bases—the organizational context itself. Abstract feeling rules and discourses are made concrete in the ongoing process of organizing. It is in and through organizations that feelings and meanings are continuously (re-)negotiated in light of the quotidian issues and occurrences of organizational life—the social quality of sensemaking. As I explored elsewhere with existing AIDS organizations (Kleres 2009) volunteers' practice involves constant emotion management such as dealing with disruptive emotions, defining the scope and retaining the limits of their volunteer work and caring emotions, etc. Crucially, organizational structures may function as mediating forums for negotiating this emotion management. In the AIDS organizations I studied there were trainings that socialized new volunteers. There were also regular supervision sessions, guided by a social worker, where volunteers could reflect on their ongoing experience with clients. Both functioned to give shape to volunteers' emotion management. Finally, organizations may put effort into screening people who are interested in volunteering to make sure they bring along compatible orientations (see also Nadai *et al.* 2005: 129–32). In sum the concrete shape and scope of civic action is negotiated in the quotidian organizational practice. These negotiations are in turn not only conditioned by various discourses but equally by concrete organizational structures that constitute and govern concrete instances of civic action. From this perspective civic organizations form "political micro-cultures" (Perrin 2005) the effects of which, however, go beyond the rules of political talk that Eliasoph (1998) and Perrin (2005) have analyzed. They shape the very emotionality of concrete instances of civic action. Ultimately, it is only through the lens of the organizational context that we can understand how civic actors feel about the cause they pursue and the work they do.

Organizations are thus instrumental in constituting and retaining the mode of civic action. This has been more widely recognized for social movements already, such as in the idea that social movements are efforts at establishing new, non-hegemonic feelings rules, which they socialize their members to adopt (e.g., Flam 2005). To the extent that civic organizations foster compliant forms of civic action—volunteerism or professionalism—they are implicated with hegemonic power structures, rather than challenging them. For this reason we may categorize them as nonprofits or NGOs rather than social movement organizations. As Ilcan and Bazok (2004: 133) state:

> Voluntary agencies not only assume the responsibility for service provision; they also train other citizens, namely the volunteers they employ, to become responsible for service provision to disadvantaged people in "the community" and therefore to have little or no opportunity to engage in social justice-oriented advocacy activities.

In line with neo-corporatist arguments, the authors coin the term "community government" for this, i.e., government through community. As I have tried to show in this book, emotions play a central role in this.

Demise

Analyzing modes of civic action does more than tell us something about different ways of constructing organizational realities. As modes of civic action involve different understandings of what organizational realities are about and how to relate to them, they are crucial for understanding the evolution of civic actors' organizing. Only by analyzing different ways of making sense of, for example, funding conflicts was it possible to understand civic organizers' decision to disband. What is more, their motives to get involved in the first place and to keep going came into focus as well.

We should be wary of describing fixed patterns of how emotions are linked to dissolution. As analysis shows, organizational demise is rather complex and any attempt to make fixed theoretical statements about it are likely to fail when applied to different contexts. Having said this, I want to highlight some selected patterns to be considered as empirical possibilities.

Some organizers were driven by strong emotional motives that bestowed a pro-active quality on their civic action. This included not only activists but also professionals. Paul at AIDS Relief D-Town (Chapter 6) was driven by solidarity and resentment. Sarah, the executive director of Migrant AIDS Group (Chapter 9), was driven by the will to professional pride. Adam at Positive Relief (Chapter 8) was driven by his wish to prove eastern AIDS organizing to the west. In each of these cases, strong emotions propelled organizers and led them, each in their own way, to cope with adverse conditions, persevering for considerable periods of time. But ultimately, this resulted in exhaustion and collapse of their engagement as their organizations' contexts remained closed to their claims and efforts.

One specific condition for this was that some emotions, especially pride, brought civic organizers into emotional dependence on powerful actors even though it also made for forms of resentment against them. Adam and Sarah were particularly representative of this. Pride is the emotional apprehension of valuation by others. Even though a claim of pride presumes a modicum of autonomy from those others, it ultimately rests on the willingness of them to grant or withhold valuation. Through the pursuit of pride, organizers fundamentally acknowledge the legitimacy of certain actors to validate them as well as the criteria they employ. In this way, the success or failure of the claim to pride rests on other actors. In both Adam's and Sarah's case, a key condition to their decision to stop was that the regional field of AIDS organizations denied validation. In its dependence on other actors, i.e., through its acknowledgment of their legitimacy, the pursuit of pride leaves organizers without intrinsic means to counter a verdict against them.

In contrast, volunteers such as Sandra and Claudia (AIDS Relief D-Town, Chapter 6) or Alfons (the organizer at Bavarian AIDS Relief driven by pity, Chapter 7) were much less entrepreneurial and "driven." Their stances based on compassion or pity meant that their civic action had rather specific objectives, such as Claudia and Sandra's desire to support Paul. When this objective vanished (because Paul left the organization) their civic work became pointless. In the specificity of its objective, their volunteer work carried equally specific, i.e., relatively easy to reach,[2] conditions for its ending.

Finally, organizational demise needs to be separated from personal disengagement. Not all interviewed organizers ended their engagement when their organization disbanded. Both Benjamin at Positive Relief (Chapter 8) and Anıl at Migrant AIDS Group (Chapter 9) continued with AIDS organizing. This had to do with the emotional bases of their engagement. For both a sense of solidarity with people affected by HIV/AIDS made for a critical distance towards their respective organizations and meant that their concern for AIDS issues did not fade with organizational demise. Erwin's professionalism (Chapter 8), depoliticized as it was, nevertheless meant that he constructed a continuing need for Positive Relief's services. Though there were other reasons for him, too, he dissented from the decision to disband and rebuild the organization.

Coda

The three modes of civic action can be understood as grammars of civic life: they are based in specific conceptions of the problem at hand and prefigure organizational realities for civic actors. In this sense they may extend the reach of dominant power structures subtly but rather effectively into the life worlds of constituent communities. As we have seen, volunteerism and professionalism functioned to neutralize potential politicizing meanings and emotions. These were often latently present in the interview text, but interviewees put discernible effort into managing these alternative versions of organizational reality. Thus modes of civic action are nothing static. They operate dynamically as they are being applied in the ongoing process of organizing and are thereby retained or altered.

Notes

1 It would be too narrow, however, to limit volunteerism to emotions like compassion and pity as this would exclude form of volunteerism that do not address others' plight.
2 The specificity of conditions for engagement arguably increases its contingency and hence the principal likelihood that conditions may at some point not be given anymore. At the same time, specific conditions make it unlikely that they are substituted.

References

Barbalet, Jack M. 1998. *Emotion, Social Theory, and Social Structure: A Macrosociological Approach*. Cambridge, New York, Melbourne, Madrid, Cape Town, Singapore, São Paulo: Cambridge University Press.
Clair, Robin Patric. 1998. *Organizing Silence: A World of Possibilities*. Albany: State University of New York Press.
Eliasoph, Nina. 1998. *Avoiding Politics: How Americans Produce Apathy in Everyday Life*. Cambridge, New York, Melbourne, Madrid: Cambridge University Press.
Flam, Helena. 1993. "Die Erschaffung und der Verfall oppositioneller Identität." *Forschungsjournal Neue Soziale Bewegungen* 2: 83–97.
Flam, Helena. 2002. "National-Global: Zentraleuropa seit 1989." Unpublished presentation at 31st Congress of the German Society of Sociology, Leipzig.
Flam, Helena. 2005. "Emotions' Map: A Research Agenda." Pp. 19–40 in *Emotions and Social Movements*, edited by H. Flam and D. King. London, New York: Routledge.
Flam, Helena. 2010. "Emotion, and the Silenced and Short-Circuited Self." Pp. 187–205 in *Conversations about Reflexivity*, edited by M. S. Archer. London, New York: Routledge.
Ilcan, Suzan and Tanya Basok. 2004. "Community Government: Voluntary Agencies, Social Justice, and the Responsibilization of Citizens." *Citizenship Studies* 8(2): 129–41.
Kleres, Jochen. 2009. "Just Being There: Buddies and the Emotionality of Volunteerism." Pp. 291–314 in *Theorizing Emotions: Sociological Explorations and Applications*, edited by D. R. Hopkins, J. Kleres, H. Flam and H. Kuzmics. Frankfurt am Main, New York: Campus.

McAdam, Doug. 1999. *Political Process and the Development of Black Insurgency, 1930–1970*. Chicago, London: University Of Chicago Press.

Nadai, Eva, Peter Sommerfeld, Felix Bühlmann and Barbara Krattiger. 2005. *Fürsorgliche Verstrickung: Soziale Arbeit zwischen Profession und Freiwilligenarbeit*. Wiesbaden: VS Verlag für Sozialwissenschaften.

Perrin, Andrew J. 2005. "Political Microcultures: Linking Civic Life and Democratic Discourse." *Social Forces* 84(2): 1049–82.

Appendix 1: reflections on fieldwork

Despite some practical constraints—chiefly related to tracking down and recruiting disbanded organizations and their organizers—I was able to include a sample of organizations that represented a certain diversity of political contexts and internal structures. For instance, AIDS Relief D-Town and Bavarian AIDS Relief (Chapters 6 and 7) both operated in relatively adverse political contexts, yet their organizers related to this in rather different ways. The former was located in a rather rural, conservative setting while the latter, despite its regional state-wide scope, drew its key actors from urban centers. In contrast, Positive Relief and Migrant AIDS Group (Chapters 8 and 9) were located in urban centers in other regional states who in turn were more open to the political inclusion of AIDS organizations.

The sample also covers a certain diversity with respect to size and internal organizational structure. AIDS Relief D-Town was a very small organization comprising only volunteers/activists and no employees. On the other end of the spectrum, Migrant AIDS Group was a mostly professional social work project even though it did try to involve some volunteers (with limited success). An organizational unit in itself, however, it was hosted by a volunteer organization. Both Migrant AIDS Group and AIDS Relief D-Town were relatively small, comprising a handful of organizers each. Positive Relief was the biggest organization in the sample with around 50 members and presented a mix of lay and professional organizers. As a membership association it had a team of employed professionals. However, it had started out as a purely non-professional organization. It thus allowed a focus on processes of professionalization—as Chapters 2 and 3 showed this was a key element in the development of AIDS service organizations. Finally, Bavarian AIDS Relief stands out as an umbrella organization of local AIDS Relief chapters in Bavaria. On closer examination, this simple fact meant that it straddled thoroughly professionalized urban chapters and their non-professional, smaller counterparts outside the urban centers. The organization itself was small in terms of actual organizers—mainly a couple of board members together with a professional employee for a period of its existence.

The organizations also represent different target groups and constituent communities. AIDS Relief D-Town (Chapter 6) had a general, inclusive target group—the general population in the region and any local with HIV/AIDS. Positive Relief (Chapter 8) was an organization by and for eastern German gay men with HIV/AIDS. Migrant AIDS Group (Chapter 9) catered to a general Turkish/Muslim migrantic clientele (although one of its organizers tried to focus on gay Turkish migrantic men). These and some additional lines of difference are also reflected among the interviewees. Interviewees from AIDS Relief D-Town were divided in terms of HIV positive vs. negative, rural/local vs. urban/non-local, gay vs. straight, and in terms of gender. At Bavarian AIDS Relief all interviewees were urban gay men. Positive Relief interviewees were HIV positive or negative, from the east or the west. Finally, at Migrant AIDS Group interviewees differed along lines of gay vs. straight, German vs. Turkish-migrantic, and gender. It is important, however, to consider these lines of difference in non-reductive ways. They give organizers potential to make sense of their experience but should not be understood as determinants of it.

I interviewed key organizers, such as board members or professional employees. As they had ceased to exist, finding organizations and interview partners within them was in many ways a difficult task and limited the scope of available empirical data. German AIDS Relief was particularly helpful in identifying some of its disbanded member organizations. Even so, identifying and tracking down their former representatives was rather difficult, time consuming and, in several cases, impossible. For example, some people had simply moved away and nobody knew where they were now living. Some also had passed away, either because of AIDS-related or other causes.

It was also challenging to actually recruit interview partners (I was not able to include a fifth organization due to my interview requests being denied). Even many participating interview partners were at first often very reluctant. The interactions before the actual interview involved a fair amount of negotiation during which interviewees tested who I had already spoken to and how I positioned myself in relation to what others might have said. This was especially the case with Positive Relief and Migrant AIDS Group. In this case it was arguably due to the fact that both disbanded after a protracted funding conflict with other AIDS organizations in the regional field. More generally, organizational demise was for several interviewees also a matter of personal failure and sometimes involved the loss of social status and unemployment. This may also explain why some potential interviewees simply declined my requests. It was also the reason that two interview partners wanted to have a first interview in order to get to know me with the option of having a second appointment, which resulted in two interviews with each informant (Adam and Erwin at Positive Relief). For similar reasons it was also difficult to ask interviewees to suggest other pertinent interviewees. There was a potential for bias in their suggestions. Therefore I also asked pertinent people outside the respective organizations to suggest possible interviewees. However, I still could not fill some gaps: Positive Relief underwent a process of professionalization that caused some internal conflicts. Unfortunately, I was unable to talk to any of the critics of professionalization.

However, interviews—explicitly, implicitly or through comparisons between interviews—provided substantial data on conflicts around professionalization.

In the end I was able to conduct a total of 16 interviews with 14 people, ranging between 50 and 190 minutes per single interview, with an average of 120 minutes per interviewee. Interviews were conducted in 2006.

Interviews started out with the same, narrative-initiating question, which was: "How did you come into contact with [name of the organization] and how did things go on from there?" This question put the focus of the narrative on the period when interviewees were involved with the organizations. It meant that many biographical background conditions never came up and are thus not part of the analysis.

Interviews were transcribed verbatim including, in particular, pauses and some selected prosodic indicators (see Appendix 2). I sometimes additionally introduced commas into quoted interview excerpts used in Chapters 6–9 so as to enhance their readability. All interviews were anonymized changing personal names and places. Translating interview excerpts for this book had to reconcile the need to produce a readable text and at the same time the objective to retain as many of the original's narrative and other linguistic features.

For this book I selected 11 of the 14 interviewees, omitting those that added relatively little to developing the typology of civic action and to understanding the process of organizational dissolution.

Appendix 2: transcription system

I have used the following, simplified transcription system (see, for example, Lucius-Hoene and Deppermann 2004):

(-), (--), (---), (1.0)	pauses of 0.25/0.5/0.75/1.0 seconds duration
text'	moderate upward inflection
?	stronger upward inflection
;	moderate downward inflection
.	stronger downward inflection
CAPITALS	emphasis
CAPITALS!	stronger emphasis
this is: so: : good	drawn-out pronunciation
<<chuckling> text>	tone of voice
<laughing>	paraverbal expressions
<<p> text text>	reduced volume
<<pp> text text>	strongly reduced volume
<st>	stammering
<<ral>text text>	acceleration
h.i.v.	pronunciation as an acronym
[inaud.]	inaudible text
[text text]	insertions by the author or replacements of names for reasons of anonymity
(text)	text that was difficult to understand
(text_a/text_b)	alternative meanings where the recording was difficult to understand

Reference

Lucius-Hoene, Gabriele and Arnulf Deppermann. 2004. *Rekonstruktion narrativer Identität. Ein Arbeitsbuch zur Analyse narrativer Interviews.* Wiesbaden: VS Verlag für Sozialwissenschaften.

Index

absurdity 112, 114–17, 127, 129–31, 135–7, 139, 140, 142
ACT UP 2, 22
activism 10, 14, 16, 22, 27, 32, 34–5, 58, 110, 112, 116–18, 121–2, 127, 129–30, 141, 150, 154–5, 163, 165, 171–3, 175–6, 178–80, 191, 194, 198, 200–1, 204, 206–8
African Americans 26, 30, 130
agency 9, 35–6, 68, 77–8, 80, 97–8, 112–13, 118, 156, 187, 195, 208
AIDS service organization 2, 16, 22–41, 35, 37, 39, 41, 52, 58, 60, 63, 68, 69, 82
ambivalence 103–4, 156, 160
anger 11, 27, 90, 92, 95–7, 99, 104, 111, 119–22, 126, 9, 155, 161–3, 173, 184, 190, 194–8, 204, 206
antagonism 111, 122, 127–8, 134, 194, 207
argumentation 88, 100, 144, 159
ASO *see* AIDS service organization

Bavarian AIDS policies 49–53, 133, 139–40, 142, 144–5, 148–9, 204
blame 26, 29, 97, 104, 119–21, 135, 139, 142, 149–50, 160, 170, 183, 190, 195–6
bureaucratization 2, 5, 34, 55, 112–14, 133, 141, 166, 173, 207

change, ecological/environmental 78–9, 82; social 74–8
cognition 11, 76–7, 79, 91–5, 101, 104
cognitive liberation 11, 122, 128–9, 204
community 16, 26–7, 30, 32, 36, 38, 52–3, 55, 68, 70–1, 111–12, 114–16, 154–63, 167, 171–4, 176, 179, 181–2, 186–7, 191, 193, 195, 198–9, 200, 203, 204, 207, 211; community government 209;

gay community 2, 5, 3–3; professional community 166, 170, 183–6, 198–9, 205
compassion 11, 97, 111, 122–3, 125–30, 133, 135, 137–9, 142, 145, 146–51, 181–2, 186, 200, 204, 205, 210–11
conflict 8–11, 16, 56, 63, 69, 72, 74, 129, 136, 140–1, 153, 160–3, 166–71, 173–6, 179, 181, 182, 184–5, 189–96, 200–1, 209, 214–15
contempt 104, 157, 159

DAH *see* Deutsche AIDS Hilfe
decoupling 72–3, 76, 158
depoliticization 7, 30, 35, 56, 122, 130, 135, 137–40, 142, 166, 171, 181, 184, 187, 189, 203–7
depression 156, 160
description 88, 100, 144
despair 172, 174
Deutsche AIDS Hilfe 14, 43, 46, 48, 51, 54–9, 61–3, 156
disappointment 11, 96, 103, 126, 139, 168, 197
disbelief 110, 112, 194
discrimination 43, 109, 13, 115, 150, 191, 196, 199
disempowerment 33, 35, 37, 123, 142, 158, 167, 175, 199, 206
distrust 11, 38
drug use 24, 26–7, 34–5, 38, 46, 55, 63–4, 69, 147, 150

emotion management 29, 30, 43, 45, 117, 119, 120, 122, 126–7, 140, 155, 159, 160–1, 167, 171, 193–4, 196–7, 208
emotional climate 12, 24, 26–7, 3–8, 43, 45, 51, 53–4, 63, 68, 70, 72, 112, 116, 122–3, 125, 154–5, 167, 175, 187, 202–3, 207

emotional liberation 11, 128, 175–6, 204
emotions and agency 97–8, 112, 118, 156; narrativity of 90–4; non-consciousness of 101–2
empathy 98, 111, 127, 140, 158
empowerment 32, 36–71, 81–2, 186, 191, 203, 207
enactment 78–80, 89, 103, 199
expert, expertise 29, 30, 33, 35, 37, 44–5, 52, 69, 113, 118, 124–5, 135, 138–40, 142–3, 149, 164–5, 167, 171, 175–6, 180–2, 185–6, 189, 191, 199, 205

fear 24, 29–31, 43, 45–6, 51–2, 54, 58–70, 96, 98, 109–10, 112, 114, 119, 122–3, 125, 136, 150, 168, 177, 183, 188, 203
feeling rules 8–9, 95, 97, 104, 111, 122, 124, 126, 128–9, 150, 177, 181–2, 186, 205, 208
field, organizational 1, 13–14, 22, 33–6, 51–2, 70, 72–3, 76, 80, 82, 134, 138, 153–4, 156–7, 161–3, 172, 174, 191, 195–6, 202, 210
formalization 2, 10, 140–2, 153
frustration 15, 113, 115, 133, 139, 163
functional dilettantism 5
funding cuts/conflict 2, 142–3, 153–4, 160–3, 166–71, 174–6, 179, 185, 189–90, 194–5, 198–200, 209, 214

gay identity 25, 32, 35, 44, 53–4, 63; liberation 53–4; movement 22, 24, 31–2, 43–4, 53–4, 56, 133, 155
Gay Men's Health Crisis 25, 27, 34
German AIDS Relief *see* Deutsche AIDS Hilfe
gestalt 91–2, 94
GMHC *see* Gay Men's Health Crisis
grassroots 2, 3, 22, 32, 37, 44, 55, 140–1, 157–8, 166, 203
grief 155
guilt 24, 26, 29, 43–4, 101, 157, 159, 160, 169

hegemony 11–12, 22, 24, 33, 37, 55, 68, 72, 127–8, 145, 149, 194–6, 203–4, 206, 209
helplessness 97, 114
homophobia 25–6, 58, 63, 155, 183, 200
hope 24, 96, 109, 113, 115, 197
hopelessness 119, 156, 172, 174
hostility 109–10, 119–21, 123, 139, 167, 182

humiliation 99, 185

identity, collective 8–10, 35
indignation 104, 122
inertia, organizational 79, 172–3, 175, 196
inferiority, feeling of 154–8, 161–3, 172, 175
intimidation 114, 125
irritation 119, 165–7
isomorphism 33–4, 73

joie de vivre 156, 159–60, 163, 171, 175

legitimacy 6, 30, 32–4, 36, 44, 46, 52–5, 71–3, 75–7, 82, 86, 94–5, 100, 134, 140, 145, 147, 149, 156–8, 163, 166, 196, 210
logic of membership 71, 143; logic of influence 71

market failure 5, 6, 22, 35–7, 63
medicalization of AIDS 58, 113–14, 159–60, 171, 199, 203
migration discourse 187, 207

narration 89, 100, 119, 142, 161, 189
narrative knowledge 87, 102; narrative segments 87–9, 91, 101, 121, 137, 148, 151, 183, 195, 198; narrative structure of 87–8, 93–6, 99–101, 164
neo-corporatism 1, 13, 33–4, 68, 72–81, 158
neo-institutionalism 1, 13, 33–4, 68, 72–81, 158
NGO *see* nonprofit organization
nonprofit organization 1–4, 12, 15–16, 27, 35–8, 44, 60, 63–4, 68–9, 82, 89, 165, 171, 177, 180, 202–4, 207–9, 211

objectivity 69, 72–4, 167, 171–2, 180–1, 188–9, 195, 205
organizational reality 15, 78, 80, 82, 103, 117, 121–3, 127, 135, 137, 148, 171, 173, 187, 211
ostracism 112, 114, 116, 119, 121–3, 126, 128, 150, 155, 204
othering 24, 29, 42–3, 45, 51, 53–4, 112–14, 123, 125, 187
outrage 97, 110–13, 115–16, 119, 122, 129, 169, 175

paradigm scenarios 91
pity 11, 111, 119, 121, 129, 133, 136, 142, 144–7, 149, 204–5, 210–11

political opportunity structures 7, 29, 35, 177
prestige 11, 15, 75, 145, 166, 176, 205
prevention, structural 56, 63
pride 11, 54, 118, 121, 127, 143, 145, 147, 150–1, 154, 156–61, 163, 165–7, 169–71, 174–7, 181–91, 197–9, 204–5, 210
private interest government 31, 70–2, 203
professionalism 2, 8, 11, 15, 32–40, 55–6, 72, 80, 109, 113, 118, 122–3, 125, 135, 137–42, 146–7, 149, 151, 153–4, 157–60, 164–71, 173–7, 179–89, 191, 194–5, 198–201, 203–15; and compassion 182, 186, 205; medical 180–1; and rationality 164, 180, 205; in social work 35–6, 164–71; *see also* professional community
professionalization 2, 15, 23, 32–3, 36–7, 55–6, 63, 73, 113–17, 125, 133–4, 136–9, 142–3, 146–9, 153–4, 157–61, 163–4, 167, 171, 173, 175–6, 182, 188, 203, 205, 213–15
public funding 34, 36, 44, 55, 64, 136, 142, 153, 160, 169, 171, 207; *see also* funding cuts
public health 2, 23, 25, 27–31, 55, 60, 204; new public health 28–30, 45, 47, 49, 51–2, 56, 64, 133; old public health 28, 30–1, 44, 45, 49, 71, 139, 200

racism 26, 30, 38, 103, 183–4, 199, 207
rationality 1, 5–8, 11–12, 15, 69–78, 80, 93–5, 129, 137–43, 147, 165–9, 171, 175–7, 180–3, 185–6, 188–9, 196, 198–9, 202, 205
reason 93, 102–3, 129
resentment 11, 112, 116, 122, 127–9, 158–60, 169, 172, 177, 183–4, 193, 196, 198, 204, 207, 210
resignation 126, 136–7, 140, 142, 161–3, 189–90, 194, 197–9
retention 73, 79, 89, 124, 129
routine 2, 16, 52, 73, 78–80, 105
rule system theory 76–8

selection 79, 89
self, short-circuited 104, 153, 206; silenced 103–4
self-help 44–5, 55–6, 109, 111–12, 115, 118, 147–8, 153–4, 172, 195, 200; self-help organization 55, 128, 147, 173
sensemaking, characteristics of 79–80; and emotions 102–5; and narrative analysis 88–9; and power 81–2; vocabularies of 80
shame 24, 26, 54, 90, 102, 104, 112, 120–1, 123, 150, 154–7, 161–3, 172, 174–5, 177, 185–7, 189–91, 194–6, 199
shock 75, 96, 110–11, 122, 166–7; moral shock 110–11
SMO *see* social movement organization
social movement 1, 4, 6–12, 104, 122, 203, 208–9
social movement organization 8, 16, 22, 203
solidarity 3, 11, 38, 51, 82, 97, 111–17, 122–3, 125, 127–30, 139–40, 145–6, 150–1, 158, 171–2, 174–6, 181–4, 186–9, 192–4, 197–9, 204, 206–7
state failure 5–6, 22, 25, 27, 35–7
stigma, stigmatization 24, 26, 30, 52, 54–5, 63, 114–15, 119–21, 139, 150, 182, 192–3
superiority, feeling of 138, 143, 146, 149, 151, 157, 162, 165, 171, 177
sympathy 6, 98, 130, 154

taken-for-grantedness 14, 33–4, 72, 74, 76–7, 80, 82, 112, 116, 128, 139, 141, 151, 174, 195, 205
third party government 5
third sector 1, 3, 7, 9, 13, 15, 22, 27, 68–9, 202
thought *see* cognition
trust 5–6, 35

volunteerism 1, 6, 7, 9, 10–12, 14, 110, 117–18, 121–3, 126–9, 131, 134–4, 137–42, 146, 149, 151, 165, 171, 179, 186, 188, 202–9, 211

Taylor & Francis eBooks

Helping you to choose the right eBooks for your Library

Add Routledge titles to your library's digital collection today. Taylor and Francis ebooks contains over 50,000 titles in the Humanities, Social Sciences, Behavioural Sciences, Built Environment and Law.

Choose from a range of subject packages or create your own!

Benefits for you
- Free MARC records
- COUNTER-compliant usage statistics
- Flexible purchase and pricing options
- All titles DRM-free.

Benefits for your user
- Off-site, anytime access via Athens or referring URL
- Print or copy pages or chapters
- Full content search
- Bookmark, highlight and annotate text
- Access to thousands of pages of quality research at the click of a button.

REQUEST YOUR FREE INSTITUTIONAL TRIAL TODAY

Free Trials Available
We offer free trials to qualifying academic, corporate and government customers.

eCollections – Choose from over 30 subject eCollections, including:

Archaeology	Language Learning
Architecture	Law
Asian Studies	Literature
Business & Management	Media & Communication
Classical Studies	Middle East Studies
Construction	Music
Creative & Media Arts	Philosophy
Criminology & Criminal Justice	Planning
Economics	Politics
Education	Psychology & Mental Health
Energy	Religion
Engineering	Security
English Language & Linguistics	Social Work
Environment & Sustainability	Sociology
Geography	Sport
Health Studies	Theatre & Performance
History	Tourism, Hospitality & Events

For more information, pricing enquiries or to order a free trial, please contact your local sales team:
www.tandfebooks.com/page/sales

The home of Routledge books

www.tandfebooks.com